EVERYDAY
osho

365 DAILY MEDITATIONS
FOR THE HERE AND NOW

OSHO

FAIR WINDS
PRESS
BEVERLY, MASSACHUSETTS

Text © 2002 Osho International Foundation

Designed and typeset by Gopa & Ted2
Editing and compilation: Prartho Sereno

First published in the U.S. in 2002 by
Fair Winds Press, a member of
Quayside Publishing Group
100 Cummings Center
Suite 406-L
Beverly , MA 01915
www.fairwindspress.com

ISBN-13: 978-1-931412-90-2
ISBN-10: 1-931412-90-1

Material in this book has been selected from
unpublished transcripts of dialogues between
Osho and hundreds of visitors and friends over
a period of twenty years.

www.osho.com

10   9   8   7

Printed in Canada

EVERYDAY osho

I.

ILLUMINATION

The moment you are illuminated, the whole of existence is illuminated.
If you are dark, then the whole of existence is dark. It all depends on you.

There are a thousand and one fallacies about meditation prevalent all around the world. Meditation is very simple: It is nothing but consciousness. It is not chanting, it is not using a mantra or a rosary. These are hypnotic methods. They can give you a certain kind of rest—nothing is wrong with that rest; if one is just trying to relax, it is perfectly good. Any hypnotic method can be helpful, but if one wants to know the truth, then it is not enough.

Meditation simply means transforming your unconsciousness into consciousness. Normally only one-tenth of our mind is conscious, and nine-tenths is unconscious. Just a small part of our mind, a thin layer, has light; otherwise the whole house is in darkness. And the challenge is to grow that small light so much that the whole house is flooded with light, so that not even a nook or corner is left in darkness.

When the whole house is full of light, then life is a miracle; it has the quality of magic. Then it is no longer ordinary—everything becomes extraordinary. The mundane is transformed into the sacred, and the small things of life start having such tremendous significance that one could not have ever imagined it. Ordinary stones look as beautiful as diamonds; the whole of existence becomes illuminated. The moment you are illuminated, the whole of existence is illuminated. If you are dark, then the whole of existence is dark. It all depends on you.

2.

AMATEURS AND EXPERTS

All great discoveries are made by amateurs.

It always happens that when you start new work, you are very creative, you are deeply involved, your whole being is in it. Then by and by, as you become acquainted with the territory, rather than being inventive and creative you start being repetitive. This is natural, because the more skilled you become in any work, the more repetitive you become. Skill is repetitive.

So all great discoveries are made by amateurs, because a skilled person has too much at stake. If something new happens, what will happen to the old skill? The person has learned for years and now has become an expert. So experts never discover anything; they never go beyond the limit of their expertise. On the one hand, they become more and more skillful, and on the other hand they become more and more dull and the work seems to be a drag. Now there is nothing new that can be a thrill to them—they already know what is going to happen, they know what they are going to do; there is no surprise in it.

So here is the lesson: It is good to attain to skill, but it is not good to settle with it forever. Whenever the feeling arises in you that now the thing is looking stale, change it. Invent something, add something new, delete something old. Again be free from the pattern—that means be free from the skill—again become an amateur. It needs courage and guts, to become an amateur again, but that's how life becomes beautiful.

3.
CHOOSE NATURE

Wherever you find that society is in conflict with nature,
choose nature—whatever the cost. You will never be a loser.

The thinking up to now has been that the individual exists for the society, that the individual has to follow what the society dictates. The individual has to fit with the society. That has become the definition of the normal human being—one who fits with the society. Even if the society is insane, you have to fit with it; then you are normal.

Now the problem for the individual is that nature demands one thing, and society demands something contrary. If the society were demanding the same as nature demands, there would be no conflict. We would have remained in the Garden of Eden. The problem arises because society has its own interests, which are not necessarily in tune with the interests of the individual. Society has its own investments, and the individual has to be sacrificed. This is a very topsy-turvy world. It should be just the other way round. The individual does not exist for the society, the society exists for the individual. Because society is just an institution, it has no soul. The individual has the soul, is the conscious center.

4.

AN ECHOING PLACE

The world is an echoing place. If we throw anger, anger comes back;
if we give love, love comes back.

Love should not be demanding; otherwise it loses wings, it cannot
fly. It becomes rooted in the earth becomes very earthly; then it is
lust and it brings great misery and great suffering. Love should not
be conditional, one should not expect anything out of it. It should
be for its own sake—not for any reward, not for any result. If there
is some motive in it, again, your love cannot become the sky. It is
confined to the motive; the motive becomes its definition, its
boundary. Unmotivated love has no boundary: It is pure elation,
exuberance, it is the fragrance of the heart.

And just because there is no desire for any result, it does not
mean that results do not happen; they do, they happen a thou-
sandfold, because whatever we give to the world comes back, it
rebounds. The world is an echoing place. If we throw anger, anger
comes back; if we give love, love comes back. But that is a natural
phenomenon; one need not think about it. One can trust: It happens on its own. This is the law of karma: Whatever you sow, you
reap; whatever you give, you receive. So there is no need to think
about it, it is automatic. Hate, and you will be hated. Love, and
you will be loved.

5.
RETROSPECTIVE WISDOM

The other is never responsible. Just watch. If you become wise in the moment, there will be no problem. But everybody becomes wise when the moment is gone. Retrospective wisdom is worthless.

When you have done evfought and nagged and bitched and then you become wise and see that there was no point in it, it is too late. It is meaningless—you have already done the harm. This wisdom is just pseudo-wisdom. It gives you a feeling "as if" you have understood. That is a trick of the ego. This wisdom is not going to help. When you are doing the thing, at that very moment, simultaneously, the awareness should arise, and you should see that what you are doing is useless.

If you can see it when it is there, then you cannot do it. One can never go against one's awareness, and if one goes against it, that awareness is not awareness. Something else is being mistaken for it.

So remember, the other is never responsible for anything. The problem is something boiling within you. And of course the one you love is closest. You cannot throw it on some stranger passing on the road, so the closest person becomes the place where you go on throwing and pouring your nonsense. But that has to be avoided, because love is very fragile. If you do it too much, if you overdo it, love can disappear.

The other is never responsible. Try to make this such a permanent state of awareness in you that whenever you start finding something wrong with the other, remember it. Catch yourself red-handed, and drop it then and there. And ask to be forgiven.

6.

GRATITUDE

Feel as grateful to existence as possible—for small things, not only for great things... just for sheer breathing. We don't have any claim on existence, so whatever is given is a gift.

Grow more and more in gratitude and thankfulness; let it become your very style. Be grateful to everybody. If one understands gratitude, then one is grateful for things that have been done positively. And one even feels grateful for things that could have been done but were not done. You feel grateful that somebody helped you—this is just the beginning. Then you start feeling grateful that somebody has not harmed you—he could have; it was kind of him not to.

Once you understand the feeling of gratitude and allow it to sink deeply within you, you will start feeling grateful for everything. And the more grateful you are, the less complaining, grumbling. Once complaining disappears, misery disappears. It exists with complaints. It is hooked with complaints and with the complaining mind. Misery is impossible with gratefulness. This is one of the most important secrets to learn.

7.
LAUGHTER

Why wait for reasons to laugh? Life as it is should be reason enough
to laugh. It is so absurd, it is so ridiculous. It is so beautiful,
so wonderful! It is all sorts of things together. It is a great cosmic joke.

Laughter is the easiest thing in the world if you allow it, but it has become hard. People laugh very rarely, and even when they laugh it is not true. People laugh as if they are obliging somebody, as if they are fulfilling a certain duty. Laughter is fun. You are not obliging anybody!

You should not laugh to make somebody else happy, because if you are not happy, you cannot make anybody else happy. You should simply laugh of your own accord, without waiting for reasons to laugh. If you start looking into things, you will not be able to stop laughing. Everything is simply perfect for laughter—nothing is lacking—but we won't allow it. We are very miserly...miserly about laughter, about love, about life. Once you know that miserliness can be dropped, you move into a different dimension. Laughter is the real religion. Everything else is just metaphysics.

8.

NONJUDGMENT

When you judge, division starts.

You may be talking in deep conversation with a friend when suddenly you feel like being silent. You want to stop talking, right in the middle of the sentence. So stop right there, and don't even complete the rest of the sentence, because that will be going against nature.

But then judgment comes in. You feel embarrassed about what others will think if you suddenly stop talking in the middle of a sentence. If you suddenly become silent they will not understand, so you somehow manage to complete the sentence. You pretend to show interest, and then you finally escape. That is very costly, and there is no need to do it. Just say that conversation is not coming to you now. You can ask to be excused, and be silent.

For a few days perhaps it will be a little troublesome, but by and by people will begin to understand. Don't judge yourself about why you became silent; don't tell yourself that it is not good. Everything is good! In deep acceptance, everything becomes a blessing. This is how it happened—your whole being wanted to be silent. So follow it. Just become a shadow to your totality, and wherever it goes you have to follow because there is no other goal. You will begin to feel a tremendous relaxation surrounding you.

9.
THE REAL ROBBERS

There is nothing to fear, because we don't have anything to lose.
All that can be robbed from you is not worthwhile, so why fear,
why suspect, why doubt?

These are the real robbers: doubt, suspicion, fear. They destroy your very possibility of celebration. So while on earth, celebrate the earth. While this moment lasts, enjoy it to the very core. Because of fear we miss many things. Because of fear we cannot love, or even if we love it is always half-hearted, it is always so-so. It is always up to a certain extent and not beyond that. We always come to a point beyond which we are afraid, so we get stuck there. We cannot move deeply in friendship because of fear. We cannot pray deeply because of fear.

Be conscious but never be cautious. The distinction is very subtle. Consciousness is not rooted in fear. Caution is rooted in fear. One is cautious so that one might never go wrong, but then one cannot go very far. The very fear will not allow you to investigate new lifestyles, new channels for your energy, new directions, new lands. You will always tread the same path again and again, shuttling backward and forward—like a freight train!

10.

CRITICAL MIND

I am not saying that a critical attitude is always harmful.
If you are working on a scientific project, it is not harmful;
it is the only way to work.

A critical mind is an absolute necessity if you are working on a scientific project. But the critical mind is an absolute barrier if you are trying to reach your own interiority, your own subjectivity. With the objective world it is perfectly okay. Without it there is no science; with it there is no religiousness. This has to be understood: When one is working objectively one has to be capable of using it, and when one is working subjectively one has to be capable of putting it aside. It should be used as a means. It should not become an idée fixe; you should be able to use it or not, you should be free.

There is no possibility of going into the inner world with a critical mind. Doubt is a barrier, just as trust is a barrier in science. A person of trust will not go very far in science. That's why in the days when religion was predominant in the world, it remained unscientific. The conflict that arose between the church and science was not accidental; it was very fundamental. It was not really a conflict between science and religion; it was a conflict between two different dimensions of being, the objective and the subjective. Their workings are different.

II.

ORGASM

There are moments, a few moments, far and few between, when ego disappears because you are in such a total drunkenness. In love it sometimes happens; in orgasm it sometimes happens.

In deep orgasm your history disappears, your past recedes, goes on receding, receding, and disappears. You don't have any history in orgasm, you don't have any past, you don't have any mind, you don't have any autobiography. You are utterly here now. You don't know who you are, you don't have any identity. In that moment the ego is not functioning, hence the joy of orgasm, the refreshing quality of it, the rejuvenation of it. That's why it leaves you so silent, so quiet, so relaxed, so fulfilled. But again the ego comes in, the past enters and encroaches on the present. Again *history* starts functioning and *you* stop functioning. The ego is your history, it is not a reality. And this is your enemy; the ego is the enemy.

Every person comes around this corner many times in life, because life moves in a circle. Again and again we come to the same point, but because of fear we escape from it. Otherwise the ego is a falsity. In fact, to let it die should be the easiest thing and to keep it alive should be the hardest thing, but we keep it alive and we think it is easier.

12.

CHAIN REACTION

All things happen together.

When you feel less guilty, immediately you start feeling happier. When you feel more happy, you feel less in conflict, more harmonious — together. When you feel together, more harmonious, suddenly you feel a certain grace surrounding you. These things function like a chain reaction: One starts the other, the other starts another, and they go on spreading.

Feeling less guilty is very important. The whole of humanity has been made to feel guilty—centuries of conditioning, of being told to do this and not to do that. Not only that, but forcing people by saying that if they do something that is not allowed by the society or by the church, then they are sinners. If they do something that is appreciated by the society and the church, then they are saints. So everybody has been fooled into doing things that society wants them to do, and not to do things that society does not want them to do. Nobody has bothered about whether this is your thing or not. Nobody has bothered about the individual.

Move into a new light, into a new consciousness, where you can unguilt yourself. And then many more things will follow.

13.
FLEXIBILITY

You are young in proportion to your flexibility. Watch a small child—so soft, tender, and flexible. As you grow old everything becomes tight, hard, inflexible. But you can remain absolutely young to the very moment of your death if you remain flexible.

When you are happy you expand. When you are afraid you shrink, you hide in your shell, because if you go out there may be some danger. You shrink in every way—in love, in relationships, in meditation, in every way. You become a turtle and you shrink inside.

If you remain in fear continuously, as many people live, by and by the elasticity of your energy is lost. You become a stagnant pool, you are no longer flowing, no longer a river. Then you feel more and more dead every day.

But fear has a natural use. When the house is on fire you have to escape. Don't try being unafraid there or you will be a fool! One should also remain capable of shrinking, because there are moments when one needs to stop the flow. One should be able to go out, to come in, to go out, to come in. This is flexibility: expansion, shrinking, expansion, shrinking. It is just like breathing. People who are very afraid don't breathe deeply, because even that expansion brings fear. Their chest will shrink; they will have a sunken chest.

So try to find out ways to make your energy move. Sometimes even anger is good. At least it moves your energy. If you have to choose between fear and anger, choose anger. But don't go to the other extreme. Expansion is good, but you should not become addicted to it. The real thing to remember is flexibility: the capacity to move from one end to another.

14.
GRACE

Grace brings beauty.
Grace simply means the aura that surrounds total relaxation.

If you move spontaneously, each moment itself decides how it will be. This moment is not going to decide for the next, so you simply remain open-ended. The next moment will decide its own being; you have no plan, no pattern, no expectation.

Today is enough; don't plan for tomorrow, or even for the next moment. Today ends, and then tomorrow comes fresh and innocent, with no manipulator. It opens of its own accord, and without the past. This is grace. Watch a flower opening in the morning. Just go on watching…this is grace. There is no effort at all—the flower just moves according to nature. Or watch a cat awakening, effortlessly, with a tremendous grace surrounding it. The whole of nature is full of grace, but we have lost the capacity to be graceful because of the divisions within

So just move, and let the moment decide—don't try to manage it. This is what I call let-go—and everything happens out of this. Give it a chance!

15.

THE SPECIAL FEAR

It's a good kind of fear when you don't know what exactly it is.
It simply means that you are on the verge of something unknown.

When your fear has some object, it is an ordinary fear. One is afraid of death—it is a very ordinary fear instinctive; there's nothing special about it. Being afraid of old age or disease, illness—these are ordinary fears, common, garden variety. The special fear is when you cannot find an object for it, when it is there for no reason at all. That makes one really scared! If you can find a reason, the mind is satisfied. If you can answer why, the mind has some explanation to cling to. All explanations help things to be explained away, they don't do anything else, but once you have a rational explanation, you feel satisfied.

It is better to see the thing as it is without asking why. Something unknown is hovering around you, as it is going to hover around every seeker. This is the fear every seeker has to pass through. I am not here to give you explanations but to push you into it. I am not a psychoanalyst—I am an existentialist. My effort is to make you capable of experiencing as many things as possible—love, fear, anger, greed, violence, compassion, meditation, beauty, and so forth. The more you experience these things, the richer you become.

16.

THE DIVIDED BODY

In a primitive society the whole body is accepted.
There is no condemnation. Nothing is lower and nothing is higher.
Everything simply is.

In accepting the body, yoga does not go far enough. It makes you very controlled, and every sort of control is a sort of repression. So you repress and then you forget all about the repression. It moves into the stomach, and near the diaphragm all those repressed things collect. The stomach is the only space where you can go on throwing things; nowhere else is there any space.

The day your control explodes, you will feel so free, so alive. You will feel reborn, because it will connect your divided body. The diaphragm is the place where the body is divided between the upper and lower. In all the old religious teachings, the lower is condemned and the upper is made to be something high, something superior, something holier. It is not. The body is one, and this bifurcation is dangerous; it makes you split. By and by you deny many things in life. Whatever you exclude from your life will take its revenge some day. It will come as a disease.

Now some medical researchers say that cancer is nothing but too much stress inside. Cancer only exists in very repressed societies. The more civilized and cultured a society, the more cancer is possible. It cannot exist in a primitive society, because in a primitive society the whole body is accepted. There is no condemnation. Nothing is lower and nothing is higher. Everything simply is.

17.

IGNORANCE

When I use the word ignorance, I don't use it in any negative sense—
I don't mean absence of knowledge. I mean something very fundamental,
very present, very positive. It is how we are. It is the very nature of
existence to remain mysterious, and that's why it is so beautiful.

All knowledge is superfluous. Knowledge as such is superfluous.
And all knowledge only creates an illusion that we know. But we
don't know. You can live someone your whole life and think that
you know the person—and you don't know. You can give birth to
a child and you can think you know the child—and you don't
know.

Whatever we think we know is very illusory. Somebody asks,
"What is water?" and you say, "H_2O." You are simply playing a game.
It is not known what water is, or what "H" is or "O." You are just
labeling. Somebody asks what this "H" is, this hydrogen, and you go
to the molecules, to the atoms, to the electrons—but you are again
just giving names. The mystery is not finished—the mystery is only
postponed, and at the end, there is still tremendous ignorance. In
the beginning we did not know what the water was; now we don't
know what the electron is, so we have not come to any knowledge.
We have played a game of naming things, categorizing, but life
remains a mystery. Ignorance is so profound and so ultimate that it
cannot be destroyed. And once you understand it, you can rest in
it. It is so beautiful, it is so relaxing... because then there is nowhere
to go. There is nothing to be known, because nothing can be
known. Ignorance is ultimate. It is tremendous and vast.

18.

BEHIND ANGER

Shift from anger to creativity, and immediately you will see a great change arising in you. Tomorrow the same things will not feel like excuses for being angry.

Out of one hundred people suffering from anger, about 50 percent suffer from too much creative energy that they have not been able to put into use. Their problem is not anger, but they will go on thinking their whole life that it is. Once a problem is diagnosed rightly, half of it is already solved.

Put your energies into creativity. Forget about anger as a problem; ignore it. Channel your energy towards more creativity. Pour yourself into something that you love. Rather than making anger your problem, let creativity be your object of meditation. Shift from anger to creativity and immediately you will see a great change arising in you. And tomorrow the same things will not feel like excuses for being angry because now energy is moving, it is enjoying itself, its own dance. Who cares about small things?

19.
SPONTANEITY

Whatever you do, just do it as totally as possible. If you enjoy walking, good! If suddenly you realize that you no longer have the urge or desire to move, then sit down immediately; not even a single step should be taken against your will.

Whatever happens, accept and enjoy it; and don't force anything. If you feel like talking, talk. If you feel like being silent, be silent— just move with the feeling. Don't force in any way, not even for a single moment, because once you force anything you are divided in two—and that creates the problem, then your whole life becomes split.

The whole of humanity has become almost schizophrenic, because we have been taught to force things. The part that wants to laugh and the part that doesn't allow you to laugh become separate, and then you are divided. You create a top dog and an underdog, so there is conflict. The rift that the conflict creates can become bigger and bigger and bigger. So the problem is how to bridge that rift, and how not to create it anymore. In Zen they have a very beautiful saying: *Sitting, just sit. Walking, just walk. Above all, don't wobble.*

20.

HOLDING BACK

Why do we hold back? There is some fear that if we don't hold back,
if we give all, then we have nothing else to give. So we give only in parts,
we keep the carrot dangling. We want to remain mysterious.

When you don't allow the other to enter into your whole being and
know it totally, it is because of the fear that once the other knows
you totally he or she may become disinterested. You keep a few corners of yourself aloof so that the other goes on wondering, "What
are those corners? What more do you have give?" And the other
goes on searching and seeking and persuading and seducing.... And
in the same way, the other is also holding back.

There is some animal understanding behind it that once the mystery is known, the thing is finished. We love the mystery, we love the
unknown. When it is known, mapped, and measured, it is finished!
Then what else is there? The adventuring mind will start thinking
of other women, other men. This has happened to millions of husbands and wives: They have looked into each other totally—
finished! Now the other has no soul because the mystery is no
longer here—and the soul exists in mystery. This is the logic in it.

But when you are truly independent, and you are surrendered
to the god of love, then you can open yourself totally. And in that
very opening you become one. When two people are open, they are
no longer two. When the walls disappear, the room is one. And
that is where the fulfillment is. That's what every lover is seeking
for, searching for, hankering after, dreaming about, desiring. But
not understanding rightly, you can go on seeking and searching in
a wrong direction.

BE LIKE A CHILD

We are separate only on the surface; deep down we are not. separate.
Only the visible part is separate; the invisible part is still one.

The Upanishads say, "Those who think they know, know not," because the very idea that you know does not allow you to know. The very idea that one is ignorant makes you vulnerable, open. Like a child, your eyes are full of wonder. Then it is difficult to decide whether the thoughts are yours or whether they are entering you from the outside, because one has lost all moorings. But there is no need to worry, because basically the mind is one, it is the universal mind. Call it God, or, in Jungian terms, call it the "collective unconscious."

We are separate only on the surface; deep down we are not. separate. Only the visible part is separate, the invisible part is still one. So when you relax and become silent, and you become more humble, more childlike, more innocent, then it will be difficult in the beginning to see whether these thoughts are yours, are coming out of the blue, or somebody else is sending his messages and you are just on the receiving end! But they are coming from nowhere. They are coming from the deepest core of your being—and that is the core of everybody else, also.

So a really original thought carries nobody's signature. It is simply there, out of the collective, out of the universal, out of the one mind—mind with a capital M. And when the individual mind, the ego mind, relaxes, the universal mind starts overflooding you.

22.

LOVE'S FRAGILITY

Don't think that love is eternal. It is very fragile, as fragile as a rose. In the morning it is there—by the evening it is gone. Any small thing can destroy it.

The higher a thing is, the more fragile it is. It has to be protected. A rock will remain, but the flower will be gone. If you throw a rock at the flower, the rock is not going to be hurt, but the flower will be destroyed.

Love is very fragile, very delicate. One has to be very careful and cautious about it. You can do such harm that the other becomes closed, becomes defensive. If you are fighting too much, your partner will start escaping; he will bcome more and more cold, more and more closed, so that he is no longer vulnerable to your attack. Then you will attack him some more, because you will resist that coldness. This can become a vicious circle. And that's how lovers fall apart, by and by. They drift away from each other, and they think that the other was responsible, that the other betrayed them.

In fact, as I see it, no lover has ever betrayed anybody. It is only ignorance that kills love. Both wanted to be together, but somehow both were ignorant. Their ignorance played tricks on them and became multiplied.

23.
ESSENTIALS

Meditation means to be oneself, and love means to share one's being with somebody else. Meditation gives you the treasure, and love helps you to share it. These are the two most basic things, and all else is nonessential.

There is an old anecdote about three travelers who go to Rome. They visit the pope, who asks of the first, "How long are you going to be here?" The man says, "For three months." The pope says, "Then you will be able to see much of Rome." In answer to how long he was going to stay, the second traveler replies that he can only stay for six weeks. The pope says, "Then you will be able to see more than the first." The third traveler says he will only be in Rome for two weeks, to which the pope replies, "You are fortunate, because you will be able to see everything there is to see!"

The travelers were puzzled, because they didn't understand the mechanism of the mind. Just think, if you had a lifespan of a thousand years, you would miss many things, because you would go on postponing things. But because life is so short, one cannot afford to postpone. Yet people do postpone—and at their own cost.

Imagine if somebody were to tell you that you have only one day left to live. What will you do? Will you go on thinking about unnecessary things? No, you will forget all that. You will love and pray and meditate, because only twenty-four hours are left. The real things, the essential things, you will not postpone.

24.
AUTHORITY

Never ask anybody what is right and what is wrong. Life is an experiment to find out.

Each individual has to be conscious, alert, and watchful, and experiment with life and find out what is good for him. Whatever gives you peace, whatever makes you blissful, whatever gives you serenity, whatever brings you closer to existence and its immense harmony is good. And whatever creates conflict, misery, pain in you is wrong. Nobody else can decide it for you, because every individual has his own world, his own sensitivity. We are unique. So formulas are not going to work. The whole world is a proof of this.

Never ask anybody what is right and what is wrong. Life is an experiment to find out what is right, what is wrong. Sometimes you may do what is wrong, but that will give you the experience of it, that will make you aware of what has to be avoided. Sometimes you may do something good, and you will be immensely benefited. The rewards are not beyond this life, in heaven and hell. They are here and now.

Each action brings its result immediately. Just be alert and watch. Mature people are those who have watched and found for themselves what is right, what is wrong, what is good, what is bad. And by finding it for themselves, they have a tremendous authority. The whole world may say something else, and it makes no difference to them. They have their own experience to go by, and that is enough.

25.
HAPPINESS

There are no outside causes of happiness or unhappiness;
these things are just excuses. By and by we come to realize that
it is something inside us that goes on changing, that has nothing
to do with outside circumstances.

How you feel is something inside you, a wheel that keeps on moving. Just watch it—and it is very beautiful, because in being aware of it, something has been attained. Now you understand that you are free from outside excuses, because nothing has happened on the outside and yet your mood has changed within a few minutes from happiness to unhappiness, or the other way around.

This means that happiness and unhappiness are your moods and don't depend on the outside. This is one of the most basic things to be realized, because then much can be done. The second thing to understand is that your moods depend on your unawareness. So just watch and become aware. If happiness is there, just watch it and don't become identified with it. When unhappiness is there, again just watch. It is just like morning and evening. In the morning you watch and enjoy the rising sun. When the sun sets and darkness descends, that too you watch and enjoy.

26.

PLAYING A ROLE

Play, but play knowingly. Play your games, whatever they are;
don't repress them. Play them as perfectly as possible, but stay fully alert.
Enjoy it, and others will also enjoy it.

When a person plays a role there is some reason in it. That role has some significance to the person. If the game is played perfectly, something from the unconscious will disappear, evaporate, and you will be freed from a burden.

For example, if you want to play like a child, that means that in your childhood something has remained incomplete. You could not be a child as you wanted to be; somebody stopped you. People made you more serious, forced you to appear more adult and mature than you were. Something has remained incomplete. That incompletion demands to be completed and it will continue to haunt you. So finish it. Nothing is wrong in it. You could not be a child that time, back in the past; now you can be. Once you can be totally in it, you will see that it has disappeared and will never come again.

27.
LABELS

Don't use the words happiness and unhappiness, because these words carry judgments. Simply watch without judging—just say, "This is mood 'A' and this is mood 'B.'"

"A" mood has gone, now "B" mood is here, and you are simply a watcher. Suddenly you will realize that when you call happiness "A," it is not so happy, and when you call unhappiness "B," it is not so unhappy. Just by calling the moods "A" and "B," a distance is created.

When you say *happiness,* much is implied in the word. You are saying you want to cling to it, that you don't want it to go. When you say *unhappy,* you are not just using a word; much is implied in it. You are saying that you don't want it, that it should not be there. All these things are said unconsciously.

So use these new terms for your moods for seven days. Just be a watcher—as if you are sitting on top of the hill, and in the valley clouds and sunrises and sunsets come, and sometimes it is day and sometimes night. Just be a watcher on the hill, far away.

28.

NEW-MOON LOVE

Let a new-moon love happen. Hold each other, be loving to each other, care, and don't hanker for the heat—because that heat was a madness, it was a frenzy; it is good that it is gone. You should think yourselves fortunate.

If love goes deeper, husbands and wives become brothers and sisters. If love goes deeper, the sun energy becomes moon energy: The heat is gone, it is very cool. And when love goes deeper, a misunderstanding can happen, because we have become accustomed to the fever, the passion, the excitement, and now it all looks foolish. It is foolish! Now when you make love, it looks silly; if you don't make love, you feel as if something is missing because of the old habit.

When a husband and wife start feeling like this, a fear arises— have you started taking the other for granted? Has he become a brother or a sister, no longer your choice, no longer your ego trip? All these fears arise. Sometimes one starts feeling that one is missing something—a sort of emptiness. But don't look at it through the past. Look at it from the future. Much is going to happen in this emptiness, much is going to happen in this intimacy—you will both disappear. Your love will become absolutely nonsexual, all the heat will be gone, and then you will know a totally different quality of love.

29.
TRUST

Always remember that at no cost should you become mistrustful.
Even if your trust allows others to deceive you, this is better than
not to trust.

It is very easy to trust when everybody is loving and nobody is deceiving you. But even if the whole world is deceptive and everybody is bent on deceiving you—and they can only deceive you when you trust—then too, go on trusting. Never lose trust in trust, whatever the cost, and you will never be a loser, because trust in itself is the ultimate end. It should not be a means to anything else, because it has its own intrinsic value.

If you can trust, you remain open. People become closed as a defense, so that nobody can deceive them or take advantage of them. Let them take advantage of you! If you insist on continuing to trust, then a beautiful flowering happens, because then there is no fear. The fear is that people will deceive—but once you accept that, there is no fear, so there is no barrier to your opening. The fear is more dangerous than any harm anybody can do to you. This fear can poison your whole life. So remain open, and just trust innocently, unconditionally.

You will flower, and you will help others to flower once they become aware that they have not been deceiving you a bit, but they have been deceiving themselves. You cannot go on deceiving a person endlessly if that person continues to trust you. The very trust will throw you back to yourself again and again.

30.
EMPTINESS

The greatest day in life is when you cannot find anything in you
to throw out; all has already been thrown out, and there is only pure
emptiness. In that emptiness you will find yourself.

Meditation simply means becoming empty of all the contents of the mind: memory, imagination, thoughts, desires, expectations, projections, moods. One has to go on emptying oneself of all these contents. The greatest day in life is when you cannot find anything in you to throw out; all has already been thrown out, and there is only pure emptiness. In that emptiness you will find yourself; in that emptiness you find your pure consciousness.

That emptiness is empty only as far as mind is concerned. Otherwise it is overflowing, full of being—empty of mind but full of consciousness. So don't be afraid of the word *empty;* it is not negative. It negates only the unnecessary luggage, which you are carrying just from old habit, which does not help but only hinders, which is just a weight, a mountainous weight. Once this weight is removed you are free from all boundaries, you become as infinite as the sky. This is the experience of God or Buddhahood or whatever word one likes. Call it dhamma, call it Tao, call it truth, call it nirvana—they all mean the same thing.

31.
EXPERIMENTATION

*Always remain open and experimentative, always ready to walk
a path you have never walked before. Who knows? Even if it proves
useless, it will be an experience.*

Edison was working on a certain experiment for almost three
years, and he had failed seven hundred times. All his colleagues and
his students became completely frustrated. Every morning he
would come to the lab happy and bubbling with joy, ready to start
again. It was too much: seven hundred times and three years
wasted! Everybody was almost certain that nothing was going to
come of the experiment. The whole thing seemed to be useless,
just a whim.

They all gathered and told Edison, "We have failed seven hundred times. We have not achieved anything. We have to stop."

Edison laughed uproariously. He said, "What are you talking
about? Failed? We have succeeded in knowing that seven hundred
methods won't be of any help. We are coming closer and closer to
the truth every day! If we had not knocked on those seven hundred
doors, we would have had no way of knowing. But now we are certain that seven hundred doors are false. This is a great achievement!'"

This is the basic scientific attitude: If you can decide that something is false, you are coming closer to the truth. Truth is not available in the market so that you can go directly and order it. It is not
ready-made, available. You have to experiment. So always remain
experimentative. And never become smug. Never think that whatever you are doing is perfect. It is never perfect. It is always possible to improve on it; it is always possible to make it more perfect.

32.
PROBLEMS

If you can function as if you have no problems, you will find that you don't have any problems! All problems are make-believe; you believe in them, and that's why they are there.

It is autohypnosis: You go on repeating that you are this way and that way, that you are inadequate or incapable. You repeat this, and it becomes a mantra; it sinks into your heart and becomes reality.

Just try to function as if you have no problems, and suddenly you will see that you have a totally different quality: you don't have any problems! And then it is up to you whether you take up the problems again or you drop them forever. A problem can be dropped so easily if you understand that it is you holding the problem, not the problem holding you. But we cannot live without problems, so we go on creating them. One feels so alone without problems—there is nothing left to be done. With the problem you feel very happy—something has to be done, and you have to think about it; it gives you an occupation.

This continuous idea that you are inadequate and you are incapable and you are this and that—this is basically very egoistic. You want to be so adequate, but why? You want to be really tremendously capable, but why? Why can't you be satisfied with all the inadequacies and limitations that are there? Once you accept them, you will see that you start to flow more easily.

33.
REMAIN IGNORANT

Don't have any attitude about fear; in fact, don't call it fear.
The moment you have called it fear, you have taken an attitude about it.

This is one of the most essential things—to stop giving things names. Just watch the feeling, the way it is. Allow it, and don't give it a label—remain ignorant. Ignorance is a tremendously meditative state. Insist on being ignorant, and don't allow the mind to manipulate. Don't allow the mind to use language and words, labels and categories, because this starts a whole process. One thing is associated with another, and it goes on and on.

Simply look—don't call it fear. Become afraid and tremble—that is beautiful. Hide in a corner, get under a blanket. Do what an animal does when it is afraid. If you allow fear to take possession of you, your hair will stand on end! Then for the first time you will know what a beautiful phenomenon fear is. In that turmoil, in that cyclone, you will come to know that there is still a point somewhere within you that is absolutely untouched.

34.
LIFE IS SIMPLE

Life is very simple. Even trees are living it; it must be simple. Why has it become so complicated for us? Because we can theorize about it.

To be in the thick of life, in the intensity and passion of life, you will have to drop all philosophies of life. Otherwise you will remain clouded in your words.

Have you heard the famous anecdote about a centipede? It was a beautiful sunny morning, and the centipede was happy and must have been singing in her heart. She was almost drunk with the morning air. A frog sitting by the side was very puzzled—he must have been a philosopher. He asked, "Wait! You are doing a miracle. A hundred legs! How do you manage? Which leg comes first, which comes second, third—and so on, up to a hundred? Don't you get puzzled? How do you manage? It looks impossible to me." The centipede said, "I have never thought about it. Let me brood." And standing there, she started trembling, and she fell down on the ground. She herself became so puzzled—a hundred legs! How was she going to manage?

Philosophy paralyzes people. Life needs no philosophy, life is enough unto itself. It needs no crutches; it needs no support, no props. It is enough unto itself.

35.
CENTERING

Don't create conflict between going astray and remaining centered. Float.
If you become afraid of going astray, there is a greater chance that you
will go astray; whatever you try to suppress becomes significant.

Whatever you try to deny becomes very attractive. So don't create any condemnation of going astray. In fact, go with it. If it is happening, allow it to happen; there is nothing wrong in it. There must be something in it, and that's why it is happening. Sometimes even going astray is good.

A person who really wants to remain centered should not worry about centering. If you worry about it, the worry will never allow you to be centered; you need an unworried mind. Going astray is good; there is nothing wrong in it.

Stop fighting with existence. Stop all conflict and the idea of conquering—surrender. And when you surrender, what can you do? If the mind goes astray, you go; if it doesn't go, that too is okay. Sometimes you will be centered, and sometimes you will not. But deep down you will always remain centered because there is no worry. Otherwise everything can become a worry. Then going astray becomes just like a sin one is not to commit—and the problem is created again.

Never create duality within you. If you decide to always be true, then there will be an attraction to being untrue. If you decide to be nonviolent, then violence will become the sin. If you decide to be celibate, then sex will become the sin. If you try to be centered, going astray will become a sin—that's how all religions have become stupidities. Accept, go astray; there is nothing wrong in it.

36.
NEEDS AND DESIRES

Desires are many, needs are few. Needs can be fulfilled; desires never.
A desire is a need gone crazy. It is impossible to fulfill it. The more you
try to fulfill it, the more it goes on asking and asking.

There is a Sufi story that when Alexander died and reached heaven, he was carrying all his weight—his whole kingdom, gold, diamonds—of course not in reality, but as an idea. He was burdened too much by being Alexander.

The gatekeeper started laughing and asked, "Why are you carrying such a burden?" Alexander said, "What burden?" So the gatekeeper gave him a scale and put an eye on one side of the scale. He told Alexander to put all his weight, all his greatness, treasures, and kingdom, on the other side. But that one eye still remained heavier than Alexander's whole kingdom.

The gatekeeper said, "This is a human eye. It represents human desire. It cannot be fulfilled, however great the kingdom and however great your efforts." Then the gatekeeper threw a little dust into the eye. The eye immediately blinked and lost all its weight.

A little dust of understanding has to be thrown into the eye of desire. The desire disappears and only needs remain, which are not weighty. Needs are very few, and they are beautiful. Desires are ugly and they make monsters of men. They create mad people. Once you start learning how to choose the peaceful, a small room is enough; a small quantity of food is enough; a few clothes are enough; one lover is enough.

37.
SECURITY

There is no security anywhere. Life is insecure, and there is no ground to it—it is groundless.

In the very asking for security, you create the problem. The more you ask the more insecure you will be, because insecurity is the very nature of life. If you don't ask for security, then you will never be worried about insecurity. As trees are green, life is insecure. If you start asking for trees to be white, there is a problem. The problem is created by you, not by the trees—they are green and you ask them to be white! They cannot perform in that way.

Life is insecure, and so is love. And it is good that it is so. Life can be secure only if you are dead; then everything can be certain. Underneath a rock there is ground. Underneath a flower there is none; the flower is insecure. With a small breeze the flower may disperse; the petals may fall and disappear. It is a miracle that the flower is there. Life is a miracle—because there is no reason for it to be. It is simply a miracle that you are, otherwise there is every reason for you not to be. Maturity comes to you only when you accept this, and not only accept, but start rejoicing in it.

38.
UNCONDITIONAL

Once you know what love is, you are ready to give; the more you give,
the more you have it. The more you go on showering on others,
the more love springs up in your being.

Love never bothers much about whether the other is worthy of receiving or not. This is a miserly attitude, and love is never a miser. The cloud never bothers about whether the earth is worthy. It rains on the mountains, it rains on the rocks; it rains everywhere and anywhere. It gives without any conditions, without any strings attached.

And that's how love is: It simply gives, it enjoys giving. Whoever is willing to receive, receives it. He need not be worthy, he need not fit any special category, he need not fulfill any qualifications. If all these things are required, then what you are giving is not love; it must be something else. Once you know what love is, you are ready to give; the more you give, the more you have. The more you go on showering on others, the more love springs up in your being.

Ordinary economics is totally different: If you give something, you lose it. If you want to keep something, avoid giving it away. Collect it, be miserly. Just the opposite is the case with love: If you want to have it, don't be miserly; otherwise it will go dead, it will become stale. Go on giving, and fresh sources will become available. Fresh streams will flow into your being. The whole of existence starts pouring into you when your giving is unconditional, when it is total.

39.
ELECTRIC MIND

Mind goes on changing from negative to positive, from positive to
negative. Those two polarities are as basic to the mind as negative
and positive poles are to electricity. With one pole, electricity cannot
exist—and mind also cannot exist.

Deep down, mind is electrical. That's why the computer can do
its work and sometimes will do it better than the human mind.
Mind is just a bio-computer. It has these two polarities and goes
on moving.

So the problem is not that sometimes you feel magic moments
and sometimes you feel dark moments. The darkness of the dark
moments will be proportionate to the magicalness of the magical
moments. If you reach a higher peak in positivity, then you will
touch the lowest in your negativity. The higher the reach of the
positive, the lower will be the depth of the negative. So the higher
you reach, the deeper abyss you will have to touch.

This has to be understood: If you try not to touch the lower
rungs, then higher peaks will disappear. Then you move on plain
ground. That's what many people have managed to do; afraid of
the depth, they have missed the peaks. One has to take risks. You
have to pay for the peak, and the price is to be paid by your depth,
your low moments. But it is worth it. Even one moment at the
peak, the magic moment, is worth a whole life in the darkest
depths. If you can touch heaven for one moment, you can be ready
to live for the whole of eternity in hell. And it is always proportionate, half and half, fifty-fifty.

40.
AT WORK

One has to remember that the people who are associates at work
are not at all concerned with your inner life. That is your work to do;
they have their own inner lives to work out.

Your work colleagues have their own negative moods, their own personal problems and anxieties, just as everybody else, including you, has. But when you are in a working situation with somebody, you need not bring these things in, because if they start bringing in all their negativities and you start bringing in all of yours, it will be a never-ending process.

If you are feeling negative, do something. For example, write out a very negative thing and burn it. Go to the therapy room, beat a pillow and throw it. Do a terrible dance! You have to work it out; it is your problem.

And once in a while it is good to ask whoever is working with you whether you have been negative, if they are feeling hurt. Because sometimes you may not know that you have been negative. Small gestures, just a word, even a silence, can be hurtful; the way you look at someone can be hurtful. So once in a while ask their forgiveness. Tell them, "Every time I ask you, you have to be honest. Just tell me, because I am a human being and sometimes things can go wrong from my side and I have to put them right."

41.
MEDIOCRITY

Never settle for any mediocrity, because that is a sin against life.
Never ask that life should be without risk, and never ask for security,
because that is asking for death.

Many people have decided to live on the plain ground, safe, not taking any risks. They never fall to the depths, they never rise to the heights. Their life is a dull affair, a drab thing, monotonous—with no peaks, no valleys, no nights, no days. They just live in a gray world, without colors—the rainbow doesn't exist for them. They live a gray life, and by and by they also become gray and mediocre.

The greatest danger is to reach to the greatest peaks of godliness and to fall to the greatest depths of hell. Become a traveler between these two, unafraid. By and by you will come to understand that there is a transcendence. By and by you will come to know that you are neither the peak nor the depth, neither the peak nor the valley. By and by you will come to know that you are the watcher, the witness. Something in your mind goes to the peak, something in your mind goes to the valley, but something beyond is always there—just watching, just taking note of it—and that is you.

Both polarities are in you, but you are neither—you tower higher than both. The ground is high and low, both heaven and hell are there, but you are somewhere far from both. You simply watch the whole game of it, the whole play of consciousness.

42.

POSTPONING

Life is very short, and much has to be learned; those people
who go on postponing go on missing.

Ask yourself constantly whether you are moving into more blissful states or not. If you are moving into more and more blissful
states, you are on the right track. Go into it more, have more of it.
And if you are feeling miserable, then look: Somewhere you have
fallen off track, gone astray. You have been distracted by something;
you are no longer natural, you are alienated from nature; hence,
misery. Look, analyze, and whatever you find to be the cause of
misery, drop it. And don't postpone for tomorrow; drop it immediately.

Life is very short, and much has to be learned; those people
who go on postponing go on missing. Today you will postpone for
tomorrow and again tomorrow you will postpone. Slowly, slowly
postponement becomes your habit. And it is always today that it
comes; tomorrow never comes. So you can go on postponing forever. Whenever you see that something is creating misery, drop it
then and there—don't hold it for a single moment. This is courage:
courage to live, courage to risk, courage to adventure. And only
those who are courageous are one day rewarded by the whole, by
light, by love, bliss, and benediction.

43.
BELIEVE IN POETRY

Life is an inexhaustible treasure,
but only the heart of the poet can know it.

Love is the only poetry there is. All other poetry is just a reflection of it. The poetry may be in sound, the poetry may be in stone, the poetry may be in the architecture, but basically these are all reflections of love caught in different mediums. But the soul of poetry is love, and those who live love are the real poets. They may never write poems, they may never compose any music—they may never do anything that people ordinarily think of as art—but those who live love, love utterly, totally, are the real poets. Religion is true if it creates the poet in you. If it kills the poet and creates the so-called saint, it is not religion. It is pathology, a kind of neurosis garbed in religious terms. Real religion always releases poetry in you, and love and art and creativity; it makes you more sensitive. You throb more, your heart has a new beat to it. Your life is no longer a boring, stale phenomenon. It is constantly a surprise, and each moment opens new mysteries. Life is an inexhaustible treasure, but only the heart of the poet can know it. I don't believe in philosophy, I don't believe in theology, but I believe in poetry.

44.
SELF-IMPROVEMENT

Self-improvement is the way to hell. All efforts to make something
out of yourself—something of an ideal—are going to create more
and more madness. Ideals are the base of all madness, and all
of humanity is neurotic because of too many ideals.

Animals are not neurotic because they don't have any ideals. Trees
are not neurotic because they don't have any ideals. They are not
trying to become somebody else. They are simply enjoying whatever they are.

You are you. But somewhere deep down you want to become a
Buddha or a Jesus, and then you go around in a circle that will be
unending. Just see the point of it—you are you. And the whole, or
existence, wants you to be you. That's why existence has created
you, otherwise it would have created a different model. It wanted
you to be here at this moment. It did not want Jesus to be here in
place of you. And existence knows better. The whole always knows
better than the part.

So just accept yourself. If you can accept yourself, you have
learned the greatest secret of life, and then everything comes on its
own. Just be yourself. There is no need to pull yourself up; there
is no need to be a different height from what you are already. There
is no need to have another face. Simply be as you are, and in deep
acceptance of it, and a flowering will happen and you will go on
becoming more and more yourself.

Once you drop the idea of becoming somebody, there is no tension. Suddenly all tension disappears. You are here, luminous, in this
moment. And there is nothing else to do but to celebrate and enjoy.

45.
HOME

Unless we find our real home we have to go on traveling,
we have to go on journeying. And the most surprising thing
is that the real home is not far away.

We make many homes, and we never look at the real home. The homes that we make are all arbitrary; they are sandcastles or palaces made of playing cards: just toys to play with. They are not real homes, because death destroys them all.

The definition of the real home is that which is eternal. Only God is eternal; everything else is temporary. The body is temporary, the mind is temporary; money, power, prestige—all are temporary. Don't make your home in these things. I am not against these things. Use them, but remember that they are just a caravansary; they are good for an overnight stay, but in the morning we have to go.

We go on missing our real home because it is very close; it is not even close, it is within ourselves. Search for it within. Those that have gone in have always found it.

46.
CONFUSION

Drop your fixed ideas. Then you will be able to enjoy confusion more. And it will not be confusion—it will be creative chaos. We need a creative chaos in the heart to give birth to dancing stars. There is no other way.

If you have fixed ideas, life is going to create much confusion for you, because life never believes your ideas. It goes on muddling things. It goes on meddling with people. It goes on playing tricks. It is not a drawing room in which you fix your furniture and it remains the same. It is a very wild phenomenon.

God is very chaotic. God is not an engineer or an architect, a scientist or a mathematician. God is a dreamer, and in a world of dreams, everything is muddled. Your boyfriend suddenly becomes a horse.... In a dream you never argue and never say, "What has happened? Just a moment before you were my boyfriend and now you have become a horse!" In a dream, you accept. Not even a suspicion about what is happening arises, because in a dream you don't carry your ideas.

But while you are awake it will be impossible for you to see that your boyfriend is turning into a horse. And boyfriends many times turn into horses! The face may remain the same but the energy becomes different. Then you feel confused.

I have never really come across any person who is confused. Rather I come across people who have fixed ideas. The more fixed the idea, the more confusion there will be.

If you want to be unconfused, drop the idea—not that confusion will change, but it will not look like confusion at all. It is just life, alive.

47.
POVERTY

Sooner or later the outer poverty is going to disappear—
we now have enough technology to make it disappear—
and the real problem is going to arise.

The really poor people are those who are missing love; and the whole earth is full of those poor people who are starved. Sooner or later the outer poverty is going to disappear—we now have enough technology to make it disappear—and the real problem is going to arise. The real problem will be inner poverty. No technology can help. We are capable of feeding people now—but who will feed the spirit, the soul? Science cannot do that. Something else is needed, and that is what I call religion. Then science has done its work; only then can true religion enter the world.

Up to now religion has been only a freak phenomenon—once in a while a Buddha, a Jesus, a Krishna appears. These are exceptional people; they don't represent humanity. They simply herald a possibility, a future. But that future is coming closer. Once science has released the potential powers of matter and human beings are physically satisfied—have shelter, have enough food, have enough education—then for the first time they will see that now a new food is needed. That food is love, and science cannot provide it. That can only be done by religion. Religion is the science of love.

48.

FORGIVING YOUR PARENTS

To forgive one's parents is one of the most difficult things,
because they have given birth to you—how can you forgive them?

Unless you start loving yourself, unless you come to a state in which you are thrilled by your being—how can you thank your parents? It is impossible. You will be angry—they have given birth to you, and they didn't even ask you first. They have created this horrible person. Why should you suffer because they decided to give birth to a child? You were not a party to it. Why have you been dragged into the world? Hence the rage.

If you come to a point where you can love yourself, where you feel really ecstatic that you are, where your gratefulness knows no limitation, then suddenly you feel great love arising for your parents. They have been the doors for you to enter into existence. Without them this ecstasy would not have been possible—they have made it possible.

If you can celebrate your being—and that is the whole purpose of my work, to help you to celebrate your being—then suddenly you can feel gratitude for your parents, for their compassion, their love. You can not only feel grateful, you also forgive them.

49.
FAILURE

You cannot be a failure; life does not allow failure.
And because there is no goal, you cannot be frustrated.

If you feel frustrated, it is because of the mental goal you have imposed on life. By the time you have reached your goal, life has left it; just a dead shell of the ideals and the goals remain, and you are frustrated again. The frustration is created by you.

Once you understand that life is never going to be confined to a goal, goal oriented, then you flow in all directions with no fear. Because there is no failure, there is no success either—and then there is no frustration. Then each moment becomes a moment in itself; not that it is leading somewhere, not that it has to be used as a means to some end—it has intrinsic value.

Each moment is a diamond, and you go from one diamond to another—but there is no finality to anything. Life remains alive… there is no death. Finality means death, perfection means death, reaching a goal means death. Life knows no death—it goes on changing its forms, shapes. It is an infinity, but to no purpose.

50.
LOVE-HATE

Whenever you love something, you hate it too.
You will find excuses for why you hate, but they are not relevant.

Never let your hate decide anything. Knowing well there is hate, always let love decide. I'm not saying to suppress hate, but never let it decide. Let it be there, let it have a secondary place. Accept it, but never let it be decisive.

Neglect it, and it dies of its own accord. Pay more attention to love; just let love decide. Sooner or later, love will take possession of your whole being, and there will be no place left for hate.

51.
SMOKELESS FLAME

Wherever you see light, feel worshipful. The temple is there.

Look at the mysteries of light. Just a small flame is the most mysterious thing in the world, and the whole of life depends on it.

The same flame is burning in you. That's why continuous oxygen is needed, because the flame cannot burn without oxygen. This is why yoga emphasizes breathing deeply, breathing more and more oxygen so that your life burns deeper and the flame becomes clearer and no smoke arises in you—so that you can attain a smokeless flame.

52.
THE DOOR

All relationship is imagination, because whenever you go out of yourself,
you go only through the door of imagination. There is no other door.

The friend, the enemy: both are your imagination. When you stop imagination completely, you are alone, absolutely alone. Once you understand that life and all its relationships are imagination, you don't go against life, but your understanding helps you to make your relationships richer. Now that you know that relationships are imagination, why not put more imagination into them? Why not enjoy them as deeply as possible? When the flower is nothing but your imagination, why not create a beautiful flower? Why settle for an ordinary flower? Let the flower be of emeralds and diamonds.

Whatever you imagine, let it be that. Imagination is not a sin, it is a capacity. It is a bridge. Just as you cross a river and you make a bridge between this shore and that, so imagination functions between two people. Two beings project a bridge—call it love, call it trust—but it is imagination. Imagination is the only creative faculty in human beings, so whatever is creative is going to be imagination. Enjoy it and make it more and more beautiful. By and by you will come to a point where you don't depend on relationships. You share. If you have something, you share it with people, but you are content as you are. All love is imagination, but not in the condemnatory sense that the word is ordinarily used. Imagination is a divine faculty.

53.
STORMS

It is good to be available to the wind, to the rain, to the sun, because this is what life is. So rather than becoming worried about it, dance!

Growth means that you are absorbing something new every day, and that absorption is possible only if you are open. Now your windows and doors are open. Sometimes the rain comes in and the wind comes in, the sun comes, and life moves within you. So you will feel a few disturbances: Your newspaper will start moving in the wind, the papers on the table will be disturbed, and if the rain starts coming in, your clothes may become wet. If you have always lived in a closed room, you will ask, "What is happening?"

Something beautiful is happening. It is good to be available to the wind, to the rain, to the sun, because this is what life is. So rather than becoming worried about it, dance! Dance when the storm comes, because silence will follow. Dance when challenges come and disturb your life, because in responding to those challenges you will be growing to new heights. Remember, even suffering is a grace. If one can take it rightly it becomes a stepping stone.

People who have never suffered and have lived a convenient and comfortable life are almost dead. Their lives will not be like a sharp sword. It will not even cut vegetables. Intelligence becomes sharp when you face challenges. Pray every day to God, "Send me more challenges tomorrow, send more storms," and then you will know life at the optimum.

54.
RELATING

The more centered you become, the more relaxed you become,
the more possibility there is to enter into a relationship deeply.

It is you who goes into a relationship. If you are not there—if you
are tense, crippled, worried, and fragmented—who is going to go
deeply into a relationship? Because of our fragmentedness, we are
really afraid of getting into the deeper layers of a relationship,
because then our reality will be revealed. Then you will have to
open your heart, and your heart is just fragments. There is not one
person inside you—you are a crowd. If you really love another and
you open your heart, the other will think you are a public, not a
person—that is the fear.

That's why people go on having casual affairs. They don't want
to go deep; just hit-and-run, just touching the surface and escaping before anything becomes a commitment. You only have sex—
and that too is impoverished, superficial. Only boundaries meet,
but that is not love at all; it may be a bodily release, a catharsis, but
it is no more than that.

We can keep our masks if a relationship is not very intimate.
Then when you smile, there is no need for you to smile, just the
mask smiles. If you really want to go deep, there are dangers. You
will have to go naked—and naked means with all the problems
inside made known to the other.

55.
GOING ASTRAY

To know something, one has to lose it.

Everybody goes astray from their inner world, the inner space, and then by and by one feels starved, hungry for it. An appetite arises, a thirst is felt. The call comes from the innermost self to come back home, and one starts traveling. That's what being a seeker is. It is going to the warm inner space that you left one day. You will not be gaining something new. You will be gaining something that was always there, but it will still be a gain because now for the first time, you will see what it is. The last time you were in that space, you were oblivious to it.

One cannot be aware of something if one has not left it. So everything is good. Going astray is also good. To sin is also good, because that is the only way to become a saint.

56.
SETTLING DOWN

Lovers become afraid when things go smoothly.
They start feeling that perhaps love is disappearing.

When love settles, everything becomes smooth. Then love becomes more like friendship—and that has a beauty of its own. Friendship is the very cream, the very essence, of love. So settle! And don't be worried, otherwise sooner or later you will start creating trouble. The mind always wants to create trouble, because then it remains important; when there is no trouble, it becomes unimportant. The mind is just like the police department. If the city is calm and quiet, they feel bad: no robbery, no riot, no murders—nothing! They are not needed for anything. When everything is silent and peaceful, the mind has a fear, because if you really settle, the mind will be no more.

Just remember this. The mind has to go, because it is not the goal. The goal is to go beyond the mind. So help each other to be silent, and keep things going smoothly. If the other starts to get panicky, try to help.

57.
IN AN EGGSHELL

When you can come out of your conditioning, you are free, you are simply a human being. And that is real freedom! Then you don't carry a crust around you. The capsule has broken.

When the bird is in the egg, it cannot fly. When we are "Indian" or "German" or "English" or "American," we are in an eggshell. We cannot fly, cannot open our wings, cannot use our tremendous freedom that existence makes available.

There are layers upon layers of conditioning. One is conditioned as a German, one is conditioned as a Christian, and so on. One is conditioned as a man and another is conditioned as a woman. I am not talking about the biological difference—that's okay, that has nothing to do with conditioning—but the man is conditioned as a man. You continuously remember that you are a man, that you are not a woman, that you have to behave like a man—that you are not to cry, that tears are not to be allowed, that that is just feminine, it is not expected of you. This is conditioning, this is a crust around you.

A really free person is neither man nor woman—not that the biological difference disappears, but the psychological difference disappears. A free person is neither black nor white—not that the black becomes white and the white becomes black. The skin remains as it was before, but the psychological color is no longer there.

When all these things drop, you are unburdened. You walk one foot above the earth; for you, gravitation doesn't function anymore. You can open your wings and fly.

58.
LEAVE GOD OUT

Have you heard the famous Mulla Nasruddin story?

Mulla had saved up to buy a new shirt. He went to a tailor's shop, full of excitement. The tailor measured him and said, "Come back in a week, and—if Allah wills—your shirt will be ready."

Mulla contained himself for a week and then went back to the shop. The tailor said, "There has been a delay, but—if Allah wills—your shirt will be ready tomorrow."

The following day Nasruddin returned. "I am sorry," said the tailor, "but it is not quite finished. Try tomorrow, and—if Allah wills—it will be ready."

"How long will it take," asked the exasperated Nasruddin, "if you leave Allah out of it?"

It is better to leave God out. Ordinarily, whenever we don't know, we say "God knows!" In fact, to hide the fact that we don't know, we say "God knows!" It is better to say, "I don't know," because the moment you say "God knows," ignorance masquerades as knowledge. It is very dangerous.

59.

SIN

To repress anything is a crime: It cripples the soul.
It gives more attention to fear than to love, and that is what sin is.

To take more note of fear is sin, to take more note of love is virtue. And always remember to take more note of love, because it is through love that one reaches the higher peaks of life, to God. Out of fear one cannot grow. Fear cripples, paralyzes: It creates hell.

All paralyzed people—psychologically paralyzed, spiritually paralyzed—live life in hell. And how do they create it? The secret is that they live in fear; they only do a certain thing when there is no fear, but then there is nothing left worth doing. All that is worth doing has certain fears around it. If you fall in love, there is fear because you may be rejected. Fear says, "Don't fall in love, then nobody will reject you." That is true—if you don't fall in love, nobody will ever reject you—but then you will live a loveless existence, which is far worse than being rejected. And if one rejects you, somebody else will accept you. Those who live out of fear think mostly of not committing mistakes. They don't commit any mistakes, but they don't do anything else, either; their life is blank. They don't contribute anything to existence. They come, they exist—they vegetate, rather—and then they die.

60.

FREEDOM

Life is insecure—that means life is free. If there is security, then there will be bondage; if everything is certain, then there will be no freedom.

If tomorrow is fixed, then there can be security, but you have no freedom. Then you are just like a robot. You have to fulfill certain things that are already predestined. But tomorrow is beautiful, because tomorrow is total freedom. Nobody knows what is going to happen. Whether you will be breathing, whether you will be alive at all, nobody knows. Hence there is beauty, because everything is in a chaos, everything is a challenge, and everything exists as a possibility.

Don't ask for consolations. If you go on asking, you will remain insecure. Accept insecurity, and insecurity will disappear. This is not a paradox, it is a simple truth—paradoxical, but absolutely true. Up to now you have existed, so why be worried about tomorrow? If you could exist today, if you could exist yesterday, tomorrow will take care of itself too.

Don't think of the morrow, and move freely. A chaos at ease—that's how a person should be. When you carry a revolution within you, every moment brings a new world, a new life…every moment becomes a new birth.

61.

DEATH

Nothing is wrong in death.
Whenever it happens, it is a great rest.

When your body is completely spent, death is the only thing needed. Then it happens; then you move into another body. You may become a tree or a bird or a tiger or something else, and you go on moving. The existence gives you a new body when the old is spent.

Death is beautiful, but never ask for it, because when you ask for it, the quality of death changes toward suicide. Then it is no longer a natural death. You may not be committing suicide, but the very asking makes you suicidal. When alive, be alive; when dead, be dead. But don't overlap things. There are people who are dying and who go on clinging to life. That too is wrong, because when death has come, you have to go, and you have to go dancing. If you are asking for death, even thinking about it, then you are alive and clinging to the idea of death. It is the same in the reverse direction. Somebody who is dying and goes on clinging to life, does not want to die. Somebody is alive and wants to die: That is nonacceptance.

Accept whatever is there, and once you accept unconditionally, then everything is beautiful. Even pain has a purifying effect. So whatever comes on your way, just be thankful.

62.

MONODRAMA

It is very difficult to be religious, because you have to be
both the experimenter and the experimented upon,
both the scientist and the experiment.
There is no separation inside. You are playing a monodrama.

In an ordinary drama there are many actors, and the roles are divided. In a monodrama you are alone. All the roles have to be played by you.

A Zen monk used to call out loudly every morning, "Bokuju, where are you?" That was his own name. And he would answer, "Yes, sir? I am here."

Then he would say, "Bokuju, remember, another day is given. Be aware and alert and don't be foolish!" He would then say, "Yes, sir, I will try my best." And there was nobody else there!

His disciples started thinking he had gone mad. But he was only playing a monodrama. And that's the inner situation. You are the talker, you are the listener, you are the commander, and you are the commanded. It is difficult, because roles tend to get mixed, to overlap. It is very easy when somebody else is the led and you are the leader. If the roles are divided, things are clear-cut. Nothing overlaps; you have to finish your role, she has to finish hers. It is easy; the situation is arbitrary.

When you play both roles, the situation is natural, not arbitrary, and of course it is more complicated. But you will learn, by and by.

63.
BALANCE

When feeling and reason are balanced, one is free.
In that very balance is freedom, in that very balance
is equilibrium, tranquility, silence.

When the head is too much—and it is too much, it is very murderous—it does not allow anything that is not profitable to exist. And all joy is profitless, all joy is just playfulness; it has no purpose. Love is play, it has no purpose; so is dance, so is beauty. All that is significant to the heart is meaningless to reason.

So in the beginning one has to put much investment into the heart so the balance is achieved. One has almost to lean too much toward the heart. One has to go to the other extreme to create the balance. By and by one comes into the middle, but first one has to go to the other extreme, because reason has dominated too much.

64.
AUTHENTICITY

When you want something not to grow, just keep your back to it—
and it dies of its own accord. Just like a plant that is neglected,
not watered, it withers away and dies. So whenever you see something
that is phony, just put it aside.

If you are just about to smile, then suddenly you realize that it
would be phony, stop, even in the middle of the smile; relax your
lips and ask the person to excuse you. Tell them it was a phony
smile, and you are sorry. If a real smile comes, then it is okay; if it
doesn't, then that is also okay. What can you do? If it comes, it
comes; if it doesn't come, it doesn't. One cannot force it.

I'm not saying to just get out of the social formalities. I am saying
be watchful, and if you have to be false, be it consciously. Knowing
that this person is your boss and you have to smile, smile consciously, knowing well that it is phony. Let the boss be deceived—
you should not be deceived by your smile, that's the point. If you
smile unconsciously, the boss may not be deceived, because it is
difficult to deceive bosses—but you may be deceived. You will pat
yourself on the back and think you were perfectly good, such a
good boy—but there you are missing.

So if sometimes you think it is necessary—because it may be
necessary; life is complex and you are not alone; there are many
things that you have to do because the whole society exists on
phoniness—then be phony consciously. But in your relationships
where you can be true, don't allow phoniness.

65.
SATORI

Many times glimpses of satori, illumination, come, but you cannot hold them. Don't be worried that you could not hold them for longer. Forget all about it. Just remember the situation in which it happened and try to move into that situation again and again.

The experience is not important. How you were feeling, the situation, that is important. If you can re-create that situation, the experience will happen again. Experience is not important. The situation is important; how were you feeling? Flowing, loving...what was the situation? Music may have been on, people may have been dancing, eating. Remember the flavor of food, or some beautiful person just by your side, a friend talking to you—and suddenly.... Just remember the aroma in which it happened, the field. Try to create that field. Just sit silently and try to create that situation again.

Sometimes it happens accidentally. The whole science of yoga developed out of accidents. The first time, people were not looking for satori; how would they know about it? The first time it happened in a certain situation, and they became aware. They started seeking it, searching for methods to reach it. Naturally they became aware that if the situation could be created again, maybe the experience would follow. This is how, by trial and error, the whole science of yoga, tantra, and Zen developed. It took centuries to develop them.

But everybody has to find in what situation his satori starts bubbling, *samadhi* starts happening. Everybody has to feel their own way. If you are just a little alert, after a few experiences you will become able to create these situations.

66.
VERBS

Authenticity is a verb. All that is beautiful in life is a verb;
it is not a noun. Truth is a verb; it is not a noun. Love is not a noun;
it is a verb. Love is in loving. It is a process.

Authenticity is one of the greatest values in life. Nothing can be compared to it. In the old terminology, authenticity is also called truth. The new terminology calls it authenticity—which is better than truth, because when we talk about truth, it seems like a thing, like a phenomenon somewhere that you have to find. Truth looks more like a noun. But authenticity is a verb. It is not something waiting for you. You have to be authentic, only then is it there. You cannot discover it. You have to create it continuously by being true. It is a dynamic process.

Let this sink into you as deeply as possible, that all that is beautiful in life is a verb; it is not a noun. Truth is a verb; it is not a noun. Language is fallacious. Love is not a noun; it is a verb. Love is in loving. It is a process. When you love, only then is love there. When you don't love, it has disappeared. It exists precisely when it is dynamic. Trust is a verb, not a noun. When you trust, it is there. Trust means trusting and love means loving. Truth means being truthful.

67.
OKAY

Okay is not enough. Okay is not an ecstatic word; it is just lukewarm.
So feel blessed—and it is a question of feeling. Whatever you feel,
you become. It is your responsibility.

This is what we mean in India when we say, "It is your own karma."
Karma means your own action. It is what you have done to yourself. And once you understand that this is what you have done to
yourself, you can drop it. It is your attitude; nobody is forcing you
to feel that way. You have chosen it—maybe unconsciously, maybe
for some subtle reasons that feel good at the time but which turn
out to be bitter, but you have chosen it.

Once you understand that it is you, why settle for okayness?
That is not much, and your life will not be a life of song and dance
and celebration. Just by being okay, how will you celebrate? Just by
being okay, how will you love? Why be so miserly about it? But
there are many people who are stuck at okayness. They have lost all
energy just because of their ideas. Okayness is like a person who is
not sick but who is also not healthy, just so-so. He is not ill, but he
is not alive and healthy. He cannot celebrate.

I will suggest that if it is too difficult for you to feel blissful, at
least feel miserable. That will be something; at least energy will be
there. You can cry and weep. You may not be able to laugh, but tears
will be possible. Even that will be life. But okayness is very cold.
And if there is a question of choosing, why choose misery when you
can choose happiness?

68.

OPENNESS

Let winds come, let the sun come—everything is welcome.
Once you become attuned to living with an open heart, you will never
close. But a little time has to be given to it. And you have to maintain
that opening, otherwise it will close again.

Openness is vulnerability. When you are open, you feel at the same time that something wrong can enter you. That is not just a feeling; it is a possibility. That's why people are closed. If you open the door for the friend to come in, the enemy can also enter. Clever people have closed their doors. To avoid the enemy, they don't even open the door for the friend. But then their whole life becomes dead.

But there is nothing that could happen, because basically we have nothing to lose—and that which we have cannot be lost. That which can be lost is not worth keeping. When this understanding becomes tacit, one remains open.

I can see that even lovers are defending themselves. Then they cry and weep because nothing is happening. They have closed all the windows and are suffocating. No new light has come in and it is almost impossible to live, but still they drag on somehow. But they don't open, because fresh air seems to be dangerous.

So when you feel open, try to enjoy it. These are rare moments. In these moments move out so that you can have an experience of openness. Once the experience is there, solid in your hands, then you can drop the fear. You will see that being open is a treasure that you were losing unnecessarily. And the treasure is such that nobody can take it away. The more you share it, the more it grows. The more open you are, the more you *are*.

69.
GOALS

Life is goal-less... and that is the beauty of it!

If there were a goal to life, things would not be so beautiful, because one day you would come to the very end, and then everything after that would just be boring. There would be repetition, repetition, repetition; the same monotonous state would continue—and life abhors monotony. It goes on creating new goals—because it has none! Once you attain a certain state, life gives you another goal. The horizon goes on and on running in front of you; you never reach it, you are always on the way—always reaching, just reaching. And if you understand that, then the whole tension of the mind disappears, because the tension is to seek a goal, to arrive somewhere.

Mind is continuously hankering for arrival, and life is a continuous departure and arrival again—but arriving just to depart once more. There is no finality to it. It is never perfect, and that's its perfection. It is a dynamic process, not a dead, static thing.

Life is not stagnant—it is flowing and flowing, and there is no other shore. Once you understand this you start enjoying the journey itself. Each step is a goal, and there is no goal. This understanding, once it settles deep into your inner core, relaxes you. Then there is no tension because there is nowhere to go, so you cannot go astray.

70.
CONTROL

Life is beyond your control. You can enjoy it, but you cannot control it.
You can live it, but you cannot control it. You can dance it,
but you cannot control it.

Ordinarily we say that we breathe, and that's not true—life breathes us. But we go on thinking of ourselves as doers, and that creates the trouble. Once you become controlled, too controlled, you don't allow life to happen to you. You have too many conditions, and life cannot fulfill any.

Life happens to you only when you are unconditionally accepting it; when you are ready to welcome it. Whatever form it takes. But a person with too much control is always asking life to come in a certain form, to fulfill certain conditions—and life doesn't bother; it just passes these people by.

The sooner you break out of the confinement of control the better, because all control is from the mind. And you are greater than the mind. A small part is trying to dominate, trying to dictate. Life goes on moving, and you are left far behind, and then you are frustrated. The logic of the mind is such that it says, "Look, you didn't control it well, that's why you missed, so control more."

The truth is just the opposite: People miss many things because of too much control. Be like a wild river, and much you cannot even dream, cannot even imagine, cannot even hope, is available just around the corner, just within reach. But open your hand; don't go on living the life of a fist, because that is the life of control. Live the life of an open hand. The whole sky is available; don't settle for less.

71.
STRONG WINDS

Those strong winds that hit hard are not really enemies.
They help to integrate you. They look as if they will uproot you,
but in fighting with them you become rooted.

Think of a tree. You can bring a tree inside the room and, in a way, it will be protected; the wind will not be so hard on it. When storms are raging outside, it will be out of danger. But there will be no challenge; everything will be protected. You can put it in a hothouse, but by and by the tree will start becoming pale, it will not be green. Something deep inside it will start dying—because challenge shapes life.

Those strong winds that hit hard are not really enemies. They help to integrate you. They look as if they will uproot you, but in fighting with them you become rooted. You send your roots even deeper than the storm can reach and destroy. The sun is very hot and it seems it will burn, but the tree sucks up more water to protect itself against the sun. It becomes greener and greener. Fighting with natural forces, it attains to a certain soul. The soul arises only through struggle.

If things are very easy, you start dispersing. By and by you disintegrate, because integration is not needed at all. You become like a pampered child. So when a challenge happens, live it courageously.

72.
START AGAIN

Just look around: Whatever you have been doing, that is not the end.
Open it up again, let the journey start again. Bring in new things—
sometimes bizarre, eccentric, sometimes almost crazy; they all help.

All inventors are thought to be crazy people, eccentric. They are, because they go beyond the limit. They find their own pathways. They never walk on the superhighway, that is not for them; they move into the forest. There is danger: They may be lost, they may not be able to come back again to the crowd, they are losing contact with the herd....

Sometimes you may fail. I am not saying that you may not fail— with the new there is always danger—but then there will be thrill. And that thrill is worth the risk—at any price it is worth it. So either bring something new into the old work so that it becomes new and growing, is not mechanical but becomes organic, or change: Change the whole thing and start doing something absolutely new. Go back to the ABCs and become a potter or a musician or a dancer or a vagabond—anything will do!

Ordinarily the mind will say that this is wrong—you are now established, you have a certain name, a certain fame, and so many people know you, your work is going well and is paying you well, things are settled, why bother? Your mind will say this. Never listen to the mind; the mind is in the service of death.

73.
LOVE

Every lover feels that something is missing, because love
is unfinished. It is a process, not a thing. Every lover is bound
to feel that something is missing. Don't interpret this wrongly.
It simply shows that love in itself is dynamic.

Love is just like a river, always moving. In the very movement is the
life of the river. Once it stops it becomes a stagnant thing; then it
is no longer a river. The very word *river* shows a process, the very
sound of it gives you the feeling of movement.

Love is a river. So don't think that something is missing; it is
part of love's process. And it is good that it is not completed. When
something is missing you have to do something about it—that is a
call from higher and higher peaks. Not that when you reach them
you will feel fulfilled; love never feels fulfilled. It knows no fulfillment, but it is beautiful because then it is alive forever and ever.

And you will always feel that something is not in tune. That too
is natural, because when two persons are meeting, two different
worlds are meeting. To expect that they will fit perfectly is to expect
the impossible, and that will create frustration. At the most there
are a few moments when everything is in tune, rare moments.

This is how it has to be. Make all efforts to create that intune-
ness, but always be ready if it doesn't happen perfectly. And don't
be worried about it, otherwise you will fall more and more out of
tune. It comes only when you are not worried about it. It happens
only when you are not tense about it, when you are not even
expecting it—just out of the blue.

74.
INSIGHT

Every insight, even if it is very hard to accept, helps.
Even if it goes against the grain, it helps.
Even if it is very ego shattering, it helps. Insight is the only friend.

One should be ready to see into any fact, without rationalizing in any way. Out of this insight, many things happen. But if you have missed the first insight into the matter, you will be puzzled and confused. Many problems will be there, but there will be no solution in sight, because from the very first step a truth has not been accepted. So you are falsifying your own being.

There are many people who have so many problems, but those problems are not real. Ninety-nine percent of problems are false. So if they are not solved, you are in trouble, and even if they are solved, nothing will happen, because they are not your real problems. When you have solved some false problems, you will create others. So the first thing is to penetrate into what is the real problem and to see it as it is. To see the false as false is the beginning of being able to see truth as truth.

75.
WITHDRAW UNLOVE

We don't love. But that is not the only problem. We unlove.
So first start dropping anything that you feel is unloving.
Any attitude, any word that you have used out of habit
but that now suddenly you feel is cruel—drop it!

Always be ready to say, "I am sorry." Very few people are capable of saying this. Even when they appear to be saying it, they are not. It may be just a social formality. To really say "I am sorry" is a great understanding. You are saying that you have done something wrong—and you are not just trying to be polite. You are withdrawing something. You are withdrawing an act that was going to happen, you are withdrawing a word that you had uttered.

So withdraw unlove, and as you do you will see many more things—that it is not really a question of how to love. It is only a question of how not to love. It is just like a spring covered with stones and rocks. You remove the rocks, and the spring starts flowing. It is there.

Every heart has love, because the heart cannot exist without it. It is the very pulse of life. Nobody can be without love; that is impossible. It is a basic truth that everyone has love, has the capacity to love and to be loved. But some rocks—wrong upbringing, wrong attitudes, cleverness, cunningness, and a thousand and one things—are blocking the path.

Withdraw unloving acts, unloving words, unloving gestures, and then suddenly you will catch yourself in a very loving mood. Many moments will come when suddenly you will see that something is bubbling—and there was love, just a glimpse. And by and by those moments will become longer.

76.
NOT INSTANT COFFEE

Love is not a thing you can do.
But when you do other things, love will happen.

There are small things you can do—sitting together, looking at the moon, listening to music—nothing directly to do with love. Love is very delicate, fragile. If you look at it, gaze at it directly, it will disappear. It comes only when you are unaware, doing something else. You cannot go directly, arrowlike. Love is not a target. It is a very subtle phenomenon; it is very shy. If you go directly, it will hide. If you do something directly, you will miss it.

The world has become very stupid about love. They want it immediately. They want it like instant coffee—whenever you want it, order it, and it is there.

Love is a delicate art; it is nothing you can do. Sometimes those rare blissful moments come...then something of the unknown descends. You are no longer on the earth; you are in paradise. Reading a book with your lover, both deeply absorbed in it, suddenly you find that a different quality of being has arisen around you both. Something surrounds you both like an aura, and everything is peaceful. But you were not doing anything directly. You were just reading a book, or just going for a long walk, hand-in-hand against the strong wind—and suddenly it was there. It always takes you unaware.

77.

TOGETHERNESS

People have completely forgotten the language of doing things together—or not doing anything but just being together.

People have forgotten how to just be. If they have nothing to do, they make love. Then nothing happens, and by and by they are frustrated by love itself. Man and woman are different—not only different, they are opposite; they cannot fit together. And that's the beauty—when they fit together it is a miracle, a magic moment. Otherwise they conflict and fight. That's natural and can be understood, because they have different minds. Their outlooks are polar opposites. They cannot agree on anything, because their ways are different, their logic is different.

To fit in a deep attunement, to fall in deep harmony, is almost miraculous. It is like a Kohinoor, a great diamond, and one should not ask for it every day. One should not ask for it as part of a routine. One should wait for it. Months, sometimes years, pass, and then suddenly it is there. And it is always out of the blue, uncaused.

Don't be worried—it will take care of itself. And don't become a seeker of love, or else you will miss it completely.

78.
CYPRESS
IN THE COURTYARD

The fact of this moment is what true religion is all about.
So if you are feeling sad, then that is the cypress in the courtyard.
Look at it... just look at it. There is nothing else to be done.

There is a very famous story about a Zen master, Chou Chou. A monk asked him, "What is true religion?"

It was a full-moon night and the moon was rising. The master remained silent for a long time; he didn't say anything. And then suddenly he came to life and said, "Look at the cypress in the courtyard." A beautiful cool breeze was blowing and playing with the cypress and the moon had just come above the branch. It was beautiful, incredible. It was almost impossible that it could be so beautiful.

But the monk said, "This was not my question. I'm not asking about the cypress in the courtyard, or about the moon or its beauty. My question has nothing to do with this. I am asking what true religion is. Have you forgotten my question?"

The master again remained silent for a long time. Then again he came to life and said, "Look at the cypress in the courtyard."

True religion consists of the here and now. The fact of this moment is what true religion is all about. So if you are feeling sad, then that is the cypress in the courtyard. Look at it... just look at it. There is nothing else to be done. That very look will reveal many mysteries. It will open many doors.

79.
DOING NOTHING

If you can do nothing, that is the best.

One needs much courage to do nothing. To do does not need much courage, because the mind is a doer. The ego always hankers to do something—worldly or otherworldly, the ego always wants to do something. If you are doing something, the ego feels perfectly right, healthy, moving, enjoying itself.

Nothing is the most difficult thing in the world, and if you can do that, that's the best. The very idea that we have to do something is basically wrong. We have to be, not to do. All that I suggest to people that they do is just to come to know the futility of doing, so that one day out of sheer tiredness they flop on the ground and they say, "Now it is enough! We don't want to do anything." And then the real work starts.

The real work is just to be, because all that you need is already given, and all that you can be you are. You don't know yet, that's true. So all that is needed is to be in such a silent space that you can fall into yourself and see what you are.

80.

TOMORROW

When you seek, the future is important, the goal is important. And when
you don't seek, the present moment is all there is. There is no future,
so you cannot postpone—you cannot say, "Tomorrow I will be happy."

Through tomorrow we destroy today; through the fictitious we
destroy the real. So you can say, "Okay, if I am sad today, there is
nothing to be worried about—tomorrow I will be happy." So today
can be tolerated, you can bear it. But if there is no tomorrow and
no future and nothing to seek for and find, there is no way to postpone—the very postponement disappears. Then it is up to you to
be happy or not to be happy. This moment, you have to decide.
And I don't think anybody is going to decide to be unhappy. Why?
For what?

The past is no more, and the future is never going to be, so this
is the moment. You can celebrate it: You can love, you can pray, you
can sing, you can dance, you can meditate, you can use it as you
want. And the moment is so small that if you are not very alert it
will slip out of your hands, it will be gone. So, to be, one has to be
very alert. Doing needs no alertness; it is very mechanical.

And don't use the word *wait*—because that means the future
has entered again from the back door. If you think that you should
just wait, then again you are waiting for the future. There is nothing to wait for. Existence is as perfect this moment as it will ever
be. It is never going to be more perfect.

81.
WORSHIP

One need not go to the church or to the temple or to the mosque;
wherever you are, be blissful, and there is the temple. The temple
is a subtle creation of your own energy. If you are blissful, you create
the temple around you.

In the temples we are just doing fake things. In the temples we offer flowers that are not ours; we borrow them, from the trees. They were already offered to God on the trees, and they were alive on the trees; you have killed them, you have murdered something beautiful, and now you are offering those murdered flowers to God and not even feeling ashamed.

I have watched. Particularly in India people don't take the flowers of their own plants: they pick them from the neighbors, and nobody can prevent them, because this is a religious country and they are picking flowers for religious purposes. People burn lights and candles, but they are not theirs; people burn incense and create fragrance, but all is borrowed.

The real temple is created by blissfulness—and all these things start happening on their own. If you are blissful you will find a few flowers are being offered, but those flowers are of your consciousness; there will be light, but that light is of your own inner flame; there will be fragrance, but that fragrance belongs to your very being. This is true worship.

82.

RIGHT AND WRONG

There is nothing right or wrong. It all depends on your standpoint.

The same thing can be right to one person and wrong to another, because it more or less depends on the person. The same thing can be right in one moment for a person, and in another moment it can be wrong, because it depends on the situation.

You have been taught in Aristotelian categories. This is right and that is wrong. This is white and that is black. This is God and that is the devil. These categories are false. Life is not divided into black and white. Much of it is more like gray.

And if you see very deeply, white is one extreme of gray, and black is another extreme, but the expanse is of gray. Reality is gray. It has to be so, because it is not divided anywhere. There are no watertight compartments anywhere. This is a foolish categorization, but it has been implanted in our minds.

So right and wrong go on changing continuously. Then what is there to do? If somebody wants to decide absolutely, he will be paralyzed; he will not be able to act. If you want to act only when you have an absolute decision about what is right, you will be paralyzed. You will not be able to act. One has to act, and to act in a relative world. There is no absolute decision, so don't wait for it. Just watch, see, and whatever you feel is right, do it.

83.
LISTENING

When friends offer advice, listen carefully.

One of the great things to be learned is listening. Listen very silently. Just don't listen indifferently. Don't listen as if you want others to stop talking and you are just listening to be polite because they are your friends. In that case it is better to tell them not to say anything because you are not in the mood to listen.

But when you are listening, really listen—be open, because your friends may be right. And even if they are wrong, listening to them will enrich you. You will learn more viewpoints, and it is always good to learn. So listen well, but always decide on your own.

Once a person has this relative understanding, things become very clear and easy. Otherwise people are very absolutist. They think in terms of absolutes: This is truth and whatever is against it is wrong. This attitude has crippled the whole earth—Hindus and Muslims and Christians are all fighting because everybody claims the absolute truth. But nobody has any claim on it. It is nobody's monopoly.

Truth is vast. Infinite are its facets and infinite are the ways to know it. Whatever we know is limited; it is just one part.

84.
PERHAPS

Hesitate more. Use the words maybe and perhaps more, and allow others the freedom to decide on their own.

Watch every word that you speak. Our language is such, our ways of speaking are such, that knowingly and unknowingly, we make absolute statements. Never do that. Say "perhaps" more. Hesitate more. Say "maybe" more, and allow others the freedom to decide on their own.

Try it for one month. You will have to be very alert, because speaking in absolutes is a deep-rooted habit, but if one is watchful, this habit can be dropped. Then you will see that arguments will drop and there will be no need to defend.

85.

SIBLING RIVALRY

The mother may love one child more, another a little less. You cannot expect that she should love absolutely equally; it is not possible.

Children are very perceptive. They can immediately see that somebody is liked more and somebody is liked less. They know that this pretension of the mother's loving them equally is just bogus. So an inner conflict, fight, ambition arises.

Each child is different. Somebody has a musical talent, somebody does not. Somebody has a mathematical talent and somebody has not. Somebody is physically more beautiful than another or one has a certain charm of personality and the other is lacking it. Then more and more problems arise, and we are taught to be nice, never to be true.

If children are taught to be true, they will fight it out, and they will drop it by fighting. They will be angry, they will fight and say hard things to one another, and then they will be finished, because children get rid of things very easily. If they are angry, they will be angry, hot, almost volcanic, but the next moment they will be holding each other's hands and everything will be forgotten. Children are very simple, but often they are not allowed that simplicity. They are told to be nice, whatever the cost. They are prohibited from being angry at each other: "She is your sister, he is your brother. How can you be angry?"

These angers, jealousies, and a thousand and one wounds go on collecting. But if you can face each other in true anger, jealousy, if you can fight it out, immediately afterward, in the wake of the fight, a deep love and compassion will arise. And that will be the real thing.

86.

DECISIONS

Respond to this moment. That's what responsibility is. Someone would like to marry you. Now you are puzzled as to whether to say yes or no, so you go to the I Ching.

It is your life—why leave it for someone who has written a book five thousand years ago to decide for you? It is better to decide on your own. Even if you err and go astray, it is still better to decide on your own. And even if you don't go astray and you have a more successful life through the *I Ching,* it is still not good, because you are avoiding responsibility.

Through responsibility, one grows. Take responsibility into your hands. These are ways of avoiding. Some people give responsibility to God, others to karma, others to destiny, others to the *I Ching.* But we become spiritual when we take the whole responsibility on our own shoulders.

The responsibility is tremendous, and your shoulders are weak, that I know. But when you take on the responsibility, they will become stronger. There is no other way for them to grow and become stronger.

87.
LIKE A BREEZE

Just as it comes, it goes; you cannot hold on to it, you cannot cling to it. The breeze comes like a whisper. It does not make noise, it does not make proclamations; it comes very silently, you cannot hear it—suddenly it is there. And that's how God comes—truth comes—bliss comes, love comes—they all come in a whisperlike manner, not with trumpets and drums. They suddenly come without even having an appointment, without even asking you, "May I come in?"—they just suddenly come. And that's how the breeze comes: One moment it is not there, another moment it is.

And the second thing: Just as it comes, it goes; you cannot hold on to it, you cannot cling to it. Enjoy it while it is there, and when it goes, let it go. Be thankful that it came. Don't hold any grudge, don't complain. When it goes, it goes—nothing can be done about it.

But we are all clingers. When love comes, we are very happy, but when it goes we are very hurt. That is being very unconscious—ungrateful—misunderstanding. Remember, it comes in one way, now it is going in the same way. It did not ask to come…why should it ask now if it can go? It was a gift from the beyond, mysterious, and it has to go in the same mysterious way. If one takes life as a breeze, then there is no clinging, no attachment—no obsession—one simply remains available, and whatever happens is good.

88.

WORK IN BALANCE

The best arrangement is to work in the world but not to be lost in it.
Work for five or six hours, and then forget all about it. Give at least two
hours to your inner growth, a few hours to your relationship, to love,
to your children, to your friends, to society.

Your profession should only be one part of life. It should not overlap into every dimension of your life, as ordinarily it does. A doctor becomes almost a twenty-four-hour doctor. He thinks about it,
he talks about it. Even when he is eating, he is a doctor. While he
is making love, he is a doctor. Then it is madness; it is insane. To
avoid this kind of madness, people escape. Then they become
twenty-four-hour seekers. Again they are making the same mistake—the mistake of being in anything for twenty-four hours.

My whole effort is to help you to be in the world and yet to be
a seeker. Of course this is difficult, because there will be more
challenge and situations. It is easier to be either a doctor or a seeker.
It will be difficult to be both, because that will give you many contradictory situations. But a person grows in contradictory situations. In the turmoil, in that clash of the contradictions, integrity
is born. My suggestion is that you work for five or six hours. Use
the remaining hours for other things: for sleep, for music, for
poetry, for meditation, for love, or for just fooling around. That
too is needed. If a person becomes too wise and cannot fool
around, he becomes heavy, somber, serious. He misses life.

89.
ACCIDENTS

Always think of the positive side of things: There was an accident, but you are still alive, so you transcended it.

Don't take too much note of accidents. Rather, take note that you survived. That is the real thing. You defeated those accidents, and you survived. So there is nothing to worry about. Always think of the positive side of things: The accident happened, but you are still alive, so you transcended it. You proved your mettle, you proved stronger than the accident.

But I can understand that fear will arise if such things happen again and again. You fall into wells, and do things like that, then the fear of death is bound to arise in the mind. But death is going to happen anyway, whether you fall into a well or not. The most dangerous place to avoid, if you want to avoid death, is your bed, because ninety-nine percent of deaths happen there—rarely in a well!

Death is going to happen anyhow; it doesn't matter how it happens. And if one has to choose between the bed and the well, I think the well is far better; it has something aesthetic about it.

90.
FEAR OF DEATH

There is no need to be afraid of death. Death is going to come; that is the only certain thing in life. Everything else is uncertain, so why be worried about the certainty?

Death is an absolute certainty. One hundred percent of people die—not ninety-nine percent, but one hundred. All the scientific growth and all the advances in medical science make no difference as far as people's deaths are concerned: one hundred percent of people still die, just as they used to die ten thousand years ago. Whoever is born, dies; there is no exception.

So about death we can be completely oblivious. It is going to happen, so whenever it happens it is okay. What difference does it make how it happens—whether you are knocked out in an accident or you just die in a hospital bed? It doesn't matter. Once you see the point that death is certain, these are only formalities—how one dies, where one dies. The only real thing is that one dies. By and by you will accept the fact. Death has to be accepted. There is no point in denying it; and nobody has ever been able to prevent it. So relax! While you are alive, enjoy it totally; and when death comes, enjoy that too.

91.
WATCHING TV

*The whole secret of meditation is to be neither for nor against, but uncon-
cerned, cool, without any likes and dislikes, without any choice.*

Meditation is a simple method. Your mind is like a TV screen.
Memories are passing, images are passing, thoughts, desires, a thousand and one things are passing; it is always rush hour. And the road
is almost like an Indian road: There are no traffic rules, and everybody is going in every direction. One has to watch the mind without any evaluation, without any judgment, without any choice,
simply watching unconcerned as if it has nothing to do with you
and you are just a witness. That is choiceless awareness.

If you choose, if you say, "This thought is good—let me have it,"
or "It is a beautiful dream, I should enjoy it a little more," if you
choose, you lose your witnessing. If you say, "This is bad, immoral,
a sin, I should throw it out," and you start struggling, again you
lose your witnessing. You can lose your witnessing in two ways:
either being for or against. And the whole secret of meditation is
to be neither for nor against, but unconcerned, cool, without any
likes and dislikes, without any choice. If you can manage even a
few moments of that witnessing, you will be surprised how ecstatic
you become.

92.
SIMPLE HEART

To be simple means shifting from the head to the heart.

Mind is very cunning; it is never simple. The heart is never cunning; it is always simple. To be simple means shifting from the head to the heart.

We live through the head. That's why our life becomes more and more complicated, more and more like a jigsaw puzzle: Nothing seems to fit. And the more we try to be clever, the more in a mess we are. That has been our history: We have gone more and more insane. Now the whole earth is almost like a madhouse. The time has come, if humanity is to survive at all, for a great shift to happen: We have to move from the head to the heart. Otherwise, the head is ready to commit suicide. It has created so much misery and so much boredom and so many problems that suicide seems the only way out. The whole earth is preparing for suicide. It is going to be a global suicide, unless a miracle happens.

And this is going to be the miracle—if it happens, this is the miracle—there will be a great shift, a radical change, in our very outlook: We will start living from the heart. We will drop the whole universe of the mind, and we will start afresh like small children.

Live from the heart. Feel more, think less, be more sensitive and less logical. Be more and more heartful, and your life will become a sheer joy.

93.
THE UNCONSCIOUS

The unconscious is nine times bigger than the conscious, so whatever
comes from the unconscious is overwhelming. That's why people are afraid
of their emotions, feelings. They hold them back, they are afraid they will
create chaos. They do, but chaos is beautiful!

There is a need for order, and there is a need for chaos too. When
order is needed, use order, use the conscious mind; when chaos is
needed, use the unconscious and let chaos be. A whole person, a
total person, is one who is capable of using both, who does not
allow any interference of the conscious into the unconscious or of
the unconscious into the conscious. There are things that you can
only do consciously. For example, if you are doing arithmetic or scientific work, you can do it only from the conscious. But love is not
like that, poetry is not like that; they come from the unconscious.
So you have to put your conscious aside.

It is the conscious that tries to hold things because it is afraid. It
seems to it that something big is coming, a tidal wave; will it be able
to survive? It tries to avoid it, it wants to escape, hide somewhere.
But that is not right. That's why people have become dull and dead.
All springs of life are in the unconscious.

94.
ELASTICITY

There are moments when people should be so relaxed,
so wildly relaxed, that they don't have any formalities to follow.

Once it happened that a great Chinese emperor went to see a great
Zen master. The Zen master was rolling on the floor and laughing,
and his disciples were laughing too—he must have told a joke or
something. The emperor was embarrassed. He could not believe his
eyes, because the behavior was so unmannerly; he could not prevent himself from saying so.

He told the master, "This is unmannerly! It is not expected of a
master like you; some etiquette has to be observed. You are rolling
on the floor, laughing like a madman."

The master looked at the emperor, who had a bow; in those old
days they used to carry bows and arrows. He said, "Tell me one
thing: Do you keep this bow always strained, stretched, tense, or
do you allow it to relax too?"

The emperor said, "If we keep it stretched continuously it will
lose elasticity, it will not be of any use then. It has to be left relaxed
so that whenever we need it, it has elasticity."

And the master said, "That's what I'm doing."

95.
POWER

If vulnerability grows along with power,
there is no fear that power will be abused.

People decide to live at the minimum so that there is no risk. When you have power, there is every risk that you will use it. When you have a sports car that can go two hundred miles per hour, there is a risk that one day you will decide to go that fast. The very thing that's possible becomes a challenge. So people live low-key lives, because if they know how much they can rise in power, how powerful they can be, then it will be difficult to resist. The temptation will be too much; they will want to go the whole way.

Patanjali, the founder of yoga, has written a whole chapter in his *Yoga Sutras* about power just to help every seeker to walk very carefully in this area, because great power will be available, and there will be great danger.

But my view is totally different. If vulnerability grows along with power, there is no fear; if power grows alone without vulnerability, then there is fear, then something can go wrong. That's what Patanjali is afraid of, because his methodology goes against vulnerability. It gives you power but no vulnerability. It makes you stronger and stronger, like steel, but not strong like a rose.

96.
BE AVAILABLE

A relationship is not something than just happens out of the blue.
You have to help it to happen.

With relationships, you can always throw the responsibility onto others: Nobody is coming to you, nobody is worth the bother, or you don't have feelings for anyone, so what can you do? But these things are very deeply related. If you move, you will start feeling. If you feel, you move more. These things go on helping each other, and one has to start from somewhere.

The world is full of so many beautiful people who are available. Everybody is seeking and searching for love. Just be available. Be a little outgoing, available; otherwise it will not happen.

With meditation there is a deep necessity for love. They are both like wings, and you cannot fly with one wing. If meditation is going well, suddenly you will see that love is missing. If love is going very well, suddenly you will see that meditation is missing. If nothing is going well, then it is okay. One settles with one's sadness, one's closedness. But when one wing has started moving, the other wing is needed.

97.
MAKING LOVE

*Love has to be cherished, tasted very slowly, so that it suffuses your being
and becomes such a possessing experience that you are no more.
It is not that you are making love—you are love.*

Love can become a bigger energy around you. It can transcend you
and your lover so that you are both lost in it. But for that you will
have to wait. Wait for the moment, and soon you will have the
knack of it. Let the energy accumulate, and let it happen on its
own. By and by, you will become aware when the moment arises.
You will start seeing the symptoms of it, the presymptoms, and
then there will be no difficulty.

If the moment does not arise in which you naturally fall into
lovemaking, then wait; there is no hurry. The Western mind is in
too much hurry—even while making love, it is something that has
to be done with and finished. That is a completely wrong attitude.

You cannot manipulate love. It happens when it happens. If it is
not happening, there is nothing to be worried about. Don't make
it an ego trip that somehow you have to make love. That is also
there in the Western mind; the man thinks he has to perform somehow. If he is not managing, he is not manly enough. This is foolish,
stupid. Love is something transcendental. You cannot manage it.
Those who have tried to have missed all its beauty. Then at the most
it becomes a sexual release, but all the subtle and deeper realms
remain untouched.

98.

MOVEMENT
AND STILLNESS

On the circumference is a dance, and at the center is absolute stillness.

Meditation is not just when you close your eyes and sit silently. In fact, deep down, when Buddha is sitting silently under his bodhi tree, not moving at all, there is a dance deep inside him—the dance of consciousness. It is invisible of course, but the dance is there, because nothing remains at rest. *Rest* is an unreal word; nothing corresponds to rest in reality.

It depends on us: We can make our life just a restlessness or a dance. Rest is not in the nature of things, but we can have a very chaotic restlessness—that is misery, that is neurosis, that is madness. Or we can be creative with this energy; then restlessness is no longer restless. It becomes smooth, graceful—it starts taking the form of a dance and a song. And the paradox is that when the dancer is totally in dance, there is rest—the impossible happens, the center of the cyclone. But that rest is not possible in any other way. When the dance is total, only then does that rest happen.

And there is a center to this whole dance. It cannot go on without a center. The periphery is dancing, the circumference is dancing—to know the center, the only way is to become a total dance. Only then, in contrast to the dance, does one suddenly become aware of something very quiet and very still.

99.
LOGIC

The modern mind has become too rational; it is caught in the net of logic. Much repression has happened because logic is a dictatorial force, totalitarian. Once logic controls you, it kills many things.

Logic is like Adolf Hitler or Joseph Stalin; it does not allow the opposite to exist, and emotions are opposite. Love, meditation, is opposite to logic. Religion is opposite to reason. So reason simply massacres them, kills them, uproots them. Then suddenly you see that your life is meaningless—because all meaning is irrational.

So first you listen to reason, and then you kill all that was going to give meaning to your life. When you have killed and you are feeling victorious, suddenly you feel empty. Now nothing is left in your hand, only logic. And what can you do with logic? You cannot eat it. You cannot drink it. You cannot love it. You cannot live it. It is just rubbish.

If you tend to be intellectual, it will be difficult. Life is simple, nonintellectual. The whole problem of humanity is metaphysics. Life is as simple as a rose —there's nothing complicated about it— and yet it is mysterious. Although there is nothing complicated about it, we are not able to comprehend it through the intellect. You can fall in love with a rose, you can smell it, you can touch it, you can feel it, you can even be it, but if you start dissecting it, you will only have something dead in your hands.

IOO.

LOW ENERGY

Don't think that anything is wrong with having low energy.
There is also nothing especially right about having high energy.

You can use high energy as a destructive force. That's what high-energy people all over the world have been doing all through the centuries. The world has never suffered from low-energy people. In fact, they have been the most innocent people. They cannot become a Hitler or a Stalin or a Mussolini. They cannot create world wars. They don't try to conquer the world. They are not ambitious. They cannot fight or become politicians. Low energy is wrong only if it becomes indifference. If it remains positive, nothing is wrong with it. The difference is like the difference between shouting, which is high energy, and whispering, which is low energy. There are moments when shouting is foolish and only whispering is right. There are a few people who are attuned to shouting and a few who are attuned to whispering.

101.

THE ONLY DUTY

One thing that one should always maintain—and it is the only duty—
is to be happy.

Make it a religion to be happy. If you are not happy, something must
be wrong and some drastic change is needed. Let happiness decide.

I am a hedonist. And happiness is the only criterion humankind
has. There is no other criterion. Happiness gives you the clue that
things are going well. Unhappiness gives you the indication that
things are going wrong and that a great change is needed somewhere.

102.

REMAIN UNEXPLAINED

Everything in life need not be explained.
We have no responsibility to explain anything to anybody.

All that is deep is always unexplained. That which you can explain
will be very superficial. There are things that you cannot explain.

If you fall in love with a person, how can you explain how you
have fallen in love? Whatever you answer will sound stupid—
because of his nose, because of her face, because of his voice. All
those things will not seem worth mentioning, but there is something there in the person. Those things may be part of why you
love the person, but that "something" is bigger than everything.
That something is more than the total.

103.
MAKING A PATH

When there has been a breakthrough, make it a point to relive it
again and again. Just sitting silently, remember it;
don't just remember it, relive it.

Start feeling the same as you felt when the breakthrough happened.
Let the vibrations surround you. Move into the same space, and
allow it to happen so it becomes, by and by, very natural to you.
You become so capable of bringing it back that any moment you
can do it.

Many valuable insights happen, but they need follow-up.
Otherwise they become just memories and you will lose contact
and will not be able to move into the same world. By and by, one
day you yourself will start disbelieving them. You may think that it
was a dream or a hypnosis or some trick of the mind. That's how
humanity has lost many beautiful experiences.

Everybody comes to beautiful spaces in life. But we never try to
make a path to those beautiful spaces so that they become as natural as eating, taking a bath, or going to sleep, so that whenever you
close your eyes you can be in that space.

104.
ALMOST MAD

To become a seeker is almost to become mad as far as the world is concerned. So you are entering into madness. But that madness is the only sanity there is!

Our misery is that we have forgotten the language of love. The reason we have forgotten the language of love is that we have become too identified with reason. Nothing is wrong with reason, but it has a tendency to monopolize. It clings to the whole of your being. Then feeling suffers—feeling is starved—and by and by you forget about feeling completely. So it goes on shrinking and shrinking, and that dead feeling becomes a dead weight; that feeling becomes a dead heart.

Then one can go on pulling oneself along somehow—it will always be "somehow." There will be no charm, no magic, because without love there is no magic in life. And there will be no poetry either; life will be all prose, flat. Yes, it will have grammar, but it will not have a song in it. It will have a structure, but it will not have substance.

The risk of moving from reason to feeling, and trying to bring a balance, is something only for those people who are really courageous—for mad people only—because the price of admittance is nothing but your reason-dominated mind, your logic-dominated mind, your mathematically dominated mind.

When that attitude is dropped, prose is no longer at the center, but poetry; purpose no longer at the center, but play; money no longer at the center, but meditation; power no longer at the center, but simplicity, nonpossessiveness, a sheer joy of life—almost a madness.

105.
CHANGING THE WORLD

You are your world, so when you change your attitude you change
the very world in which you exist. We cannot change the world—
that's what politicians have been trying to do down through the ages,
and they have utterly failed.

The only way to change the world is to change your vision, and
suddenly you will live in a different world.

We don't live in the same world, and we are not all contemporaries. Somebody may be living in the past—how can he be your
contemporary? He may be sitting by your side and thinking of the
past; then he is not your contemporary. Somebody may be in the
future, already in that which is not yet. How can he be your contemporary?

Only two people who live in the now are contemporaries, but
in the now they are no more—because *you* are your past and
your future. The present is not of you, it has nothing to do with
you. When two people are absolutely in the here and now, they are
not—then God is. We live in the same world only when we live in
God. You may live with another person for years, and you live in
your world and she lives in hers—hence the continuous clash
of two worlds colliding. By and by, one learns how to avoid this
collision. That's what we call living together: trying to avoid the
collision, trying not to come to a clash. That's what we call family,
society, humanity… all bogus! You cannot really be with a man or
a woman unless you both live in God. There is no other love, no
other family, and no other society.

106.
THE UNPLANNED LIFE

There is no planning in existence. An unplanned life has tremendous beauty, because there is always some surprise waiting in the future.

The future is not just going to be a repetition; something new is always happening, and one can never take it for granted.

Secure people live a bourgeois life. A bourgeois life means getting up at seven-thirty, taking your breakfast at eight, at eight-thirty catching the train to the town, returning home at five-thirty, taking your tea, reading your newspaper, watching TV, having supper, making love to your partner without any love, and going to bed. Again the same thing starts the next day. Everything is settled, and there is no surprise: The future will be nothing but the past repeated again and again. Naturally there is no fear. You have done these things so many times that you have become skillful. You can do them again.

With the new comes fear, because one never knows whether one will be able to do it. One is doing always for the first time, so one is always shaky, uncertain about whether one is going to make it or not. But in that very thrill, in that adventure, is life—aliveness, let us say, rather than life, because *life* has also become a dull and dead word—aliveness, the flow.

107.
OUTLANDISH LOVE

Only fools know what love is, because love is a kind of madness.

Perhaps you have never reached the peaks of love, and you have a great longing for it. You have been in love, but it has never been outlandish, it has never been fantastic, it has never been far out. It has been lukewarm. It was not like a fire that consumes. You were in it, but you were not destroyed by it; you managed yourself. You have been clever in it, you have not been a fool. And only fools know what love is, because love is a kind of madness.

If you are too clever, you can allow only so far and then you stop. Your whole mind says, "Now this is too much. Going beyond this point is dangerous." Love knows only one experience that is satisfying, and that is to go to the very peak, to the ultimate peak, even once. Then there is a great change in energy. To know love once at the climax is enough; then there is no need to go into it again and again. The experience simply changes your whole being. So be less clever. Forget about cleverness; be more muddle-headed!

108.

MUDDLE-HEADED

Lao Tzu says: I am a muddle-headed man. When everybody is clear,
only I am unclear; when everybody seems to be intelligent, I am stupid.

What Lao Tzu means is that he does not calculate about his life—
he lives it. He lives like any animal, like any tree, like any bird.
He lives it simply, without figuring out what it is and where it is
leading. Anywhere is good; even nowhere is good.

Put your mind aside. It will be difficult, but it can be done. This
is one of the crucial problems for the modern mind—putting cleverness aside. You need to be a little more wild. That will bring great
innocence to you; that will make you ready to jump into a great
love. It need not be with anybody in particular, but it should be just
a passionate love—for life, for existence, or for any human being.
It could be for painting, poetry, dance, music, drama, anything—but
a great, passionate love that becomes your whole life, in which you
are so totally absorbed that nothing is left outside: so you and your
love become one. That will be the transformation for you.

Fear is there, but don't choose fear. Those who choose fear
destroy themselves. Let the fear be there; in spite of it, go into love.

109.
CIRCLE OF LIMITATION

If we believe we are limited, we function as limited human beings. Once we drop that foolish belief, we start functioning as unlimited beings.

You have drawn your own circle. It happens with gypsies. Gypsies are continually moving—they are wandering people. So when the older people go into a town, they draw circles around their children and tell them, "Sit here. You cannot leave. It is a magic circle." And the gypsy child cannot get out of it—it's impossible! Then he grows and grows and becomes an old man; and even then, if his father draws a circle, the old man cannot get out of it. Now he believes—and when you believe, it works.

Now you will say that this cannot be done to you. If somebody draws a circle, you will immediately jump out of it; nothing will happen. But from his very childhood, this old gypsy man has been conditioned for it. It functions for him, it is a reality for him, because reality is that which affects you. There is no other criterion for reality.

So limitation is a concept. People have wrong beliefs and then they function wrongly. When they function wrongly they search for a reason why. They come across the belief and go on emphasizing it: "I am functioning wrongly because of this." This becomes a vicious circle. Then they are *more* limited. Drop that idea completely. It is just a circle that you or others have helped you to draw around yourself.

110.

HIGHER THAN SEX

*People have forgotten completely that sex is nothing compared
to the merger that happens when you are simply lying together
in deep love, in deep reverence, in prayer.*

When physical energy is not sexually involved, it rises to higher
altitudes. It can reach to the very ultimate, to *samadhi,* awakening.
But people have forgotten completely. They think that sex is the
end. But sex is only the beginning. Whenever you love someone,
make it a point to first lie together in deep love, and you will reach
to subtler and deeper orgasms. That's how, by and by, real celibacy
arises. What we call in India *brahmacharya,* real celibacy, is not
against sex: It is higher than sex, it is deeper than sex. It is more
than sex. Whatever sex can give, it gives, but it gives more also. So
when you know how to use your energy on such a high level, who
bothers about the lower spaces? Nobody!

I'm not saying to drop sex. I am saying sometimes to allow yourself pure, loving spaces where sex is not a concern. Otherwise you
are pulled back to earth, and you can never fly into the sky.

III.

THE THREAD

This is the work of the meditator: to find the thread.

The world is in a constant flux, it is riverlike. It flows, but behind all this flow, change, flux, there must be a thread running that keeps everything together. Change is not possible without something remaining absolutely unchanging. Change can exist only together with a nonchanging element, otherwise things will fall apart.

Life is like a garland: You don't see the thread that runs through the flowers. but it is there, holding them together. If the thread were not there, the flowers would fall apart; there would be a heap of flowers but no garland. And existence is not a heap, it is a very well-knit pattern. Things are changing, but some unchanging element keeps a cosmic law behind it all. That cosmic law is called *sadashiva,* the eternal God, the timeless God, the nonchanging God. And that is the work of the meditator: to find the thread.

There are only two types of people. One gets too enchanted by the flowers and forgets the thread. He lives a life that cannot have any lasting value or significance, because whatever he does will vanish. Today he will make it, tomorrow it will be gone. It will be making castles of sand or launching boats of paper. The second type of person searches for the thread and devotes his whole life to that which always abides; he is never a loser.

112.

KNOWLEDGE

The most important thing to remember is that knowledge is not wisdom, and it cannot be; not only that, but it is antiwisdom, it is the barrier that prevents wisdom from arising.

Knowledge is the false coin, the pretender. It pretends to know. It knows nothing, but it can befool people—it is befooling millions of people—and it is so subtle, that unless one is really intelligent one never becomes aware of this fact. And it is so deep-rooted, because from our childhoods we have been conditioned in it.

To know means to accumulate, to collect information, to collect data. It does not change you—you remain the same; just your collection of information becomes bigger and bigger. Wisdom transforms you. It is really *in-formation,* not just "information"—it forms your inner being in a new way. It is transformation. It creates a new quality of seeing, knowing, being. So it is possible for a person to be not at all informed and yet be wise. It is also possible for a person to be very much informed and still be very unwise.

In fact, that's what has happened in the world: People have become more educated, more literate. Universal education is available, so everybody has become knowledgeable, and wisdom has been lost. Knowledge has become so easily available from paperbacks—who bothers about wisdom? Wisdom takes time, energy, devotion, dedication.

113.
BRAVERY

You have been taught very egoistical ideals—"Be brave."
What nonsense! How can an intelligent person avoid fear?

Everybody is afraid—they have to be. Life is such that one has to be. And people who become fearless become fearless not by becoming brave—because brave people have only repressed their fear; they are not really fearless.

A person becomes fearless by accepting his or her fears. It is not a question of bravery. It is simply seeing into the facts of life and realizing that fears are natural. One accepts them! The problem arises when you want to reject them. You have been taught very egoistical ideals—"Be brave." What nonsense! How can an intelligent person avoid fear? The bus driver goes on honking, and you stand in the middle of the road unafraid, or a bull comes charging at you, and you stand there unafraid—this would be stupid! An intelligent person has to jump out of the way. Or if there is nobody on the road, and then too you are afraid and start running, there is a problem; otherwise, fear is natural.

It is not that there will be no fears in life. You will come to know that ninety percent of your fears are just imagination. About ten percent are real, so one has to accept them. Become more responsive, sensitive, and alert, and this will be enough. You will become aware that you can use your fears as stepping stones.

114.
CHANGE

This is my observation, that one should never make an effort
to change anything, because that effort is going to make things
difficult rather than easy.

Your mind is attached to something, and now the same mind tries
to detach itself. At the most it can repress, but it can never become
a real detachment. For the real detachment to happen, the mind has
to understand why the attachment is there. There is no need to be
in a hurry to drop it; rather, see why it is there. Just look into the
mechanism, how it works, how it has come in: what circumstances,
what unawareness has helped it to be there. Just understand everything around it. Don't be in a hurry to drop it, because people who
are in a hurry to drop things don't give themselves enough time to
understand them.

Once you understand, suddenly you see that it is slipping out of
your hands; so there is no need to drop it. Nothing is there for any
reason other than a misunderstanding. Something has been misun-
derstood; hence it is there. Understand it rightly and it disappears.
All that is creating trouble is just like darkness. Bring light to it—
and simply light, because with the very presence of light, darkness
no longer exists.

115.
UNDERSTANDING

The basic problem of why you are here will disappear only
when you have reached to the very core of your being, never before.

Unless you meditate deeply, understanding will not arise. Nobody else can give it to you; you have to earn it. Through arduous effort, struggle, sacrifice, you have to earn it, only then problems will disappear.

The basic problem of why you are here will disappear only when you have reached to the very core of your being, never before. At the core you will know that you have always been here. It is not a question of why you are here. You have always been here in different forms.

The form has been changing, but you have always been here. The form will go on changing but you will always remain here. You are part of this whole. The river falls into the ocean, and again the ocean rises and becomes clouds. Again it becomes a river and falls into the ocean, then becomes clouds again. It goes on... it is a wheel. You have been here many times. You will be here many times. In fact you have been here for eternity, and you will be here for eternity. There is no beginning and no end to existence: It is eternal.

I can say that to you, but it will not bring understanding. When you go deep within yourself and you open the innermost shrine of your being, when you enter into that shrine, suddenly you will realize that you have always been here.

116.

BEYOND LANGUAGE

All that is great is beyond language.

When there is so much to say, it is always difficult to say it. Only small things can be said, only trivia can be said, only the mundane can be said. Whenever you feel something overwhelming, it is impossible to say it, because words are too narrow to contain anything essential.

Words are utilitarian. They are good for day-to-day, mundane activities. They start falling short as you move beyond ordinary life. In love they are not useful; in prayer they become utterly inadequate.

All that is great is beyond language, and when you find that nothing can be expressed, then you have arrived. Then life is full of great beauty, great love, great joy, great celebration.

117.
A REAL MARRIAGE

The whole process of tantra is joining opposites together,
helping polarities dissolve into one being.
And when one is whole, one is holy.

The man and the woman cannot meet eternally; their meeting can only be momentary. That is the misery of love, and the joy too. The joy, the ecstasy, is because of the momentary meeting. At least for a moment one feels whole; nothing is missing; everything falls into one harmony. There is great joy, but soon it is lost.

Tantra says, use this as a key—that the meeting with the outer can only be momentary. But there is an inner woman, an inner man; the meeting with the inner can be permanent, eternal. So learn the secret from the outside and apply it inside. No man is just man and no woman is just woman. This is one of the greatest insights of tantra… because a man is born out of man and woman, out of the meeting of these two polarities. He carries something from the father and something from the mother. It is also the case with the woman. So deep down each of us is the opposite, too; if the conscious mind is man, then the unconscious is woman, and vice versa.

Unless you learn the art of meeting with the other inside, love will remain a misery, and joy a vicious circle, and you will be torn apart. That inner meeting is possible just as the outer meeting is possible. But the inner meeting has one thing special about it: It need not end; it can be a real marriage.

118.

FRIENDSHIP

The first friendship has to be with oneself, but very rarely will you find a person who is friendly toward himself or herself. We are enemies to ourselves, while hoping in vain that we can be friends to someone else.

We have been taught to condemn ourselves. Self-love has been thought of as a sin. It is not. It is the foundation of all other loves. It is only through self-love that altruistic love is possible. Because self-love has been condemned, all other possibilities of love have disappeared from the earth. This has been a very cunning strategy to destroy love.

It is as if you were to say to a tree, "Don't nourish yourself through the earth; that is sin. Don't nourish yourself from the moon and the sun and the stars; that is selfishness. Be altruistic—serve other trees." It looks logical, and that is the danger. It looks logical: If you want to serve others, then sacrifice; service means sacrifice. But if a tree sacrifices, it will die, it will not be able to serve any other tree; it will not be able to exist at all.

You have been taught, "Don't love yourself." That almost has been the universal message of the so-called organized religions. Not of Jesus, but certainly of Christianity; not of Buddha but of Buddhism—of all organized religions, that has been the teaching: Condemn yourself, you are a sinner, you are worthless.

And because of this condemnation the tree of the human being has shrunk, has lost luster, can no longer rejoice. People are dragging themselves along somehow. People don't have any roots in existence—they are uprooted. They are trying to be of service to others and they cannot, because they have not even been friendly to themselves.

119.
SHRUNKEN HEART

Whenever you allow any doubt, you will become tense in the heart—
because the heart relaxes with trust and shrinks with doubt.

Ordinarily people are not aware of this dynamic. In fact, they continuously remain shrunken and contracted at the heart, so they have forgotten how it feels to be relaxed there. Knowing no opposite, they think that everything is okay, but out of one hundred people, ninety-nine live with a contracted heart.

The more you are in the head, the more the heart contracts. When you are not in the head, the heart opens like a lotus flower... and it is tremendously beautiful when it opens. Then you are really alive, and the heart is relaxed. But the heart can only be relaxed in trust, in love. With suspicion, with doubt, the mind enters. Doubt is the door of the mind; doubt is the bait for the mind.

Once you are caught in doubt, you are caught with the mind. So when doubt comes, it is not worth it. I'm not saying that your doubt is always wrong. Your doubt may be perfectly right, but then too it is wrong, because it destroys your heart. It is not worth it.

120.

JOY

Joy is the antidote to all fear. Fear comes if you don't enjoy life.
If you enjoy life, fear disappears.

Be positive and enjoy more, laugh more, dance more, sing more. Become more and more cheerful, enthusiastic about small things, even very small things. Life consists of small things, but if you can bring the quality of cheerfulness to small things, the total will be tremendous.

So don't wait for anything great to happen. Great things do happen—it is not that they don't—but don't wait for the something great to happen. It happens only when you start living small, ordinary, day-to-day things with a new mind, with new freshness, with new vitality, with new enthusiasm. Then by and by you accumulate, and that accumulation one day explodes into sheer joy.

But one never knows when it will happen. One has just to go on collecting pebbles on the shore. The totality becomes the great happening. When you collect one pebble, it is a pebble. When all the pebbles are together, suddenly they are diamonds. That's the miracle of life.

There are many people in the world who miss because they are always waiting for something great. It can't happen. It happens only through small things: eating your breakfast, walking, taking a bath, talking to a friend, just sitting alone looking at the sky or lying on your bed doing nothing. These small things are what life is made of. They are the very stuff of life.

121.

DARKNESS

Never be bothered by negatives.
You burn the candle, and the darkness goes on its own.

Don't try to fight with the darkness. There is no way, because the darkness does not exist—how can you fight with it? Just light a candle, and the darkness is gone. So forget about the darkness, forget about the fear. Forget about all those negative things that ordinarily haunt the human mind. Just burn a small candle of enthusiasm.

First thing in the morning, get up with a great enthusiasm, with a decision that today you are really going to live with great delight—and then start living with great delight. Have your breakfast, but eat it as if you are eating God. Then it becomes a sacrament. Take your bath, but remember that God is within you; you are giving a bath to God. Then your small bathroom becomes a temple, and the water showering on you is a baptism.

Get up every morning with great decisiveness, with certainty, with clarity, a promise to yourself that today is going to be tremendously beautiful and you are going to live it tremendously. And each night when you go to bed, remember again how many beautiful things have happened today. Just the remembrance helps them to come back again tomorrow. Just remember, and then fall asleep remembering those beautiful moments that happened today. Your dreams will be more beautiful. They will carry your enthusiasm, and you will also start living in dreams with a new energy. Make every moment sacred.

122.

BETWEEN PLEASURE
AND PAIN

The only state in which one can become a permanent dweller
is the space that is neither this nor that.

In this space is a quality of silence and tranquility. Of course, in
the beginning it feels very tasteless, because there is no pain and no
pleasure. But all pain and all pleasure is just excitement. The excitement that you like, you call pleasure. The excitement that you don't
like, you call pain. Sometimes it happens that you can start liking
a certain excitement and it may become pleasure, and you can start
liking another excitement and it may turn into pain. So the same
experience can become pain or pleasure; it depends on your likes
and dislikes.

Relax in the space between pleasure and pain. That's the most
natural state of relaxation. Once you start being in it, feeling it, you
will learn the taste of it. That is what I call the taste of Tao. It is just
like wine. In the beginning it will be very bitter. One has to learn.
And it is the deepest wine there is, the greatest alcoholic beverage
of silence, of tranquility. One becomes drunk with it. By and by you
will understand the taste of it. In the beginning it is tasteless,
because your tongue is too full of pain and pleasure.

123.
PEACE

Whenever you remember, be deeply relaxed and feel peaceful,
as many times in the day as possible. After a few days you will feel,
without any doing on your part, that peace has been established.
It will follow you like a shadow.

There are many levels of peacefulness. There is one that you can produce just by feeling it, just by giving yourself the deep suggestion that you are peaceful; that is the first layer. The second layer is that of which you suddenly become aware. You don't create it. But the second happens only if the first is present.

The second is the real thing, but the first helps to create the way for it to come. Peace comes—but before it comes, as a prerequisite, you have to create a mental peace around you. The first peace will just be mental; it will be like an autohypnosis; it is created by you. Then one day you will suddenly see that the second peace has surfaced. It has nothing to do with your doing, or with you. In fact, it is deeper than you. It comes from the very source of your being, the unidentified being, the undivided being, the unknown being.

We know ourselves only on the surface. A small place is identified as you. A small wave is named, labeled, as you. Just within that wave, deep down, is the great ocean. So whatever you are doing, always remember to create peace around it. This is not the goal; it is just the means. Once you have created peace, something of the beyond will fill it. It will not come out of your effort.

124.
FAITH AND TRUST

Faith is a dead trust. In fact, you don't trust but you still believe,
that's what faith is. But trust is something alive. It is just like love.

All faiths have lost what you call prayer, they have lost what you call meditation. They have forgotten the whole language of ecstasy. They have all become intellectuals: creeds, dogmas, systems. There are many words, but the meaning is missing, the significance is lost. And that is natural. It has to be so.

When a Jesus is alive, religion walks on the earth, and those few who are fortunate enough to recognize him, to walk a few steps with Jesus, will be transformed. It is not that you become a Christian—that's superficial—but something of Christ enters you. Something transpires between you and Christ. You become prayerful. You have different eyes to see with, a different heart beating. Everything remains the same, but you change.

The trees are green but now in a different way. The greenery has become alive. You can almost touch the life surrounding you. But once Jesus is gone, whatever he has said becomes formulated, systematized. Then people become Christian intellectually, but the living God is no longer present.

Faith is a dead trust. In fact, you don't trust but you still believe, that's what faith is. But trust is something alive. It is just like love.

125.
DOUBT AND NEGATIVITY

Doubt means that you don't have any position; you are ready to inquire,
with an open mind. Doubt is the best point from where to begin.

Doubt is not bad. Negativity is a totally different thing. Negativity
means you have already taken a position—against. Doubt means
you don't have any position; you are ready to inquire, with open
mind. Doubt is the best point from where to begin. Doubt simply
means a quest, a question; negativity means you already have a prejudice, you are bigoted. You have already decided. Now all that you
have to do is somehow to prove your prejudice right. Doubt is
immensely spiritual. But negativity is something sick.

126.
EGO

Do you worry that if you accept yourself, you will become egoistic?
Forget about the ego!

Accept yourself. We will see about the ego later; first accept yourself
totally. Let the ego come; the ego is not such a big problem, and the
bigger it is, the easier it is burst. It is like a balloon—it becomes big,
then with just a prick it is gone! Let the ego be there, that is allowed,
but accept yourself, and things will start changing. In fact total
acceptance means acceptance of the ego. too. Start by accepting.

The world needs a few great egoists too. We need all kinds of
people!

127.
PREPARING THE WAY

There is nothing you can do. Enlightenment happens when it happens,
but by your doing you prepare the way.

You cannot force enlightenment to happen. It is not a cause and
effect thing. But you do something; you prepare the way for it. You
can do something that can hinder the way—it happens when it
happens, but if you are not ready, you may bypass it, and you may
not even recognize it.

Many people come near the first glimpses of satori, *samadhi*,
enlightenment, in the natural course of life, but they cannot recognize it because they are not ready for it. It is as if a very great diamond is given to someone who has never heard of diamonds. He
will think it is a stone, because he has no way to recognize it.

One has to become a sort of jeweler so that one can recognize.
When it happens, it happens only then. There is no way to force or
manipulate it. You cannot make it happen, but if it happens you
will be ready to recognize it. If you stop meditations your readiness
will disappear. Continue meditations so that you are ready, you are
throbbing, waiting, so that when it passes by your side you are open
to receive it.

128.

ASLEEP IN A TRAIN

*Just the other day I was reading a sentence of Jean-Paul Sartre.
He says that life is like a child who is asleep in a train and is
awakened by an inspector who wants to check the ticket, but the
child has no ticket and no money to pay for one.*

The child is also not at all aware of where he is going, what his destination is and why he is on the train. And last but not the least, the child cannot figure it out, because he never decided to be on the train in the first place. Why is he there?

This situation is becoming more and more common to the modern mind, because we are somehow uprooted, and meaning is missing. One simply feels, "Why? Where am I going?" You don't know where you are going, and you don't know why you are in the train. You don't have a ticket and you don't have the money to pay for it, and still you cannot get out of the train. Everything seems to be chaos, maddening.

This has happened because the roots in love have been lost. People are living loveless lives, somehow pulling themselves along. So what to do?

I know that everybody one day feels like a child in a train. Yet life is not going to be a failure, because in this big train there are millions of people fast asleep, but there is always somebody who is awake. The child can search and find somebody who is not asleep and snoring, someone who has consciously entered the train, someone who knows where the train is going. Being in the vicinity of that person, the child also learns the ways of becoming more conscious.

129.
SUFFERING

Nobody wants to suffer, but we carry the seeds of suffering within us.
The whole point of working on ourselves is to burn those seeds.
The burning itself may cause a little suffering, but it is nothing
compared to a whole life of misery.

Once the seeds of suffering are destroyed, your whole life will become a life of delight. So if you are just avoiding suffering, and avoiding facing suffering that is inside you, you are creating a situation in which you will be full of suffering your whole life.

Once the wounds you are carrying come to the surface they start healing. It is a healing process. But I know that when you have a wound you don't want anybody to touch it. You don't really want to know that you have it. You want to hide it, but by hiding it, it is not going to heal. It has to be opened to the sunrays, to the winds.

It may be painful in the beginning, but when it heals, you will understand. And there is no other way to heal it. It has to be brought to consciousness. Just the very bringing to consciousness is the process of healing.

130.
INTERPRETATION

Thinking is nothing but a habit of interpreting. When thinking disappears the lake of the mind is silent, calm, and quiet. Then there are no more waves, no more ripples—nothing is distorted, the moon is reflected perfectly.

Thinking is like ripples in a lake, and because of the ripples, the reflection cannot be true; the moon is reflected, but the ripples distort it. God is reflected in everybody, we mirror God, but our mind is so full of thoughts, waverings, clouds, that whatever we come to see is no longer the same; it is not *that which is.* The mind has imposed its own thoughts on it, it has interpreted it, and all interpretation is a distortion. Reality needs no interpretation; it needs only reflection. There is no point in interpreting; the interpreter goes on missing the point.

If you see a rose, it is there: there is no need to interpret it, there is no need to dissect it, there is no need to know about its meaning. It *is* its meaning. It is not a metaphor; it does not stand for something else. It is simply there! It is reality, it is not a symbol. A symbol needs to be interpreted, a dream needs to be interpreted. So psychoanalysis is right, because it interprets dreams, but philosophers are not right, because they interpret reality. A dream is symbolic, it stands for something else. An interpretation may be helpful to find out what it stands for. But a rose is a rose; it stands only for itself. It is self-evident.

131.
NOISE

Life is noisy, and the world is too crowded. But to fight with noise is not the way to get rid of it; the way to get rid of it is to accept it totally.

The more you fight, the more nervous you will be, because the more you fight, the more it will disturb you. Open up, accept it; noise too is part of life. And once you start accepting it, you will be surprised: it will no longer disturb you. Disturbance does not come from the noise; it comes from our attitude toward the noise. The noise is not the disturbance; it is the attitude that is the disturbance. If you are antagonistic to it, you are disturbed; if you are not antagonistic to it, you are not disturbed.

And where will you go? Wherever you go some kind of noise is bound to be there; the whole world is noisy. Even if you can find a cave in the Himalayas and sit there, you will miss life. Noise will not be there, but all the growth possibilities that life makes available will not be there, either, and soon the silence will look dull and dead.

I am not saying don't enjoy silence. Enjoy silence; but know that silence is not against noise. Silence can exist in noise. In fact, when it exists in noise only then is it real silence. The silence that you feel in the Himalayas is not your silence; it belongs to the Himalayas. But if in the marketplace you can feel silence, you can be utterly at ease and relaxed, it is yours. Then you have the Himalayas in your heart, and that's the true thing!

132.
CHANGING CLIMATES

Seasons change. Sometimes it is winter, sometimes it is summer.
If you are always in the same climate, you will feel stuck.

One has to learn to like that which is happening. That is what I call maturity. One has to like that which is already there. Immaturity is living always in "oughts" and "shoulds" and never living in the "is'"—and "is" is the case. "Should" is just a dream.

Whatsoever is the case is good. Love it, like it, and relax into it. When sometimes intensity comes, love it. When it goes, say goodbye. Things change... life is in flux. Nothing remains the same, so sometimes there are great spaces and sometimes nowhere to move. But both are good. Both are gifts from existence. One should be so grateful that whatever happens, one is grateful, thankful. Just enjoy it. This is what is happening right now. Tomorrow it may change; then enjoy that. The day after tomorrow something else may happen. Enjoy that. Don't compare the past with futile future fantasies. Live the moment. Sometimes it is hot, sometimes very cold, but both are needed; otherwise life will disappear. It exists in polarities.

133.
NOTHING HAPPENING

Feeling quiet is also a happening—
and it is a greater happening than other things that are noisy.

When you are crying or shouting, you feel that something is happening. When you are not crying, not shouting, not screaming, just feeling a deep silence, you think nothing is happening. You don't know that this too is a great happening, greater than the others. In fact, those other moments have paved the way for this one. This is the goal. They are just the means. But in the beginning it will look empty, everything gone. You are sitting, and nothing is happening.

Nothing is happening, and "nothing" is very positive. It is the most positive thing in the world. Buddha has called that nothing nirvana, the ultimate. So allow it, cherish it, and let it happen more, welcome it. When it happens just close your eyes and enjoy it so it comes more often. This is the treasure. But in the beginning, I can understand, it happens to everybody. There are many things people call explosions. When they disappear and the real thing comes, they don't have any notion of what it is and they simply miss their explosions. They would like those explosions to happen again. They may even start forcing them, but they will destroy the whole thing.

So wait. If something explodes on its own, it is okay, but don't force it. If silence is exploding, enjoy it. You should be happy about it! This is the misery of the world—people don't know what is what, so sometimes they are happy when they are miserable and sometimes when they should be happy, when happiness is really close, they become miserable.

134.
BELIEVE IN THE EYES

Never believe anything unless you have experienced it. Never form any prejudice, even if the whole world is saying that something is so, unless you have encountered it yourself.

The great Indian mystic Kabir said, "Never believe in the ears—just believe in the eyes. All that you have heard is false. All that you have seen is true."

This saying should be carried as a constant remembrance, because we are human beings and we tend to speak fallacies. We are part of this whole mad world, and that madness is inside every human being. Don't let it overpower you. One has to remember continuously. It is arduous, because prejudices are very comfortable and easy; you don't have to pay for them. Truth is costly, precious; you have to pay much. In fact, you have to put your whole life at stake; then you arrive at it. But only truth liberates.

So looking at other people and the functioning of their mind, always remember that the same type of mind is hidden in you also. So never listen to it. It will persuade you; it will argue, it will try to convince you. Just tell it, "I will see for myself. I am still alive. I can encounter whatever is needed."

135.
AUSTERITY

They have a word in Latin for listening, obedire. The English word obedience comes from that. If you rightly listen, it creates obedience.

If you rightly see, it brings its own discipline. The basic question is that inside, one should be perfectly empty while listening, perfectly empty while seeing, perfectly empty while touching. no prejudice for or against, staying uninvolved, and having no subtle leanings, because that leaning destroys the truth. Having no leanings at all, allowing truth to be, not forcing it to be something else but allowing it, whatever it is.

This is the austere life of the religious person. This is real austerity: to allow truth to have its own say—not disturbing, not coloring, not manipulating, not managing it in some way according to one's own beliefs. When truth is allowed to be itself, naked and new, a great discipline arises in you—obedience. A great order arises in you.

Then you are no longer in chaos; for the first time you start gathering a center, a nucleus, because truth known immediately becomes your truth. Truth known as it is immediately transforms you. You are no longer the same person. The very vision, the very clarity, and the very experience of what truth is, is a sudden mutation. It is the revolution that real religion is all about.

136.
GOING INTO FEAR

Whenever there is fear, never try to escape from it. In fact, take hints from
fear. Those are the directions in which you need to travel. Fear is simply a
challenge. It calls you: "Come!"

Whenever something is really good, it is also scary, because it
brings you some insights. It forces you toward certain changes. It
brings you to a brink from where, if you go back, you will never
forgive yourself. You will always remember yourself as a coward.
If you go ahead, it is dangerous. That's what is scary. Whenever
there is some fear, always remember not to go back, because that
is not the way to solve it. Go into it. If you are afraid of the dark
night, go into the dark night—because that is the only way to overcome it. That is the only way to transcend the fear. Go into the
night; there is nothing more important than that. Wait, sit there
alone, and let the night work. If you fear, tremble. Let the trembling be there, but tell the night, "Do whatever you want to do. I
am here." After a few minutes you will see that everything has settled. The darkness is no longer dark, it has come to be luminous.
You will enjoy it. You can touch it—the velvety silence, the vastness, the music. You will be able to enjoy it, and you will say, "How
foolish I was to be afraid of such a beautiful experience!"

137.
COUNTERFEIT

First one has to realize that one is carrying a counterfeit, a false coin.
Of course, it makes you sad. You feel as if you have lost something—
but you never had it in the first place.

People simply think they have compassion. Compassion is a very
rare quality. Sympathy is possible, but compassion is a very high-
level thing. But when you come to feel that you don't have any
compassion, now there will be a possibility of your having it.

That is the trouble with false things: If your pocket is full of false
coins and you think that you are rich, why worry? Once you come
to know that you are a beggar and all coins are false, suddenly you
become sad because all the money is lost. But now you can find out
where and how one gets real money.

Right now you cannot make the distinction between what is real
and what is unreal. Only when a very integrated consciousness arises,
will you be able to make it. It is not that a few things are real in your
life and a few things are unreal. In this state, when you are unaware,
everything is unreal like a dream, but everything looks real.

In another state, when you become awakened, become a Buddha, then everything is real; nothing is unreal. So it is not that a
few things are real and a few unreal. If you are not aware, then
everything is unreal. If you are aware, everything is real. But you
will be able to know what was unreal only when you are awake,
not before that.

138.

BECOME POETIC

A poet comes to know certain things that are revealed
only in a poetic relationship with reality.

The poet is foolish as far as worldly cleverness is concerned. He will never rise in the world of wealth and power. But in his poverty he knows a different kind of richness in life that nobody else knows.

Love is possible to a poet, and God is possible to a poet. Only one who is innocent enough to enjoy the small things of life can understand that God exists, because God exists in the small things of life: he exists in the food you eat, he exists in the walk that you go for in the morning. God exists in the love that you have for your beloved, in the friendship that you have with somebody. God does not exist in the churches; churches are not part of poetry, they are part of politics.

Become more and more poetic. It takes guts to be poetic; one needs to be courageous enough to be called a fool by the world, but only then can one be poetic. And by being poetic I don't mean that you have to write poetry. Writing poetry is only a small, nonessential part of being poetic. One may be a poet and never write a single line of poetry, and one may write thousands of poems and still not be a poet.

Being a poet is a way of life. It is love for life, it is reverence for life, it is a heart-to-heart relationship with life.

139.
ANXIETY

Create a distance between you and your personality.
All your problems are concerned with your personality, not with you.
You don't have any problems; nobody really has any problems.
All problems belong to the personality.

This is going to be the work—that whenever you feel anxiety, just remember that it belongs to the personality. You feel a strain, just remember that it belongs to the personality. You are the watcher, the witness. Create distance. Nothing else is to be done.

Once the distance is there, you will suddenly see anxiety disappearing. When the distance is lost, when you have become closed again, again anxiety will arise. Anxiety is getting identified with the problems of the personality. Relaxation is not getting involved, but remaining unidentified with the problems of the personality.

So, for one month, watch. Whatever happens, remain far away. For example, you have a headache. Just try to be far away and watch the headache. It is happening somewhere in the body mechanism. You are standing aloof, a watcher on the hills, far away, and it is happening miles away. Just create a distance. Create space between you and the headache and go on making the space bigger and bigger. A point will come when you will suddenly see that the headache is disappearing into the distance.

140.
AWARENESS FIRST

When awareness grows, and you become clearly alert,
acceptance is a natural consequence.

Acceptance is an outgrowth of awareness. Greed is there; watch it. Ambition is there; watch it. A lust for power is there; watch it. Right now don't complicate things by the idea of accepting it, because if you try to accept and you cannot, you will start repressing. That's how people have repressed. They cannot accept, so the only way is to forget about things and put them in the dark. Then one is okay, one feels that there is no problem.

First, forget about acceptance. Just be aware. When awareness grows, and you become clearly alert, acceptance is a natural consequence. Seeing the fact, one has to accept it because there is nowhere else to go. What can you do? It is there just like your two eyes. They are not four, only two.

Once you accept something, if it is real, only then can it remain. If it is unreal, it will dissolve. Love will remain; hate will dissolve. Compassion will remain; anger will dissolve.

141.

UNHAPPINESS

People say they would like to be happy, but they really don't want to be. They are afraid that they will be lost.

Whenever you become aware of something, you are separate from it. If you are happy, you are separate and happiness is separate. So being really happy means becoming happiness rather than becoming happy. You dissolve, by and by. When you are unhappy, you *are* too much. The ego comes into focus when one is unhappy. That's why egoistic people remain very unhappy, and unhappy people remain very egoistic. There is an interconnection.

If you want to be egoistic, you have to be unhappy. Unhappiness gives you the background and the ego, comes out of it very clear, crystal-clear, like a white dot on a black background. The happier you are, the less you are. That's why many people want to become happy but really they are afraid to. Its my observation that people say they would like to be happy but they really don't want to be. They are afraid that they will be lost. Happiness and egos can't go together. The happier you are, the less you are. There comes a moment when only happiness is, and you are not.

142.
THE TWO DOORS

It is not a question of choosing between truth and illusion,
because all doors that are outside you lead to illusion.

The truth is within you. It is in the very heart of the seeker. So if
on one door is written "illusion" and on another is written "truth,"
don't bother to choose between them. Both are illusory. *You* are
truth. Truth is your very consciousness.

Become more alert and more conscious. It is not a question of
choosing between doors. The darkness is there because you are
unconscious, so no light from the outside can help. I can give you
a lamp right now, but it won't help. By the time you have reached
your room, it will be out.

You have to become more conscious, more and more conscious
and alert, so your inner flame, only that, will enlighten your surroundings. In that light you will see that all doors have disappeared.
The door that was illusion and the door that was truth—both have
disappeared. They were both in conspiracy. In fact, they both lead
to the same place. They just give you an illusion of choice. So no
matter what you choose, you always choose the same thing. They
both lead to the same passage. Eventually you end up in illusion. So
that is not the problem. The problem is how to become more alert.

143.
LOOKING INTO DARKNESS

Sometimes when you come into your room it looks dark. But then you sit and rest, and by and by the darkness disappears. The room is full of light. It is not that something has happened. It is just that your eyes have become accustomed to looking into the darkness.

It is said that thieves start seeing in the dark more clearly than anybody else, because they have to work in darkness. They have to enter unfamiliar houses, and on every step there is danger. They may stumble upon something. By and by, they start seeing in the dark. Darkness is not so dark for them. So don't be afraid. Be like a thief. Sit with closed eyes and look into the darkness as deeply as possible. Let that be your meditation.

Every day for thirty minutes sit in the corner, close your eyes, and create darkness—as dark as you can imagine—and then look into that darkness. If it is difficult just think of a blackboard in front of you, so dark and so black. Soon you will be able to imagine more darkness. You will be tremendously surprised that the more you look into darkness, the clearer your eyes will become.

And if fear is there, allow it. In fact, one should enjoy it. Let it be there; start trembling. If the fear starts a certain vibration in you, just allow it. Get as frightened as possible. Be almost possessed by fear... and see how beautiful it is. It is almost like a bath; much dust will be washed away. When you come out of that trembling, you will feel very alive, throbbing with life, pulsating with a new energy, rejuvenated.

144.
LOVING YOURSELF

We always think in terms of loving somebody else. The man thinks
to love the woman, the woman thinks to love the man; the mother
thinks to love the child, the child thinks to love the mother; friends
hink to love each other. But unless you love yourself it is impossible
to love anybody else.

You can love somebody else only when you have love within you.
You can share something only when you have it. But the whole
humanity has lived under this wrong ideology, so we take it for
granted—as if we already love ourselves and now the whole question is of how to love our neighbor. It is impossible! That's why
there is so much talk about love, and the world remains ugly and
full of hatred, war and violence and anger.

It is a great insight to come to—that you don't love yourself. It
is really hard to love oneself, because we have been taught to condemn ourselves and not to love. We have been taught that we are
sinners. We have been taught that we are not of any worth. Because
of that it has become difficult to love. How can you love a worthless person? How can you love somebody who is already condemned?

But it will come. If the insight that you do not love yourself has
come, there is nothing to be worried about. One window has
opened. You will not be inside the room for long—you will jump
out. Once you know the open sky, you cannot remain confined in
a stale world. You will come out of it.

145.
PRISONS

You are a tremendous freedom with no boundaries to your being.
All boundaries are false. That's why only in love do we become
healthy and whole, because love takes away all boundaries, all
labels; it does not categorize you. It accepts you, whoever you are.

Nobody is really ill. In fact, the society is ill, individuals are victims. Society needs therapy; individuals simply need love. The society is the patient and needs hospitalization.

Individuals suffer because you cannot catch hold of society; it remains invisible. When you try to catch hold of it, an individual is found and then becomes responsible—and he is simply suffering, he is a victim. He needs understanding, not therapy; love, not therapy. Society has not given him understanding, has not given him love. Society has given him straitjackets, prisons. Society has forced him into a pigeonhole, categorized him, labeled him—"this is you, this is your identity."

You are freedom and you have no identity. You cannot be labeled, and that's your beauty and glory—that you cannot say who you are. You are is always in the making. By the time you have asserted that you are this or that, you have moved. You are deciding each moment what to be — to be or not to be. Each moment there is a fresh decision, a fresh release of life. A sinner can become a saint in a single moment, and a saint can be a sinner in a single moment. The unhealthy can become healthy, and the healthy can become unhealthy in a single moment. Just a change of decision, just a change of insight, of vision, and everything changes.

146.
ILLUSIONS
OF CONTENTMENT

Only in Buddhahood is there contentment; all other forms of contentment are just consolations just illusions created by the mind.

To live constantly in discontent is so painful that the mind creates illusions of contentment; those illusions keep people going, they help people. If you take away all the illusions, a person will not have any reason to live for even a single moment more. They are needed. In unawareness illusions are a must, because through illusions we create pseudo-meanings in life, and naturally until the real has happened, we have to go on creating these pseudo-meanings. When we become fed up with one pseudo meaning, we create another. We become fed up with money, move into politics; we get fed up with politics and move into something else. Even so-called religion is nothing but a subtle illusion.

The real religion has nothing to do with so-called religions—Christianity, Hinduism, Islam. The real religion is the shattering of all illusions. It is to live in discontent, in deep suffering, in utter pain, and to search for the real thing.

The path is of great pain and only a few attain, because, in the first place, people can't start out on it. In the first place, they can't accept the pain of life—but that pain is the source of all growth. Seeing the naked truth of it all—not avoiding, not escaping, looking into it through and through—that is the beginning of intelligence, the beginning of mindfulness, the beginning of awareness.

147.
PURITY

The purity that resides in the heart is incorruptible; what you do does not affect it at all.

Even the greatest sinner remains pure at the deepest core of being. So even the deepest sinner remains a saint; the sin can only touch the periphery, the circumference. It cannot go to your core, because doing remains on the surface; only being is at the core.

And when you start looking at people's being, then nobody is a sinner, nobody has ever been a sinner. It is impossible. Purity is so absolute that all that we do is not more than dreams; that is the Eastern approach. The Eastern approach doesn't bother much about your doing. It says that whatever you have done, you can simply go within and have a contact with the being, which remains crystal clear and always pure, unpolluted. On the periphery are just faces—saint and sinner, good and bad, the famous and the notorious. They are just acts, as if a drama were being enacted. Somebody has become a Jesus and somebody has become a Judas. Both are needed: Jesus cannot be without Judas, and what will Judas be without Jesus? They are both necessary for the whole Christ story to happen. But behind the stage they sit together and drink tea and smoke.

That's the reality. This whole world is a vast stage, and a great drama is being enacted. So don't worry about it. Whatever part has been given you, fulfill it as joyously as possible, and always remember that deep down you remain pure.

148.
LOVE SOMETHING BIGGER

Love something higher, something bigger, something in which you will
be lost; you can be possessed by it, but you cannot possess it.

Love can create great trouble and it can also create great joy. One
has to be very, very alert, because love is our basic chemistry. If one
is alert about one's love energy, then everything goes right.

Always love something higher than yourself, and you will never
be in trouble; always love something bigger than yourself. People
tend to love something lower than themselves, something smaller
than themselves. You can control the smaller, you can dominate the
smaller, and you can feel very good with the inferior, because it
makes you look superior—then the ego is fulfilled. And once you
start creating ego out of your love, then you are bound for hell.

Love something higher, something bigger, something in which
you will be lost and that you cannot control; you can only be possessed by it, but you cannot possess it. Then the ego disappears, and
when love is without ego, it is prayer.

149.
HEART AS METHOD

If you want to come down from the head, you will have to pass through the heart—that is the crossroads. You cannot go to the being directly; you will have to pass through the heart. The heart has to be used as a method.

Thinking, feeling, being—these are the three centers. But certainly feeling is closer to being than thinking, and feeling functions as a method. Feel more, and then you will think less. Don't fight with thinking, because fighting with thinking is again creating other thoughts of fighting. Never fight with thoughts; it is futile.

Rather than fighting with the thoughts, move your energy into feeling. Sing rather than think, love rather than philosophize, read poetry rather than prose. Dance, look at nature, and whatever you do, do it through the heart. The heart is the neglected center: Once you start paying attention to it, it starts functioning. When it starts functioning, the energy that was moving in the mind automatically starts moving through the heart. And the heart is closer to the energy center. The energy center is in the navel—so to pump energy to the head is hard work, in fact.

That's why all the education systems exist: to teach you how to pump the energy from the center straight to the head and how to bypass the heart. So no school, no college, no university, teaches how to feel. They destroy feeling, because they know that if you feel you cannot think. But it is easy to move from the head to the heart, and it is even easier to move from the heart to the navel. In the navel you are simply a being, a pure being—with no feeling, no thinking; you are not moving at all. That is the center of the cyclone.

150.
NO OPPOSITE

In Sanskrit we have three terms: one for suffering, one for joy,
and one that transcends both: anand, or bliss.

Anand is neither suffering nor the so-called joy. It is a totally different kind of joy that has no memory of suffering at all, that is completely uncontaminated by the opposite. It is pure oneness, and there is no duality.

Ordinarily it is difficult even to conceive of this state. Unless you taste it, it is difficult even to understand it. Because all that we can understand needs at least two things; the opposite is a must. We can understand the figure only because of the background. We call this moment night because of the day, we call somebody good because of the bad, we call somebody beautiful because of the ugly. The opposite is a must; the opposite defines it.

But *anand* means the state in which there is no opposite, when you have come to the one, when there is no possibility of the other. The ocean of bliss has only one shore. It is very illogical—because how can there be only one shore? The state of bliss is illogical. Those who are too attached to logic can never achieve it. Only for crazy people does it open its door.

151.
CRITICISM

Whenever you are ready to criticize something, first decide what you are going to give as a positive alternative to it.

If you can't think of an alternative to your criticism, wait. Don't make the criticism, because it is futile. If you say that this medicine is not right, maybe you are right, but then where is the right medicine? Criticism never brings revolution. Criticism is good as part of a positive program. So first decide about the positive program and then, keeping an eye on the positive program, criticize. Then your criticism will be very valuable, appreciated even, by those whom you are criticizing. Nobody will feel offended by it, because while you are criticizing, you are continuously keeping some positive alternative in mind and then proposing something.

152.
SLEEP

Sleep is divine, more divine than any other time. And if one falls asleep meditating, the meditation keeps resounding down into the layers of one's unconscious.

Have you ever noticed? Whatever is your last thought in the night will be your first thought in the morning. Watch it—the last, the very last, when you enter into sleep. You are standing just on the threshold—the last thought will always be the first thought when you again stand on the threshold and you are coming out of sleep.

That's why all the religions have insisted on praying before one goes to sleep, so the last thought remains of prayer, and it sinks into one's heart. The whole night it remains like an aroma around you—it fills your inner space, and in the morning when you awake, again it is there. Eight hours of sleep can be used as meditation. Nowadays people don't have much time, but these eight hours of sleep can be used as meditation time. My whole approach is that everything can be used and should be used—even sleep!

153.
NIGHTMARES

Whenever your mind is doing something that goes against your nature, the unconscious gives you the message—first politely, but if you don't listen, nightmarishly.

A nightmare is nothing but the shouting of the unconscious, a cry of desperation that you are going too far away from yourself and you will miss your whole being. Come back home! It is as if a child is lost in the woods and the mother screams and shouts the name of the child. That is exactly what a nightmare is. So start befriending your dreams.

By and by you will see that you and your unconscious are coming closer and closer together. The closer you come, the fewer dreams you will have, because then there is no need for the dream. The unconscious can deliver its message even when you are awake. There is no need for it to wait for when you are asleep; it can give you its message any time.

The closer and closer you come, the more the conscious and unconscious start overlapping. That's a great experience. You feel, for the first time, one. No part of your being is denied. You have accepted your wholeness. You start becoming whole.

154.
JUDGING

Judging has to be dropped.
It is an illness that will never allow you any peace.

When you judge, you can never be in the present—you are always comparing, always moving backward or forward, but never here and now. Because the here and now is simply there; it is neither good nor bad. And there is no way to tell whether it is better, because there is nothing with which to compare. It is simply there in all its beauty.

But the very idea to evaluate it has something of the ego in it. The ego is a great improver; it lives on improvement. It keeps torturing you: "Improve, improve!" And there is nothing to improve.

Whenever a judgment comes, drop it then and there. Drop it. It is a habit. Don't torture yourself unnecessarily.

155.
BEFRIEND YOUR DREAMS

Learn to befriend your dreams. Dreams are a communication
from the unconscious. The unconscious has a message for you.
It is trying to create a bridge to your conscious mind.

Analysis is not needed to understand dreams, because if you analyze the dream, then the conscious again becomes the master. It
tries to dissect and analyze, to force meanings that are not the
meanings of the unconscious. The unconscious uses poetic language. The meaning is very subtle; it cannot be found by analysis.
It can only be found if you start learning the language of the dream.
So the first step is to befriend the dream.

When you have a dream that seems to be significant—maybe
violent, nightmarish, but you feel that there is some import in it—
in the morning, or even in the middle of the night, before you forget the dream, sit in your bed and close your eyes. Befriend the
dream; just tell it, "I am with you, and I am ready to come to you.
Lead me wherever you want to lead me; I am available." Just surrender to the dream. Close your eyes and move with it, enjoy it;
let the dream unfold. You will be surprised at what treasures a
dream is hiding, and you will see that it keeps on unfolding.

156.
ALONENESS

*Aloneness has in it both a sort of sadness, sorrow and a very deep peace
and silence. It depends on you how you look at it.*

It can be very difficult to have one's own space. But unless you have
your own space, you will never become acquainted with your own
being. You will never come to know who you are. Always engaged,
always occupied in a thousand and one things—in relationships, in
worldly affairs, anxieties, plans, future, past—one continuously
lives on the surface.

When you are alone you can start settling, sinking inward.
Because you are not occupied, you will not feel the way you have
always been feeling. It will be different; that difference also feels
strange. And certainly one misses one's lovers, one's friends, but
this is not going to be forever. It is just a small discipline.

And if you love yourself deeply and go down into yourself, you
will be ready to love others even more deeply, because one who
does not know oneself cannot love very deeply. If you live on the
surface, your relationships cannot have depth. It is your relationship, after all. If you have depth, then your relationship will
have depth.

157.
VIOLENCE

Nobody is born violent; one learns it.
One is infected by a violent society, and one becomes violent.
Otherwise every child is born absolutely nonviolent.

There is no violence in your being itself. Rather, we are conditioned by situations. We have to defend ourselves against so many things, and offense is the best method of defending. When a person has to defend himself many times, he becomes offensive, he becomes violent, because it is better to hit first than to wait for somebody to hit you. The one who hits first has more chances of winning.

That's what Machiavelli says in his famous book, *The Prince*. It is the Bible of politicians. He says that attack is the best method of defense. Don't wait; before somebody attacks you, you should attack. When you are attacked, Machiavelli says that it is already too late. You are already on the loser's side.

Hence people become violent. Very soon they come to understand that otherwise they will be crushed. The only way to survive is to fight, and once they learn this trick, by and by their whole nature becomes poisoned by it. But it is not natural, so it can be dropped.

158.
HUMILIATION

Be humble, then nobody can humiliate you.
Be egoless, then nobody can hurt you.

Sometimes it happens that others just find excuses to throw out their anger, but that's no reason for you to get disturbed. There are only two possibilities: Either the other person is right, then you feel humiliated; or the other is wrong, then they are being ridiculous, so the whole situation is humorous and one can enjoy it.

If you feel that the other person is right, accept whatever is being said and be humble. If you are humble you can never be humiliated; that is the point. You are already standing in the last row; you cannot be thrown backward. You are not trying to become the first, so nobody can obstruct you. That is the whole Taoist attitude toward life. Be humble, then nobody can humiliate you. Be egoless, then nobody can hurt you.

159.
WORSHIP

The attitude of worship is something that has to be felt within.
People have completely forgotten what worship really means.

Worship is approaching reality with a child's heart—not calculating, not cunning, not analyzing, but full of awe, of a tremendous feeling of wonder. It is a feeling of mystery surrounding you, the presence of the hidden, that things are not as they appear to be. It is to know that the appearance is just the periphery, that beyond the appearance something of tremendous significance is hiding.

When a child runs after a butterfly, he is worshipful. Or when he suddenly comes across a path and sees a flower—just an ordinary grass flower, but the child stands there in deep wonder. Or when he comes across a snake and is surprised and full of energy. Each moment brings some surprise. The child takes nothing for granted; that is the attitude of worship.

Never take anything for granted. Once you start taking things for granted, you are settling. Your child is disappearing, your wonder is dying, and when there is no wonder in the heart, there can be no worship. Worship means that life is so mysterious that there is really no way to understand it. It surpasses understanding; all our efforts fail. And the more we try to know, the more unknowable it seems.

160.

LIKES AND DISLIKES

The day you decide not to ask for things you like but rather to like things that happen, that day you become mature.

We can always keep wanting what we likes. But that will make you always miserable, because the world does not run according to your likes and dislikes. There is no guarantee that what you want, life also wants; there is no guarantee. There is every possibility that life is destined toward something that you don't know anything about at all.

When sometimes the thing you like does happen, you will still not feel very happy, because whatever we demand, we have already lived in fantasy. So it is already secondhand. If you say that you would like a certain man to be your lover, then in many dreams and in many fantasies you have already loved that man. And if it happens, then the real man is going to fall short of your fantasy; he is going to be just a carbon copy, because reality is never as fantastic as fantasy. Then you will be frustrated.

But if you start liking that which is happening—if you don't put your own will against the whole, if you simply say okay—whatever happens, you simply say yes—then you can never be miserable. Because no matter what happens, you are always in a positive attitude, ready to receive it and enjoy it.

161.

INDEPENDENCE

A person who says, "Whatever happens, I am going to remain happy; it will not make any difference to me. I will find a way to be happy whatever the circumstance," is independent.

No politics can make any difference. No change in the state of the outside world can make any difference. Poor or rich, a beggar or a king, the independent person remains the same. His or her inner climate does not change.

This is the goal of all meditation—to attain such tranquility, such stillness, that it is unconditional. Only then it is yours. Then whatever happens, let it happen—you remain happy. You remain tremendously happy. Drop your will, and you will see that the things that you were hankering for start happening on their own. Suddenly things start running smoothly. Everything fits together.

162.

SURRENDER

*Deep down you would like to move in a total surrender where all
your worries are dissolved and you can simply rest. But you are afraid;
everybody is afraid of surrendering.*

Ordinarily we think we are somebody—and we are nothing! What
have you got to surrender?—just a bogus ego, just an idea that you
are somebody. It is just a fiction. When you surrender the fiction,
you become the real. When you surrender that which you don't
really have, you become that which you are. But we cling, because
for our whole lives we have been trained to be independent. For
our whole lives we have been trained, programmed to fight, as if
the whole of life is nothing but a struggle to survive.

Life is known only when you start surrendering. Then you stop
fighting and start enjoying. But in the West, the concept of the ego
is very strong, and everybody is trying to conquer something.
People even talk of conquering nature. Absolutely foolish! We are
part of nature; how can we conquer it? We can destroy it we cannot conquer it. That's the whole of nature is destroyed by and by;
the whole ecology is disturbed.

There is nothing to conquer. In fact, one has to move with
nature, in nature, and to allow nature to be.

163.
BEING HURT

Millions of people have decided not to be sensitive. They have grown thick skins around themselves just to avoid being hurt by anybody. But it is at great cost. Nobody can hurt them, but nobody can make them happy either.

When you start becoming open, both things become available: Sometimes it will be cloudy, and sometimes there will be sun. But if you remain closed off in your cave, then there is no cloud and no sun either. It is good to come out, to dance with the sun, and yes, sometimes to feel sad with the clouds too—and sometimes it will be very windy. When you come out of the cave, all things are possible, and one of the things is that people can hurt you…but that is only one of the things.

Don't think about it too much, otherwise you will become closed again. There are millions of possibilities; think of those things too. You will be happier; you will be more loving. You will be more available, and other people will be more available to you. You will be able to laugh, you will be able to celebrate. There are a thousand and one possibilities. Why choose only one thing, that people will hurt you?

164.
THE ALCHEMY OF LOVE

Love is divine. If anything is divine on the earth, it is love—
and love also makes everything else divine. Love is the true alchemy
of life, because it transforms base metal into gold.

There are ancient stories, many stories in almost all the languages of the world, that somebody kisses a frog and the frog becomes a prince. The frog had been cursed; he was simply waiting for some kiss to be showered on him. He was waiting for love to come and transform him.

Love transforms—that is the message of all those stories. The stories are beautiful, very indicative, symbolic. It is only love that transforms the animal into the human; otherwise there is no difference between humans and other animals. The only difference, the possible difference, is love. And the more you live through love, as love, the more humanity is born in you. The ultimate, the omega point, is when one has *become* love. Then not only is the animal transcended, even the human is transcended. Then one is divine, one is God. The whole of human growth is love's growth. Without love we are animals. With love we are human. And when love has become your natural being, your very flavor, you are God.

165.
WILD

Love is wild, and the moment one tries to domesticate it, it is destroyed.
Love is a whirlwind of freedom, of wildness, of spontaneity.

You cannot manage love and control it. Controlled, it is dead. Love can be controlled only when you have already killed it. If it is alive, it controls you, not otherwise. If it is alive, it possesses you. You are simply lost in it, because it is bigger than you, vaster than you, more primal than you, more foundational than you.

In the same way God also comes. The same way love comes to you, God comes. God is also wild, wilder than love. A civilized God is no God at all. The God of the church, the God of the temple is just an idol. God has disappeared from those places long ago, because God cannot be imprisoned. Those places are graveyards of God.

If you want to find God, you will have to be available to the wild energy of life. Love is the first glimpse, the beginning of the journey. God is the climax, the culmination, but God comes as a whirlwind. It will uproot you, it will possess you. It will crush you to pieces. It will kill you and resurrect you. It will be both—the cross and the resurrection.

166.
STRENGTH

One can become too attached to having a shelter or protection,
but that will not give you strength. Strength always comes when
you face situations that are hard.

In the old days people used to move to monasteries and to the Himalayas and to the faraway caves, and they attained to a certain peace there. But that peace was cheap, because whenever these people would come back to the world, it would immediately be shattered. Their peace was so fragile, they would become afraid of the world. So their isolation was a kind of escape, not growth.

Learn to be alone, but never get too attached to your aloneness. Remain capable of relating with others. Learn to meditate, but don't move so far to an extreme that you become incapable of love. Be silent, peaceful, still, but don't get obsessed by this stillness, or you will not be able to face the marketplace.

It is easy to be silent when you are alone. It is difficult to be silent when you are with people, but that difficulty has to be faced. Once you are able to be silent with people, you have attained; now nothing can destroy it.

167.
PARTICIPATION

There are things that you can know only if you participate.

From the outside you know only superficial things. What is happening to the inside person? Somebody is crying and tears are flowing. You can watch, but it will be very superficial. What is happening to his heart? Why is he crying? It is difficult even to interpret—because he may be crying out of misery, he may be crying out of sadness, he may be crying out of anger, he may be crying out of happiness, he may be crying out of gratitude.

And tears are just tears. There is no way to analyze a tear chemically to find out from where it comes—from deep gratitude, from a blissful state, or from misery—because all tears are the same. Chemically they don't differ, and they look the same rolling down the cheeks. So it is almost impossible, as far as the deeper realms are concerned, to conclude from the outside. A person cannot be observed. Only things can be observed. You can know from the within. That means that you have to know those tears yourself; otherwise you will never really know them. Much can be learned by observation, and it is good that you watch, very good. But that is nothing compared to what you can learn by participating.

168.

HIBERNATION

Sometimes you are cold; sometimes you are not. Don't create a problem out of it. When cold, be cold, and don't feel guilty about it.

There is no need to remain warm for twenty-four hours. That would be tiring. One needs a little rest. When you are cold, the energy is moving inward; when you are warm, the energy is moving outward. Of course, other people would like you always to be warm, because then your energy moves toward them. When you are cold, your energy is not moving toward them, so they feel offended. They will tell you that you are cold. But it is for you to decide.

In those cold moments you hibernate, you go within your being. Those are meditative moments. So this is my suggestion—when you feel cold, close the doors from relationships and moving with people. Feeling that you are cold, go home and meditate. That is the right moment to meditate. With energy itself moving in, you can ride on it and go to the very innermost core of your being. There will be no fight. You can simply move with the current. And when you are feeling warm, move out. Forget all about meditation. Be loving. Use both states, and don't worry about it.

169.
SCRIPTURES

There are many scriptures, and much great philosophy,
but they are all rubbish! They exist just to let the foolish people
get occupied; they are not for the real seeker.

What I am saying is absolutely alive, new, fresh, and young. It is not traditional at all, it is a totally different phenomenon—it has to be. Because scriptures that were written three thousand years ago were meant for the people for whom it was written. That psychology no longer functions in the world. I am responding to you; those scriptures responded to their people. Those scriptures were not written for you. There is a gap of three, four, five thousand years between you and those scriptures. They are utterly irrelevant. Relying on them would be as absurd as somebody who studies physics stopping at Newton and never getting to Albert Einstein.

But scriptures can't respond to living people; they can't grow. That's why in the old days many masters insisted that their sayings should not be written down, so that they could keep on growing. The masters would give their message to their disciples, and the disciples would live in a different world. The masters would be gone, and the disciples would be teaching something to other people in their own right. They would make many changes, because the people have changed, situations have changed. But once you write a book it becomes fixed; it becomes frozen. Nobody can change it, and if somebody does, then the followers of the book will become very angry.

170.
SADNESS

When sad, be really sad, sink into sadness. What else can you do?
Sadness is needed. It is very relaxing, a dark night that surrounds you.
Fall asleep into it. Accept it, and you will see that the moment you
accept sadness, it starts becoming beautiful.

Sadness is ugly because of our rejection of it; it is not ugly in itself. Once you accept it, you will see how beautiful it is, how relaxing, how calm and quiet, how silent. It has something to give that happiness can never give.

Sadness gives depth. Happiness gives height. Sadness gives roots. Happiness gives branches. Happiness is like a tree going into the sky, and sadness is like the roots going down into the womb of the earth. Both are needed, and the higher a tree goes, the deeper it goes, simultaneously. The bigger the tree, the bigger will be its roots. In fact, it is always in proportion. That's its balance.

You cannot bring the balance. The balance that you bring is of no use. It will be forced. Balance comes spontaneously; it is already there. In fact, when you are happy, you become so excited that it is tiring. Have you watched? The heart immediately moves then into the other direction, gives you a rest. You feel it as sadness. It is giving you a rest, because you were getting too excited. It is medicinal, therapeutic. It is just as in the day you work hard and in the night you fall deeply asleep. In the morning you are fresh again. After sadness you will be fresh again, ready to be excited.

171.
UNENLIGHTENED LOVE

Love does not necessarily mean freedom. It should—that is the ideal.
Always remember, if you love somebody with awareness, only then will
it be a blessing.

Love can be destructive in many ways, because love is not necessarily enlightened. A mother lovesthe child and the whole world is suffering because mothers love their children. Ask the psychiatrists, the psychologists. They say that every neurosis can be reduced to the mother-child relationship. Many people in the insane asylums are suffering from nothing but love. Fathers love their sons, priests love, politicians love. Everybody is loving, but love is not necessarily enlightened.

When love is enlightened, it is compassion. Then it is of a totally different quality. It gives you freedom. Its whole function is to give freedom, absolutely. And not only that it talks about freedom—it makes every effort to make you free and to destroy all the hindrances on the path of freedom.

So love can exist, but if it is not very alert, then it is destructive. Love alone is not enough, otherwise the world would already have become a paradise. You love your partner, your partner loves you, but what happens finally? Nothing but destruction. Your love is okay, but you are not okay. Something is there deep down in the unconscious that goes on creating things you are not aware of.

I don't say that love should be denied, but love should not come first. Awareness should come first. Love has to follow like a shadow.

172.
PLAY

Once you become capable of playing roles, you become free of them.

What is the difficulty in playing a role? The difficulty comes because you are fixed with another role and you think that is your personality. You have been playing one role, and you have become so identified with it that a different role seems impossible. You will have to loosen yourself from the past and move into your new role. But it is good to move into new roles. And just think—it is just a role, a game that you are playing.

Your essence has no personality. Your essence has no roles. It can play all the roles, but it has no character. That's what makes inner freedom beautiful. So just be an actor. In one film the actor is playing one role, in another film another role. Maybe in the morning she is in one role, and in the evening she is in another. She simply slips from one role to another—and there is no problem, because she knows it is just acting.

All of life should be like that. One should be so capable of slipping in and out of roles in that nothing holds one. You will start feeling a freedom arising in you, and you will start feeling your real essence. Otherwise you are always confined in a role.

173.
A GAME

Play your role, enjoy it; it is fun. But take it lightly.
It is not worth worrying about.

Whatever role you have to play in a certain circumstance, play it to your utmost ability, play it totally. But once it is finished, whether you have succeeded or failed is irrelevant. Don't look back; move ahead. There are other roles you have to play. Failure and success are unimportant. What is important is the awareness that everything is a game.

When your whole life becomes full of this awareness, you are freed, nothing binds you, you are no longer tethered to anything. Then you are no longer imprisoned by anything. You use masks, but you know that they are not your original face. And you can remove the mask, because now you know it for what it is. It is removable. And now you can know your original face too. The one who is aware that life is a game comes to know the original face. And to know one's original face is to know all that is worth knowing.

174.
FUTILITY

Everything is futile. One has to understand this. If you don't understand it, you will always remain in illusion. Everything is futile, and in life there is no progress, no improvement, because life is eternally there. Life is already perfect.

All that you try to do to make life more perfect is futile, but it takes time to realize it. When you are feeling stuck, you can do two things. You can change your lifestyle, and then for a few days again you will be on a honeymoon, with hopes and desires and ambitions, and the possibility of tomorrow again will become alive. But after a few days you realize that tomorrow never comes. Again you are stuck, and the whole thing again becomes a routine.

It is just like when you love a woman or a man. The honeymoon over, the love is over. By the end of the honeymoon, you are again seeking and searching for another. You can go on in this way from one honeymoon to another, but it is not going to help. You have to realize that there is nothing to achieve in life. Life is not goal oriented. Life is eternally here now. It is already perfect. It cannot be improved upon.

Once you realize this, then there is no future, no hope, no desire, and no ambition. You live this moment; you enjoy and delight in it.

175.
SOMETHING TO SHARE

Love is a relationship between you and somebody else. Meditation
is a relationship between you and you. Love is outgoing, meditation
is ingoing. Love is a sharing. But how can you share love if you don't
have it in the first place? What will you share?

People have anger, people have jealousies, people have hatred, so
in the name of love they start sharing these things, because that's
what they have. Once the honeymoon is over and you put down
your masks, and the reality is revealed, then what will you share?
You will share that which you have. If anger, then anger, if possessiveness, then possessiveness. Then there is fighting and conflict
and struggle, and each tries to dominate the other.

Meditation will give you something you can share. Meditation
will give you the quality, the energy that can become love when you
are related to somebody. Ordinarily you don't have that quality.
Nobody has it. You have to create it. Love is not something you are
born with. It is something that you have to create; it is something
that you have to become. It is a struggle, an effort, and a great art.

When you have overflowing love within you, then you can share.
But that can happen only when you can relate to yourself. And
meditation is nothing but learning to relate to yourself.

176.

PLANETARY BEING

The earth is undivided. India and Pakistan and England and Germany
exist only on maps, and those maps are created by the politicians,
the power-mad people. This whole earth is yours.

There is no need to identify with anything. Why become confined
to small territories? Why be confined by politics? Claim the whole
heritage of the earth. It is your earth. Be a planetary being rather
than a national one. Forget about India and England and think of the
whole globe. Think of each and everyone as brothers and sisters;
they are!

When you are an Indian you are against others. You have to be,
otherwise how will you define your Indianhood? You are against
China, against Pakistan, and against this and against that; all
identifications are basically *against*. When you are for something,
you are against something else, naturally. Don't be for and
against—just be. There are better things to think about. You don't
ask, "With what disease should I identify myself—tuberculosis or
cancer?" You don't ask that. These national identities are just like
tuberculosis and cancer.

In a better world there will be no countries, in a higher world
there will be no religions. To be human is enough, and one has even
to go beyond that one day; then one becomes divine. Then even this
earth is too small to contain you, then the stars are also yours, this
whole universe is yours. And when one becomes universal, one
has arrived.

177.
NOW WHAT?

While you are doing something—carving something, painting
something, sculpting something—you are lost in it. That is your joy,
your meditation. But when it is finished, naturally you come back
to the mind, and the mind can start asking, "What is the point?"

It is said about Gibbon that when he finished his history of the world, he wept. It had been thirty years' work; day and night, year in, year out, he worked and worked. He had only four hours of sleep and twenty hours of work each day. When it was finished, he wept. His wife could not believe it, his disciples could not believe it.

They said, "Why are you weeping?" Everybody was happy that the work was complete, when the greatest record of history was complete. But he was crying, "Now what will I do? I am finished!" And he died within three years; there was nothing else for him to do. He had always been a young man; the day his work was finished he became old. It happens to every creator: A painter is so passionately in the painting that when it is finished, the feeling arises, "Now what? Why did I do it?" Great awareness is needed to see that the joy of painting is in painting itself. There is no result—the end and the means are not separate.

If you are enjoying something, *that* is the point of it; don't ask for anything else. What more do you need? The attainment is in the very process. You have grown through it; that is the attainment. You have become deeper through it; that is the attainment. You have come closer to the center of your being; that is the attainment. If you are aware, the feeling of pointlessness will disappear.

178.
RESPONSIBILITY

From this moment start thinking in terms of yourself being the cause
of your life and your world. This is the meaning of being a seeker:
to take total responsibility for one's own being.

Misery has no outer cause; the cause is inner. You go on throwing the responsibility outside yourself, but that is just an excuse.

Yes, misery is triggered from the outside, but the outside does not create it. When somebody insults you, the insult comes from the outside, but the anger is inside you. The anger is not caused by the insult, it is not the effect of the insult. If there were no anger energy in you, the insult would have remained impotent. It would have simply passed, and you would not have been disturbed by it.

Causes don't exist outside human consciousness; causes exist inside you. You are the cause of your life, and to understand this is to understand one of the most basic truths. To understand this is to start a journey of transformation.

179.
MISERY

Nature intends everybody to be an emperor. Nature creates only kings and queens, but we never accept that; it looks too good to be true.

Bliss is the only criterion of whether you are arriving closer to truth or not. The closer you come to truth, the more blissful you become; the farther away from truth, the more miserable. Misery is nothing but distance from truth; bliss is closeness, intimacy. And when one has become one with truth, there is ultimate bliss, which cannot be taken away, because all distance has disappeared, all space between you and truth has disappeared.

The truth exists at the central core of our being, but we exist on the periphery. We live on the porch of a palace and have forgotten the palace completely. We have decorated our small porch and we think that is all there is. We are self-condemned beggars. Nature intends everybody to be an emperor,. Nature creates only kings and queens, but we never accept that; it looks too good to be true. We are happy in our misery. Misery gives something, and that is the ego. Misery gives ego, and bliss takes it away.

We would like to *be* even if we are miserable; we don't want to disappear. And that is the gamble. One has to disappear; only then are bliss and truth possible.

180.

PSYCHOLOGICAL DISEASE

Human pathology exists because we have to transcend.
If you cannot transcend humanity, you will become pathological.
You have an inner capacity to go beyond, but if you don't allow it,
it will turn on you and become destructive.

All creative people are dangerous people, because if they are not allowed creativity they will become destructive.

Human beings are the only animals on the earth who are creative; no other animal is so dangerous because no other animal creates. They simply live, they have a programmed life, they never go off the track. A dog lives like a dog and dies like a dog. He never tries to become a Buddha, and of course he never goes astray and becomes an Adolf Hitler. He simply follows the track. He is very conservative, orthodox, bourgeois; all animals except human beings are bourgeois.

Human beings have something of the freak in them. They want to do something, to go somewhere, to be; and if it is not allowed, if they cannot be a rose, then they would like to be a weed—but they would like to *be* something. If they cannot become buddhas, they will become criminals. If they cannot create poetry, they will create nightmares. If they cannot bloom, they will not allow anybody else to bloom.

181.

REMEMBRANCE

All is divine! Let this be your first fundamental—
it can change you utterly.

It is natural that you will forget that all is divine many times; don't be worr about that. The moment you remember again, let it be there. Don't repent that you forgot for one hour. That is natural. It is such an old habit; for many lives we have lived in the habit. So it is natural. Don't feel guilty about it. If you can remember even for a few seconds out of twenty-four hours, that will do—because truth is so potential, so powerful, that a small drop of it is enough to destroy your whole world of untruth. Just one ray of light is enough to destroy the darkness of thousands of years.

So it is not a question of quantity, remember. It is not a question of your remembering twenty-four hours a day—how can you? But one day you will suddenly see that the impossible has become the possible.

182.
FLUIDITY

It is good to be involved in many things. A person who has been
doing one thing, and only one thing, becomes very fixed,
and change becomes difficult.

It is very good that people go on changing from this to that job; that
keeps them fluid. In a better world, everything will be more mobile
than it is, and people should be changing continually so that
nothing becomes a fixation—a fixation is a disease.

Each new job, each new project, brings a new quality to your
being—it makes you richer.

183.
PHILOSOPHY

It almost always happens that when you are missing something you start
thinking about it, you start creating a philosophy about it.

It is my observation that people who have not loved write books
about love; it is a kind of substitute. People who have not been able
to love write poetry, they write very great love poetry, but they
don't have any experience of love, so all their poetry is just specu-
lation. They may have great flights of imagination, but this has
nothing to do with the reality of love. Love's reality is totally
different; it has to be experienced.

184.
ORGANIC UNITY

If you are not integrated, whatever you are doing cannot
have real integration; it can only be put together superficially.
And the result of that putting together will be just a mechanical
unity, not an organic unity.

You can put a car together—but you cannot put a flower together
in the same way; a flower has to be grown. It has an organic unity,
an inner unity—it has a center, and the center comes first, then the
petals. In a mechanical unity, parts come first, then the whole. In
an organic unity, the whole comes first and then the parts.

One can write poetry with no poetry in it. And one can write a
story without any center—much ado about nothing, a tale told by
an idiot, full of fury and noise, signifying nothing.

The significance comes from the person, the poet; it is not in the
poetry. If the poet has something overflowing, then the poetry
becomes luminous, then it has a glow, it has a subtle unity. It throbs
with life, it has a heart, it beats…you can hear the beat of the heart.
Then it lives and grows and it goes on growing. It is almost like
when a child is born to you; you may die, but the child keeps on
growing. The real poetry will go on growing even when the poet
is gone. That's how a Kalidas or a Shakespeare goes on living. The
poetry has something organic in it; it is not just put together.

185.

THE GREAT AMBITION

Every human being is love unborn, hence the misery, the anguish.
The seed cannot be contented as the seed. It wants to become a tree,
it wants to play with the wind, it wants to rise to the sky—
it is ambitious!

Each human being is born with a great ambition—the ambition to
flower in love, to bloom in love. So I see each human being as a possibility, as a potentiality, as a promise. Something that has not happened has yet to happen, and unless it happens there can be no
contentment, no peace; there will be agony, suffering, misery.

Only when you have come to a blooming where you feel that
now you are fulfilled—now you have become that for which you
were born, you have attained your destiny, now there is nothing left
anymore—only when ambition completely disappears because it is
fulfilled, is a person in bliss, never before.

186.

THE REAL QUESTION

The real question is just a capsule in which the answer is hidden,
a hard shell that protects the soft answer within. It is just a crust
that surrounds a seed.

Ninety-nine questions out of a hundred are rubbish, and because of
these ninety-nine questions you cannot manage to ask the really
valuable question. Because these ninety-nine clamor around you,
shout, are very noisy, they don't allow the real question to arise in
you. The real question has a very silent, still, small voice, and these
unreal ones are great pretenders. Because of them you cannot ask
the right question and you cannot find the right answer.

So to know rubbish as rubbish is a great insight. Then it starts
slipping out of your hands—because you cannot hold it long if
you know it is rubbish. The very understanding that it is rubbish
is enough for your hands to start becoming empty, and when your
hands are empty of the rubbish, only the one, the real question,
is left.

And the beauty is that if only the real question is left, the answer
is not far away. It is just inside the question. The very center of the
question is the answer.

187.

INTROVERT-EXTROVERT

There are two types of slaves: the extroverts and the introverts.

A person who is not free to move according to the moment and the situation is a slave. There are two types of slaves: the extroverts and the introverts. The extroverts are the slaves of the outer. They cannot go in; they have completely forgotten the route. If you talk about going in, they simply look at you, bewildered. They don't understand what you are talking about; they think that you are talking nonsense.

A person who has become too introverted starts losing related-ness, responsibility, and activity and misses much. He becomes closed in himself; he is like a grave. The extrovert becomes the politician, the introvert becomes an escapist—and both are ill, both are neurotic.

The really healthy person is not fixed anywhere. Going in and going out are just like inhaling and exhaling, just like the breath coming in and going out.. You are free in both. By being free in both you are beyond both, you have a transcendence. You are a total person.

188.

VULNERABLE & STRONG

There are people who feel strong only when they are not vulnerable;
but that strength is just a facade, a camouflage. Then there are people
who are vulnerable but feel weak.

Those who feel weak when they are vulnerable cannot feel vulnerable for long: Sooner or later that weakness will make them so afraid that they will close up. So the right approach is to feel vulnerable *and* strong. Then you can remain vulnerable and each day your strength will grow, and you will become courageous enough to become more and more vulnerable.

A really brave person is absolutely open—that is the criterion of courage. Only a coward is closed, and a strong person is as strong as a rock and as vulnerable as a rose. It is a paradox—and all that is real is paradoxical.

So always remember: When you feel something paradoxical, don't try to make it consistent, because that consistency will be false. Reality is always paradoxical: On the one hand you feel vulnerable, on the other hand you feel strong—that means a moment of truth has arrived. On the one hand you feel you don't know anything, on the other hand you feel you know all—a moment of truth has arrived.

On the one hand you always feel one aspect, and on the other hand the exact opposite aspect, and when you have both these aspects together, always remember that something true is very close by.

189.

SCHIZOPHRENIA

Guilt always creates schizophrenia. If guilt goes very deep,
it can create a real split.

There is no division between the world and spirituality. But a division arises because of the phenomenon of guilt. So guilt has to be dropped. Not that you have to bring spirituality and the world together; they *are* together. There is no way to separate them. You have to understand your guilt and drop it, otherwise guilt always creates schizophrenia. If guilt goes very deep, it can create a real split. A person can really become two—so much so that one may not be aware of the other at all. The split can become so great that the two aspects never meet; there is no encounter.

You have to understand your guilt. Just move as naturally as possible and don't categorize something as "spiritual" and something else as "worldly." The very categorization is wrong, because then division starts. Once you label something as spiritual, suddenly you have condemned the world. When you say something is worldly, the division has come in. There is no need.

You don't divide when you see the moon in the night and you enjoy it, and then one day you see a child smiling and you enjoy that. Which is spiritual and which is material? You see a flower opening and something opens in you and you delight in it. The food is being cooked and it smells delicious, and suddenly there is joy in it. Which is spiritual and which is worldly?

190.
ALCHEMY

Meditation is alchemical; it transforms your whole being.
It destroys all limitations, all narrowness; it makes you wide.

Meditation helps you to get rid of all boundaries: the boundaries of religion, nation, race. Awareness helps you not only to get rid of all kinds of logical and ideological confinements, imprisonments, but also it helps you to transcend the limitations of the body, the mind. It makes you aware that you are pure consciousness and nothing else.

The body is only your house; you are not it. Mind is only a mechanism to be used. It is not the master; it is just a servant. As you become aware that you are neither the body nor the mind, you start expanding, you become wider and wider. You start becoming oceanic, skylike. That transformation brings glory and victory to you.

191.
HANKERING
FOR THE POSSIBLE

When you desire the possible, the impossible can also happen.
When you desire the impossible, even the possible becomes difficult.

There are two types of people, low energy and high energy. There is nothing good in being high energy or bad in being low energy. That's how two types exist. The low-energy people move very slowly. They don't leap. They don't explode. They simply grow as trees grow. They take more time, but their growth is more settled, more certain, and falling back is difficult. Once they have reached a certain point, they will not easily lose it again.

High-energy people move quickly. They jump. They leap. With them, the work goes very fast. That's good, but there is one problem with them: They can lose whatever they achieve as easily as they achieved it. They fall back very easily because their movement has been jumping, not a growth. Growth needs very slow ripening, seasoning, time.

Low-energy people will be defeated in a worldly competition. They will always lag behind. That's why they have become condemned. There is such competition in the world. They will fall out of the rat race; they will not be able to remain in it. They will be pushed out, thrown out. But as far as spiritual growth is concerned, they can grow more deeply than high-energy people because they can wait and be patient. They are not in too much of a hurry. They don't want anything instantly. Their expectation is never for the impossible; they only hanker for the possible.

192.
BREAKING BRIDGES

It is always good to break bridges with the past. Then one retains
an aliveness, an innocence, and one never loses one's childhood.
Many times one needs to break all the bridges, to be clean and
to start again from ABC.

Whenever you begin a thing, you are again a child. The moment
that you start thinking that you have arrived, it is time to break the
bridges again, because that means that a deadness is settling in.
Now you are becoming just an entity, a commodity in the market.
And anyone who wants to be creative has to die every day to the
past, in fact every moment, because creativity means a continuous
rebirth. If you are not reborn, whatever you create will be a repetition. If you are reborn, only then can something new come out
of you.

It happens that even great artists, poets and painters, come to a
point at which they keep repeating themselves again and again.
Sometimes it has happened that their first work was their greatest.
Kahlil Gibran wrote *The Prophet* when he was only twenty or
twenty-one, and it was his last great work. He wrote many other
books, but nothing reaches the peak of the first book. In a subtle
way, he goes on repeating *The Prophet*.

So an artist, a painter or a poet, a musician or a dancer, one who
has to create something new every day, has a tremendous necessity
to forget the yesterdays so completely that there is not even a
remembrance of them. The slate is clean and out of that newness,
creativity is born.

193.
THE NEGLECTED HEART

We have passed over our hearts, we have entered our heads
directly without moving through the heart.
We have chosen a shortcut. The heart has been neglected, ignored—
because the heart is a dangerous phenomenon.

The heart is uncontrollable, and we are always afraid of anything that is uncontrollable. The head is controllable. It is within you, and in your hands; you can manage it. The heart is bigger than you, The head is within you. The same is not the case with the heart; you are within the heart. When the heart awakens, you will be surprised to find that you are just a tiny spot within it. The heart is bigger than you, it is vast. And we are always afraid of being lost in something vast.

The function of the heart is mysterious, and mystery naturally makes one apprehensive. Who knows what is going to happen? And how is one going to cope with it? One is never prepared as far as the heart is concerned. With the heart, things happen unexpectedly. Strange are its ways, hence man has decided to bypass it, to just go directly to the head and contact reality through the head.

194.
COMPARISON

My suggestion is that you enjoy music, enjoy poetry, enjoy nature,
but avoid the temptation to dissect it. And don't make comparisons,
because comparing is futile.

Don't compare a rose to a marigold. They are both flowers, so certainly they have certain similarities, but that is where their similarities end. They are unique too. A marigold is a marigold…the gold of it, such a dancing gold. The rose is a rose…that rosiness, that liveliness. Both are flowers, so you can find similarities, but there is no point in going into them. You may lose track of the uniqueness, and the uniqueness is beautiful. There are people who go on finding similarities: what is similar in the Koran and the Bible, what is similar in the Bible and the Vedas. These are stupid people; they waste their time, and they will waste other people's time. Always look at the unique and avoid the temptation to compare, because comparison will make whatever you are looking at mundane, mediocre.

Jesus turned water into wine. That is the miracle of a poet, that is poetry—turning water into wine. Ordinary words become so intoxicating when they come from a poet that one can be drunk. But then there are professors, pundits, and scholars who do just the opposite: They are experts in turning wine into water. They are the real anti-Christs! Don't do that. If you can't turn water into wine, it is better not to do anything.

195.
ETERNITY

Eternity is not the continuity of time forever. That is the meaning
in the dictionaries: forever and forever. But forever is part of time—
prolonged time, indefinitely prolonged, but it is still time.
Eternity is jumping out of time; it is nontemporal, it is no-time.

The present moment is the door to eternity. The past and future are part of time. The present is not part of time—the present is just between the two, between the past and the future. If you are absolutely alert, only then are you in the present; otherwise you keep missing it. If you are not alert, by the time you are alert it is already gone, it has become the past; it is so swift.

So between the past and the future there is a door, a gap, an interval—now—that is the door to eternity. Only in eternity is bliss possible: in time, at the most, pleasure; at worst, pain—but both are fleeting. Their nature is not different. Pain comes and goes, pleasure comes and goes. They are momentary, water bubbles.

Bliss has no counterpart. It is not a duality of pleasure and pain, day and night. It is nondual, it knows no opposite. It is a transcendence. Try to be more and more in the present. Don't move too much in imagination and memory. Whenever you find yourself wandering into memory, into imagination, bring yourself back to the present, to what you are doing, to where you are, to who you are. Pull yourself back again and again to the present. Buddha has called it recollecting oneself; in that recollection by and by you will understand what eternity is.

196.
ZERO POINT

We have become accustomed to ups and downs: When we are up, we feel
good, when we are down we feel bad. But just in the middle is a point
that is neither up nor down; that is the neutral point.

Sometimes the neutral point is very frightening, because if one
feels bad one knows what the case is; if one feels good one knows
what is the case. But when one cannot feel either, one is simply in
a kind of limbo and one is afraid. But that point is very beautiful.
If you can accept it, that point will give you immense insight into
your life. When you are up, the up disturbs you; all pleasures bring
fever, excitement. And when you are down, again you are disturbed
in a negative way. When you are up, you want to cling to that state;
when you are down you want to get out of it. Something is there
to work on and to remain occupied with, but when you are just in
the middle, all fever is gone; it is a zero point.

Through that zero point one can have immense insight into oneself because all is silent. There is no happiness, there is no unhappiness, so there is no noise of any kind, there is utter quiet. Buddha
used this point very deeply in his work with all his disciples. It was
a must, everybody had to attain it first, and then the real work
started. He calls it *upeksha*—another name for neutrality.

197.
VULNERABILITY

Existence in the body is very precarious. Any moment, with just
a little more oxygen or a little less, and you are gone!
A little less sugar in the blood and you are gone… a little dysfunction
in the brain and you are gone!

Life exists in vulnerability, it exists in danger, insecurity. There is no security, and there cannot be. Security is only for dead people. They are very strong. Can you kill a dead person?—you cannot. Can you destroy a dead person—you cannot. Dead people are very strong!

The higher the quality of life, the more fragile. Look at a rose, look at a poem, look at a song, look at music—it vibrates for a second and then is gone! Look at love: One moment it is there, next moment it is not. Look at meditation. As you go higher you will find that things become more and more vulnerable. So there is nothing wrong with vulnerability; it is understanding how life is. To pretend to be strong is foolish. Nobody is strong, nobody can be strong; it is just an ego game. Even Alexander the Great is not strong—one day comes and all his strength is gone.

So just learn to accept your vulnerability, and then there will be a very deep understanding and a deep flow of energy. You will not feel it as a problem. It is not a problem; it is something very significant.

198.
DIFFERENT ANGLES

It is always good to feel the other from different angles, because people have multiple aspects.

We all carry a world within us, and if you really want to know a person you have to know him or her from all the angles possible. Then two people can remain charmed by each other for infinity, because then no role is ever fixed. And after a few days when you are again in the roles of wife and husband, for a change sometimes, then it is beautiful, it is something new! Then it feels as if you are meeting after many days.

Change is always good. Always find new ways and means to relate with a person, new situations. Never get into a routine. Then the relationship is always flowing. There are always surprises; it is good to surprise and to be surprised by the other; then the relationship is never dead.

199.
TRUTH

*Truth is achieved only through awareness. It is not a mind process
at all. You are not to think the truth; rather, you have to stop all thinking
to know truth; you have to forget all about truth to know truth.*

You have to unburden yourself of all the theories, hypothesizes,
philosophies, and ideologies that you have learned. The process of
achieving the truth is a process of unlearning, it is a process of
unconditioning. Slowly, one has to get out of the mind, to slip out
of the mind; and one has to become just a pool of consciousness,
a pure awareness. Just a sheer watchfulness: Do nothing, just
watch, watch all that is happening in the outside world and in the
inside world.

When one can just watch without any judgment interfering,
without any old ideas coming in, then truth is revealed. And the
miracle is that it does not come from somewhere else to you, it
does not descend from above; it is found within you—it is your
intrinsic nature. It is really a great revelation to know truth, because
you are it and you have never lost it—even for a single moment.
You have always been it. It is impossible to lose it, because it is
your nature and your nature cannot be lost. That's why we call it
nature. That which cannot be lost is the very definition of nature.
That which can be lost is not nature but nurture. Truth is your
nature, your very being, your very existence, your very center.

200.

INSECURITY

The human being is a fragile flower. Any stone can crush you.
Any accident, and you are gone. Once you understand it....

When you feel very afraid, what to do? The night is dark, the path unknown, no light to light the path, nobody to guide you, no map, so what to do? If you like crying and weeping, cry and weep, but that helps nobody. Better to accept it and grope in the dark. Enjoy while you are alive. Why waste this time in hankering after security, when security is not possible. This is the wisdom of insecurity. Once you understand it, accept it, you are freed from fear.

It always happens when soldiers go to war that they are very afraid, because death is waiting for them. Maybe they will never come back again. They tremble, they cannot sleep, they have nightmares. They dream again and again that they have been killed or crippled. But once they reach the front, all fear disappears. Once they see that death is happening, people are dying, other soldiers are dead, that their friends may be dead, that bombs are falling and bullets passing—within twenty-four hours they settle, and all fear is gone. They accept reality; they start playing cards while bullets are passing. They drink tea, and they enjoy it as they have never enjoyed it before, because this may be their last cup. They joke and laugh, they dance and sing. What to do? When death is there, it is there.

This is insecurity. Accept it, then it disappears.

201.

WORDS

Words are not just words. They have moods, climates of their own.

When a word settles inside you, it brings a different climate to your mind, a different approach, a different vision. Call the same thing a different name, and you will see: Something is immediately different.

There are feeling words and there are intellectual words. Drop intellectual words more and more. Use more and more feeling words. There are political words and there are religious words. Drop political words. There are words that immediately create conflict. The moment you utter them, argument arises. So never use logical, argumentative language. Use the language of affection, of caring, of love, so that no argument arises.

If one starts being aware in this way, one sees a tremendous change arising. If one is a little alert in life, many miseries can be avoided. A single word uttered in unconsciousness can create a long chain of misery. A slight difference, just a very small turning, and it creates a lot of change. One should become very careful and use words when absolutely necessary. Avoid contaminated words. Use fresh words, noncontroversial, which are not arguments but just expressions of your feelings.

If one can become a connoisseur of words, one's whole life will be totally different. If a word brings misery, anger, conflict, or argument, drop it. What is the point in carrying it? Replace it with something better. The best is silence. The next best are singing, poetry, love.

202.

NO WORDS

If it is possible, live an experience and don't fix it with any words, because that will make it narrow.

You are sitting...it is a silent evening. The sun has gone, and the stars have started appearing. Just be. Don't even say, "This is beautiful," because the moment you say that it is beautiful, it is no longer the same. By saying *beautiful,* you are bringing in the past, and all the experiences that you said were beautiful have colored the word.

Why bring in the past? The present is so vast, and the past is so narrow. Why look from a hole in the wall when you can come out and look at the whole sky?

So try not to use words, but if you have to, then be very choosy about them, because each word has a nuance of its own. Be very poetic about it.

203.
DEVICES AND PRINCIPLES

All religions are basically nothing but methods of awakening.
But all the religions have gone astray because of doctrines.
Those doctrines are not important; those doctrines are nothing
but props to the methods. They are arbitrary.

Christians believe in only one life. This belief is a device to make people aware. You will be surprised, because ordinarily we think it is a principle. It is not a principle; it is just a device to force the idea to hit home. It is a way of hammering: "Don't lose time in unnecessary things. Don't go on chasing after power, money, prestige, because you have only one life. Death is coming. So be alert, be watchful, and see what you are doing." This is a device; it is not a principle.

But that's where things go wrong: Christians thought it was a principle, so they started making a great philosophy out of it. Then certainly it is against Hinduism, because Hinduism says that there are many lives—a long chain of lives, zillions of lives. Now there is a problem: If these are principles, then there is a conflict. Then only one can be right, not both.

But that idea too is a device created for a different kind of people who have known much, who have seen many changes, and who have noted the fact that history repeats itself. But the goal is the same. The East says, "You have been doing these things again and again and again for many lives. Are you going to continue this vicious circle, this boring repetition? Already you have been here for a very long time, doing the same stupid things again and again. It is time—become alert!"

204.

JUST THIS

It is the very essence of meditation: just this. To remain aware of just this is meditation—watching it, observing it, with no condemnation, with no evaluation, just remaining like a mirror.

The mind can live only in the past and through the past, or in the future and through the future. The present moment becomes its grave: The mind cannot exist in this-ness. And to be in a no-mind state is to be in meditation.

This can become one of the greatest secrets. It can become the very key that unlocks the door of the divine. When something is passing through the mind, remember: *just this.* Don't say it is good, don't say it is bad; don't compare it. Don't desire that something be otherwise. Whatever is, is, and whatever is not, is not.

Everybody creates much misery out of this tension. People try to attain that which is not and tend to forget that which is.

For example, when you cry, just deep inside make it a meditation. Just say deep down, *just this.* Don't evaluate it, don't think it should not be. Don't think about what others will think. Let it be, and you just be a cool, distant watcher. Crying is neither good nor bad—nothing is ever good or bad; things simply are. If we don't judge, the mind starts disappearing. And to see reality without the mind is to see the truth.

205.
BEYOND THERAPY

Therapy suggests that you slowly unburden yourself. What I am teaching is beyond therapy, but therapy does prepare you.

Therapy's work is limited: It helps you to be sane, that's all. My work goes beyond therapy, but therapy has to prepare the way. Therapies clean the ground; then I can sow the seeds. Just cleaning the ground is not going to make the garden. That's where therapy is missing in the West. You go to the therapist—he or she cleans the ground, helps you to unburden, and then you start accumulating the same things again, because the garden is not really prepared. What are you going to do with clean ground? You will gather all kinds of rubbish again.

Therapy prepares the ground, and then roses can be grown in you. So the therapist is right: aggression, anger, sadness, despair, love—everything has to be expressed, accepted. Then my work starts; then I can tell you how to drop the ego. Now there is no need to carry it.

206.

UNION

*Start making as many contacts with existence as possible. Sitting by
a tree, hug the tree and feel that you are meeting and merging with it.
Swimming, close your eyes and feel you are melting into the water;
let there be a union.*

Find ways and means wherever you can to relax and unite with
something. The more you unite your energy with some other
energy, in any form—a cat, a dog, a man, a woman, a tree—the
closer home you will be. It is pleasant work; in fact, it is ecstatic
work.

Once you have come to feel it, once you have come to know the
knack of it, you will be surprised at how much you have missed in
your life. Each tree that you have passed could have given you a
great orgasm, and each experience—a sunset, a sunrise, the moon,
the clouds in the sky, the grass on the earth—could have been
ecstatic experiences. Lying down on the lawn, feel you are becoming one with the earth. Melt into the earth, disappear into it; let the
earth penetrate you.

This is a meditation: Attain union in as many ways as possible.
God has ten thousand doors, and from everywhere he is available.
But he is available only in the state of union. That's why sometimes it happens that lovers come to know of meditation in deep
orgasm. That is one of the ways of creating union, but that is only
one of the ways; there are millions. If one goes on searching, there
is no end to it.

207.

YES

Say yes to life; drop as many no's as possible. Even if you have to say no, say it, but don't enjoy saying it. And if it is possible, say it also in the form of yes. Don't miss a single opportunity of saying yes to life.

When you say yes, say it with great celebration and joy. Nourish it; don't say it reluctantly. Say it lovingly, say it with enthusiasm, with zest; pour yourself into it totally. When you say yes, become yes!

You will be surprised to know that ninety-nine out of a hundred no's can be dropped very easily. We say them only as part of our ego; they were not needed, they were not inevitable. The one no that remains will be very significant; that one need not be dropped. But even when saying that essential no, one has to be very reluctant, very hesitant, because no is death, and yes is life.

208.

DOMINATION

The idea of dominating arises out of an inferiority complex;
people dominate because they are afraid,
because they are uncertain about themselves.

There is a very famous Eastern story.... A blind man is sitting under a tree. A king comes, touches the feet of the blind man, and says, "Sir, where is the way to the capital?" Then the prime minister of the king comes, and without touching the blind man's feet he says, "Mister, where is the way to the capital?" Then comes an orderly. He hits the old blind man on the head and says, "You fool, where is the way to the capital?" The king's party had lost its way. When they had all gone, the blind man started laughing. Somebody else was sitting by his side, and he asked, "Why are you laughing?"

The blind man said, "Look, the first man must have been a king, the second man must have been the prime minister, and the third was a poor constable."

The man was puzzled; he asked, "How could you know? You are blind." The blind man said, "Just by their behavior.... The king was so certain of his superiority that he could touch my feet. The orderly was feeling so inferior that he had to hit me. He must be in a poor situation."

There is no need to dominate; there is no need at all.

209.
FOOLISHNESS

Those moments when you feel that what you are doing is foolish are very rare moments of wisdom.

To be seeking is foolish, because that which we are seeking we already have. To meditate is foolish, because meditation is a state of nondoing. To ask is foolish, because the answer cannot come from the outside—it can only come from your own heart. In fact, it cannot come as an answer, it will come as a growth. It will be a blossoming, a blooming of your being.

But those moments when you feel that what you are doing is foolish are very rare moments of wisdom. You cannot always feel foolish, otherwise you will become enlightened! In the Zen tradition this incident is repeated again and again, in every age with every master: Somebody comes and says he wants to know how to become a Buddha and the master hits him very hard—because the question is foolish. Sometimes it has happened, if he is really ready and on the verge, that with the first hit of the master the person has become enlightened. He was able to see in that hit that it was foolish to ask how to be a Buddha, because he was one already!

These things are going to happen to every seeker by and by. While you are meditating, suddenly there is a ray of light and you see that it is foolish. But those are very rare moments of wisdom. It is only a wise man who can feel foolish. Fools never feel that they are foolish; they think that they are wise. That is the definition of a foolish man: he thinks he is wise. And a wise man is one who has come to know that everything is foolish.

210.

CHILDREN

Think of each child as a miracle. Respect children, revere them; don't take them for granted.

Each child is a meeting of the sky and the earth. Each child is a miracle. Something happens that should not ordinarily happen: the meeting of matter and consciousness, the meeting of the visible and the invisible. So think of each child as a miracle. Respect, children, revere them; don't take them for granted.

The moment we take a child for granted, we start murdering him or her. And each child is murdered; that's what is happening all over the world and has happened through the ages: it has been a great massacre. It is not only that Herod killed all the children in Israel, it is happening every day; it was happening before Herod, and it has been happening since him.

Each child passes through a psychic murder; the moment the child is not respected and is thought to belong to you like a possession, the child has been killed, effaced. The child has to be respected as a God, because the child is the coming of God into the world again. Each child is a statement from God that he is not yet tired, that he is not yet weary of humankind, that he still hopes, that he will continue to create new human beings, whatever we become. Sinners and saints, whatever we do, he still hopes that the real human being will be created. God has not failed yet! That is the declaration in each child's coming onto the earth, into existence.

211.

IRRESPONSIBILITY

When you start becoming responsible toward yourself, you start dropping your false faces. Others start feeling disturbed, because yhey have always had expectations and you were fulfilling those demands. Now they feel that you are becoming irresponsible.

When say that you are being irresponsible, they are simply saying that you are getting out from under their domination. You are becoming freer. To condemn what you are doing, they call it "irresponsible."

In fact, your freedom is growing. And you are becoming responsible, but responsibility means the ability to respond. It is not a duty that has to be fulfilled in the ordinary sense. It is a responsiveness, a sensitivity.

But the more sensitive you become, the more you will find that many people think that you are becoming irresponsible—and you have to accept that—because their interests, their investments, will not be satisfied. Many times you will not fulfill their expectations, but nobody is here to fulfill anybody else's expectations.

The basic responsibility is toward oneself. So a meditator first becomes very very selfish. But later on, when one has become more centered, rooted into one's own being, energy starts overflowing. But it is not a duty. It is not that one has to do it. One loves to do it; it is a sharing.

212.

INEXPRESSIBLE

Whenever something really happens, it is always inexpressible.

When nothing happens, you can talk much about it. But when something really happens, then to talk is almost impossible. One simply feels helpless.

So blessed are the moments when something happens and one cannot say what is happening and what has happened, when one is at a loss and loses all articulateness.

Then something has really happened!

213.
HAPPY CONFUSION

Clarity is of the mind. Happiness is of the total. All that is alive
is always confusing. Only dead things are clear.

Don't seek clarity, otherwise you will start clinging to your misery,
because misery is very clear. You go to a doctor, and if you have
any disease he can diagnose it in a very clear-cut way. He can diagnose if you have cancer or a thousand and one different diseases.
But if you are healthy, the doctor has nothing to diagnose. In fact,
medical science has no way to define what health is. At the most
they can say that you are not ill, but they cannot be very definite
about what health is. Health cannot be pigeonholed.

Happiness is bigger than health. Health is the happiness of the
body, happiness is the health of the soul. So don't be bothered
about clarity. We are not doing arithmetic here; forget all about
it. Confusion is chaotic, certainly, even frightening—but the
adventure is there and the challenge. So take the challenge.

Focus more on happiness and forget about confusion, because
confusion is bound to be there. When you are moving in new territory that you have never tasted before, your old patterns will be
confused. Listen to happiness; let it be the indicator. Let happiness
decide your direction, and then move into that.

214.
CHARACTER

A person of soul has no character.

A person is an opening. Tomorrow who knows whom you will be? Even you cannot say who you will be, because you have not known tomorrow yet and what it brings. So people who are really alert never promise anything, because how can you promise? You cannot say to somebody, "I will love you tomorrow also," because who knows?

Real awareness will give you such humbleness that you will say, "I cannot say anything about tomorrow. We will see. Let tomorrow come. I hope that I will love you, but nothing is certain." And that is the beauty.

If you have character you can be very clear, but when you live in freedom it can be very confusing to you, and to others also. But this confusion has a beauty in it because it is alive, throbbing always with new possibilities.

215.
ENERGY

When the tree is overflowing with vitality it blooms and flowers.
Flowers are a luxury. Only when you have too much and you cannot
contain it, do they burst forth.

Spirituality is a flowering—it is the ultimate luxury. If you are overflowing with vitality, only then does something like a golden flower bloom in you. William Blake was right when he said, "Energy is delight." The more energy you have, the more delight you will have.

Despair comes because energy goes on leaking, and people have forgotten how to contain it. In a thousand and one thoughts, worries, desires, imagination, dreams, memories, energy is leaking. And energy is leaking in unnecessary things that can be easily avoided. When there is no need to talk, people go on talking. When there is no need to do anything, they cannot sit silently; they have to "do."

People are obsessed with doing, as if doing is a sort of intoxicant; it keeps them drunk. They remain occupied so that they don't have time to think about the real problems of life. They keep themselves busy so that they don't bump into themselves. They are afraid—afraid of the abyss that is yawning within. This is how energy goes on leaking, and this is why you never have too much of it.

One has to learn to drop the unnecessary. And ninety percent of ordinary life is unnecessary; it can easily be dropped. Be almost telegraphic, keeping just the essential, and you will have so much energy left that one day you will suddenly start blooming, for no reason at all.

216.

MEDITATION

There is a meditation that simply happens—
it is not our part to do. On our part, only one thing is needed:
that if it happens we do not hinder it.

The meditation that you can manage will remain a mind game. It is your mind that is in control; it is the mind that is doing the meditation. But this meditation cannot take you beyond the mind. How can it, if the mind is the doer of it? Then it is manipulated by the mind and remains something in your hands.

The real meditation is that which is not in your hands; on the contrary, you are in its hands. But techniques can help; they bring you to a point of frustration. They bring you to a point of hopelessness, they bring you to a point of helplessness. They bring you to a point where, out of despair, seeing the vicious circle of your doing, you see that doing leads nowhere.... Again and again you come to the same point, you are back to your mind. One day, this insight dawns: that your doing is really your undoing. In that very moment is let-go.

Then all doing disappears, all effort disappears. Something descends from the beyond. That is liberation. And even a single moment of that glimpse is enough. You are never the same again— you cannot be the same again.

217.
THE NEW

Just remember that change is life.
In each moment remain available to the new.

When people cling to the old, change stops. Change comes with the new. With the old there is no change, but people cling to the old because it seems secure, comfortable, familiar. You have lived with it, so you know it, you have become skillful in it, knowledgeable about it. With the new again you will be ignorant. With the new you may commit mistakes; with the new, who knows where it will lead? Hence fear arises, and out of this fear you cling to the old. And the moment you start clinging to the old, you have stopped flowing.

Remain available to the new. Always go on dying to the past. It is finished! Yesterday is yesterday, and it can never come back. If you cling to it you will be dead with it; it will become your grave. Open the heart to that which is coming. Welcome the rising sun, and always say good-bye to the setting sun. Feel grateful—it has given so much—but out of gratefulness, don't start clinging to it.

If you can remember this, your life will keep growing, maturing. Each new step, each new adventure, brings new richness. And when the whole of life is a movement, by the time death arrives one is so rich, and has known something so tremendously of the ultimate, that death cannot take anything away. Death comes only to poor people—those who have not lived.

218.

BUDDHAHOOD

Nothing is missing; all is as it should be. Everyone is already perfect. Perfection has not to be achieved; it is already there. The moment you accept yourself, it is revealed.

If you don't accept yourself, you keep chasing shadows, mirages, faraway mirages. And they only look beautiful when you are very far away from them. The closer you come, the more you find that there is nothing, only sand; it was a mirage. Then you create another mirage. And this is how people waste their whole life.

Just accept yourself as you are. Nothing has to be condemned, nothing has to be judged. There is no way to judge, no way to compare, because each person is unique. There has never been a person like you, and there will never be again, so you are alone; comparison is not possible. And this is the way existence wants you to be, that's why you are this way. Don't fight with existence, and don't try to improve on yourself; otherwise you will create a mess. That's how people have created a mess out of their lives.

So this is my message to you: Accept yourself. It will be hard, very hard, because the idealistic mind is always watching and saying, "What are you doing? This is not the right thing to do! You have to become great, you have to become a Buddha or a Christ— what are you doing? This does not look like a Buddha, you are behaving like a fool. Are you mad?"

Accept yourself. In that acceptance is Buddhahood.

219.
SONG OF LIFE

Life can be a song, but one can miss it; it is not inevitable.
The potential exists, but it has to be actualized. Many people think
that the day they were born all was finished. Nothing is finished.

The day one is born, things only start; it is the beginning. Birth has to happen millions of times in your whole life: You have to go on being born again and again and again.

People have such potential, so many aspects; they are multi-dimensional. But people never explore their own being, hence life remains sad, poor. That is real poverty. The outer poverty is not a big problem; it will be solved. Technology has come to the point at which poverty is going to disappear from the earth; the time has come for that. But the real problem is the inner poverty. Even rich people live very poor lives. Their bodies are stuffed with food, but their souls are starving. They have not yet known the song of life, they have not heard anything about it. They go on existing somehow, managing, pulling themselves along, dragging, but there is no joy.

Great song is possible, great richness is possible, but one has to start exploring. And the best way to explore the song of one's life is to love; that is the very methodology. Just as logic is the methodology of science, love is the methodology of the spirit. Just as logic makes you capable of going deeper and deeper into matter, love makes you capable of going deeper and deeper into consciousness. And the deeper you go, the deeper songs are released. When one has reached the very core of one's being, the whole of life becomes a celebration, an utter celebration.

220.

KEEP THE SANCTITY

Each person has to have his or her own inner space. Then there is joy in meeting, there is longing and passion in meeting.

My feeling is that it is always good to separate your work from your love. They don't go well together. Your work problems start affecting your love, and your love problems start affecting your work; things become multiplied. Love in itself is enough; it is a world. Don't load it up with anything else; it is already complicated. Keep things separate, and your work will be easier, your love life will be smoother.

A husband and wife should not be together twenty-four hours a day.; that too is hard. We lose interest. The wife becomes taken for granted, the husband becomes taken for granted. You don't have your own space. You keep overlapping, you keep crowding each other, and sooner or later it becomes a stress.

Better to keep the sanctity of the person. Each person has to have his own inner space, her own inner space. Then it is good to meet sometimes. Then there is joy in meeting, there is a longing and a passion in meeting. One tends to forget the person who is too close twenty-four hours, the obvious tends to be forgotten. Work separately, and your closeness will grow, your intimacy will grow.

DARK NIGHT OF THE SOUL

We all learn how to be happy and to laugh and joke. That's how
the whole society goes on a merry-go-round. But everybody is carrying
a deep, dark night within them, and nobody is even aware of it.

When you enter a meditative state you will first enter this dark
night of the soul. If you can pass through it—and there is no difficulty in passing through it—then for the first time you will become
aware that your happiness was not true. False happiness will go
and real sadness will come, and only after real sadness will real
happiness surface. Then you will know that the false happiness was
even worse than the real sadness, because at least in that sadness
there is a reality. If you are sad—but truly and sincerely sad—that
sadness will enrich you.

It gives you a depth, an insight. It makes you aware of life and its
infinite possibilities and of the limits of the human mind, the small-
ness of human consciousness encountering the infinity all around,
the fragile life always surrounded by death. When you are really sad
you become aware of all these things. You become aware that life
is not just life—it is death too.

If you really want to be happy, don't just go on pretending,
playing the game of being happy. As unhappiness comes, soon you
will see that it will darken, it will become intense. But when the
night is dark, the morning is very close. Once you stop fighting,
once you accept it, it will give you a silence, a deep humming. Of
course it is sad, but it is beautiful. Even the night has its own beauty,
and those who cannot see the beauty of the night will miss much.

222.

FOOD

When a child is born, his first love and his first food are the same thing—the mother. So there is a deep association between food and love; in fact, food comes first and then love follows.

The first day the child cannot understand love. He understands the language of food, the natural primitive language of all animals. The child is born with hunger; food is needed immediately. Love will not be needed until long after—it is not so much of an emergency. One can live without love one's whole life, but one cannot live without food—that's the trouble.

By and by he feels that whenever the mother is very loving, she gives her breast in a different way. When she is not loving, but angry or sad, she gives the breast very reluctantly or does not give it at all. So the child becomes aware that whenever the mother is loving, whenever food is available, love is available. This awareness is in the unconscious.

When you are missing a life of love you eat more—it becomes a substitute. And with food things are simple, because food is dead. You can go on eating as much as you want—food cannot say no. One remains a master with food. But in love you are no longer the master. So I will say forget about food, go on eating as much as you want. But start a life of love, and immediately you will see you are not eating so much. Have you watched? If you are happy you don't eat too much. A happy person feels so fulfilled that he feels no space inside. An unhappy person goes on throwing food into himself.

223.
THE GOD OF LOVE

Surrender to something higher than both of you—
that is the God of love.

The very myth that there is a God of love is beautiful, it is a tremendous understanding. Then two lovers can surrender to the God and they remain independent. And when you are independent there is beauty—otherwise you become just a shadow, or your partner becomes a shadow. If your partner becomes a shadow, in that very moment you will start losing interest—who loves a shadow? If you become a shadow your partner will start losing interest in you. We want to love real human beings, not shadows.

There is no need to become anybody's shadow. You remain yourself, and your partner remains herself or himself. In fact, by surrendering to the God of love, you become authentic. And you are never as authentic as when you become authentic for the first time. Two authentic beings can love, and can love deeply, and then there is no need to hold back.

Let me underline this idea: When you are surrendered to the God of love, then it is not very important whether your partner remains with you or leaves you or whether you leave. One thing is important: that love remains. Your surrender is toward love, not toward your partner. So the only thing is not to betray love. Lovers can change; love can remain. Once you have understood that, there is no fear.

224.

CELEBRATE!

Small things have to be celebrated—sipping tea has to be celebrated.
Zen people have created a tea ceremony. That is the most beautiful
ritual ever to have evolved.

There are many religions, and many rituals have been born, but
there is nothing like the tea ceremony—just sipping tea and
celebrating it! Just cooking food and celebrating it! Just taking a
bath—lying down in the tub and celebrating it or standing under
the shower and celebrating it. These are small things—if you go on
celebrating them, the total of all your celebrations is what God is.
If you ask me what God is, I will say the total of all celebrations—
small, mundane celebrations.

A friend comes and holds your hand. Don't miss this opportunity—because God has come in the form of the hand, in the form
of the friend. A small child passes by and laughs. Don't miss this,
laugh with the child—because God has laughed through the child.
You pass through the street and a fragrance comes from the fields.
Stand there a moment, feel grateful—because God has come as
fragrance.

If one can celebrate moment to moment, life becomes religious—and there is no other religion, there is no need to go to
any temple. Then wherever you are is the temple, and whatever
you are doing is religion.

KEEP JUMPING

One day it is going to happen. I can see it, just below the horizon.
Any moment the sunrise is possible. But keep jumping; don't fall asleep.

Somebody asked Rothschild, "How did you become so rich?" He answered, "I always waited for my opportunity, and when it came I simply jumped on it." The man said, "I am also waiting for an opportunity, but I only know when it has gone! It is such a rare moment that it comes and by the time I am ready to jump on it, it is gone."

Rothschild laughed and he said, "Keep jumping, otherwise you will miss! That's what I have been doing all my life—jumping. An opportunity may come or not—that is not the point; I keep on jumping. When it comes, it finds me always jumping. It comes and goes in a moment, and if you are thinking about it you will miss it."

So keep jumping—that's all that meditation is about. Some day the coincidence will happen. You will be jumping and the right moment will be close by. Something clicks, and something happens. It is a happening; it is not a doing. But if you are not jumping, you will miss it. It is difficult and sometimes boring too, because you come again and again to the same space, and it becomes circular. But keep jumping.

226.

MEDICINAL USE

*Whenever there is pressure from the outside, direct entry into meditation
becomes difficult. So before meditation, for fifteen minutes, do something
to cancel the pressure.*

For fifteen minutes, simply sit silently and think of the whole world
as a dream—and it is! Think of the whole world as a dream and that
there is nothing of any significance in it.

Second, remember that sooner or later everything will
disappear—you also. You were not always here, you will not always
be here. So nothing is permanent. And third: You are just a witness. This is a passing dream, a film. Remember these three
things—that this whole world is a dream and everything is going
to pass, even you. Death is approaching and the only reality is the
witness, so you are just a witness. Relax the body, witness for
fifteen minutes, and then meditate. You will be able to get into it,
and then there will be no trouble.

But whenever you feel that this meditation has become simple,
stop it; otherwise it will become habitual. It has to be used only in
specific conditions when it is difficult to enter meditation. If you do
it every day, it will lose the effect, and then it will not work. So use
it medicinally. When things are going wrong, do it so it will clear
the way and you will be able to relax.

DOING GOOD

Do whatever is needed in life; just remain aloof from it.
Let it happen on the periphery; the center remains unattached to it.

One has to do things, so one goes on doing them, but one should not be disturbed by them. It is exactly an act, a performance. Once this is understood you can be anywhere, in any kind of work, and keep your cool; you can keep yourself absolutely uncontaminated.

The problem is that down the ages we have been taught to do good, not to do bad, to do this, not to do that. We have been given commandments, do's and don'ts. I don't give you any commandment. I'm not concerned with what you do—my whole concern is with your being.

If you are silent, blissful, centered, do whatever is needed to be done, and there is no problem. If you are not centered, if you are not collected, integrated inside, if you are not in a meditative state, then even doing good is not going to help. That's why so many people who go on doing good are nothing but do-gooders. Their ultimate result is harm.

The emphasis has to be not on the doing but on being, and being is a totally different phenomenon. It doesn't matter whether you are an attorney or a doctor or an engineer or a prostitute or a politician; it doesn't matter what you are doing. All that matters is: Are you centered in your being? And that will change many things.

228.

DYING AND MEDITATION

Once you know that you are going to die within days,
 immediately this world—the money, the bank, the business,
this and that—becomes useless. Now everything is no more
than a dream, and you are already awakening.

Once you someone learns that he is going to die within a certain
time period—the person is already dead in a way, and he starts
thinking about the future—then meditation is possible. Once a
person knows he is going to die, he will drop much rubbish of his
own accord. Immediately his whole vision is transformed.

If you have to leave tomorrow, you start packing your suitcases
and you are no longer worried about this room in the hotel. In fact
you are no longer here; you are managing your suitcases and things,
and you are thinking about the journey. The same happens to a person when you tell him that he is going to die, that death is certain
and cannot be avoided and he should not go on fooling around;
now the decisive moment has come and he has already wasted
enough life. Immediately the person turns his back on the world
and starts peeking into the darkness of the future.

At that moment, if you tell him about meditation he will be
willing to do it—and that can be one of the greatest gifts.

229.
NECESSARY EVIL

When you live with blind people, live like a blind person.
You cannot change the whole world.

I know bureaucracy exists, but it has to exist because people are absolutely irresponsible. There is no way suddenly to drop the bureaucracy and the court and the law and the police officers. There is no way, because you will not be able to live for a single moment. It is a necessary evil. One just has to learn to live with people who are not alert, who are fast asleep, who are snoring. It may be disturbing to you, but nothing can be done about it.

At the most, the one thing you can do is not to enforce the same stupid behavior that has been forced on you by society. Don't force it on anybody else. You may have a wife, a husband, children—don't force it on them or on your friends. That's all you can do. But you have to live in society and you have to follow the rules.

So don't just condemn things. Try to understand. There are many evils that are needed; they are necessary. The choice is not between right and wrong. In real life the choice is always between a bigger evil and a lesser evil, a bigger wrong and a lesser wrong.

230.
LIFE AND DEATH

These two—the life and death meditations—can help you tremendously.

In the night before you go to sleep, do this fifteen-minute meditation. It is a death meditation. Lie down and relax your body. Just feel like dying and that you cannot move your body because you are dead. Create the feeling that you are disappearing from the body. Do it for ten, fifteen minutes, and you will start feeling it within a week. Meditating that way, fall asleep. Don't interrupt it. Let the meditation turn into sleep, and if sleep overcomes you, go into it.

In the morning, the moment you feel you are awake—don't open your eyes—do the life meditation. Feel that you are becoming more wholly alive, that life is coming back and the whole body is full of vitality and energy. Start moving, swaying in the bed with eyes closed. Just feel that life is flowing in you. Feel that the body has a great flowing energy—just the opposite of the death meditation. With the life meditation you can take deep breaths. Just feel full of energy, that life is entering with the breathing. Feel full and very happy, alive. Then after fifteen minutes, get up.

These two—the life and death meditation—can help you tremendously.

231.
SHORTCUT

One thing has to be remembered about meditation: It is a long journey,
and there is no shortcut. Anyone who says there is a shortcut
is befooling you.

Meditation is a long journey because the change is very deep and
is achieved after many lives, many lives of routine habits, thinking,
desiring, and the mind structure. Those you have to drop through
meditation. In fact, it is almost impossible but it happens.

Becoming a meditator is the greatest responsibility in the world.
It is not easy. It cannot be instant. So from the beginning never
start expecting too much, and then you will never be frustrated.
You will always be happy, because things will grow very slowly.

Meditation is not a seasonal flower that blooms after weeks. It
is a very big tree. It needs time to spread its roots.

232.
FEET

Feel more and more in your feet.

Sometimes just stand on the earth without shoes and feel its coolness, its softness, its warmth. Whatever the earth is ready to give in that moment, just feel it and let it flow through you. And allow your energy to flow into the earth. Be connected with the earth.

At most people breathe down to the navel but not beyond that, so half the body is almost paralyzed, and because of it, half of life is also paralyzed. Then many things become impossible ... because the lower part of the body functions like roots. The legs are the roots, and they connect you with the earth. So people are hanging like ghosts, unconnected with the earth. One has to move back to the feet.

Lao Tzu used to say to his disciples, "Unless you start breathing from the soles of your feet, you are not my disciples." Breathing from the soles of your feet—and he is perfectly right. The deeper you go, the deeper goes your breath. It is almost true that the boundary of your being is the boundary of your breath. When the boundary increases and touches your feet, your breath almost reaches to the feet—not in a physiological sense, but in a psychological sense—then you have claimed your whole body. For the first time you are whole, of one piece, together.

233.
OLD MIND

If you listen to your likings, you are listening to your old mind.
One has to do some things against one's likings, and then one grows.

Growth is not as smooth as people think. It is painful... and the greatest pain comes when you have to go against your likes and dislikes.

But who is this that goes on saying, "This I like and this I don't like"? This is your old mind, not you. If it is allowed, there is no way to change. The mind will tell you to stay in the old rut, because it likes that. So one has to come out of it. Sometimes one has to be against likings and dislikings.

Whenever one changes an old style, it is painful, it hurts. It is like learning a new skill. You know the old very well, so everything goes easily. When you learn a new skill, it is difficult. And it is not only learning a new skill, it is learning a new being. It is going to be hard. The old has to die for the new to be born. The old has to go for the new to come. If you go on clinging to the old, there is no space for the new to come in.

234.
IDEALS

Whenever people are taught great ideals, they start feeling dirty and guilty. Because those ideals are foolish and impossible; nobody can fulfill them.

With ideals, no matter what you do, you always fall short, you are always a failure, because the ideal is impossible. It is inhuman. They call it "superhuman"—it is in human! But it becomes a a self-torture, and then whatever you do is wrong. That's what can create trouble for you. So drop ideals and just be.

Become a realist. Once you become a realist, everything seems to be just beautiful and perfect. When you don't have any ideal of perfection, everything is perfect because there is nothing with which to compare and condemn it.

I don't see anything to condemn. But for centuries the mind has been conditioned to condemn. That's a great strategy in the hands of the politician and the priests—they create guilt inside you, and then they can manipulate you. To manipulate a human being is the worst crime one can commit.

235.
EXPECTATIONS

If there is no desire, if you have no idea what should happen,
then things happen.

People who have great desires can never feel grateful, because
whatever happens is always tiny compared to their desires. And
because you can't feel grateful, much more that could have happened cannot happen, because it happens only through gratefulness. So you get trapped in a vicious circle: You desire much, and
because of that you cannot feel grateful. Whatever happens you
can't take any note of; you simply ignore it. And then you become
more and more closed.

If there is no desire, if you have no idea what should happen,
then things happen. Those things are already happening, but now
you take note of them. You feel tremendously thrilled because this
has happened and you had not expected anything. If you are expecting that when you go on the road you will find a thousand dollars
lying there, and you only find a ten-dollar bill, you will say, "What
am I doing here?" But if you had not expected that thousand dollars, a ten-dollar bill is good. And if you are grateful, then from the
same source from where the ten dollars have come, ten million
can come. But you remain open in gratefulness.

236.
HEARING AND LISTENING

The art of divine listening—that's what meditation is. If one can learn how to listen rightly, one has learned the deepest secret of meditation. Hearing is one thing—listening is altogether different; they are worlds apart. Hearing is a physical phenomenon; you hear because you have ears. Listening is a spiritual phenomenon. You listen when you have attention, when your inner being joins with your ears.

Listen to the sounds of the birds, the wind passing through the trees, the river in flood, the ocean roaring, and the clouds, the people, the faraway train passing by, the cars on the road—each sound has to be used. And listen without imposing anything on what you listen to—don't judge; the moment you judge, listening stops.

The really attentive person remains without conclusions; he or she never concludes about anything. Because life is a process—nothing ever ends. Only the foolish person can conclude; the wise will hesitate to make conclusions. So listen without conclusions. Just listen—alert, silent, open, receptive. Just be there, totally with the sound that surrounds you.

And you will be surprised: One day suddenly the sound is there, you are listening, and yet there is silence. It is true silence that happens through sound.

237.

PEEPING TOMS

People have become completely passive. You listen to music, you read
a book, you see a film—you are never a participant anywhere,
just a watcher, a spectator. The whole of humanity has been reduced
to being spectators.

It is as if somebody else is making love and you are watching—
and that is what's happening. The whole of humanity has become
peeping toms. Somebody else is doing the things, and you are a
watcher. Of course you are outside it, so there is no involvement,
no commitment, no danger. But how can you understand love by
watching somebody else make love?

My feeling is that people have become spectators to such a
degree that when they make love they are watchers. People have
started making love in the light—all lights on, mirrors all around,
so you can watch yourself making love. There are people who have
fixed cameras in their bedrooms so that pictures can be taken automatically, so later on they can see themselves making love.

When you participate, something irrational starts working. Make
love and just be like wild animals. If you listen to music, dance—
once the music has become a dance, reason is put aside. And reason
can only be a spectator, it can never be a participant. It is always on
the safe side, watching from somewhere where there is no danger.

So every day find something you can do without thinking about
it. Dig a hole in the earth; that will do. Perspire in the hot sun, and
dig—just be the digger. In fact, be not the digger but the digging.
Lose yourself completely in it. Become a participant, and suddenly
you will see a new energy arising.

238.
BREATHING

Once breathing is perfect everything else falls into place.
Breathing is life. But people ignore it, they don't pay it any attention.
And every change that is going to happen is going to happen
through the change in your breathing.

Everybody breathes wrongly because the whole society is based on very wrong conditions, notions, attitudes. For example, a small child is weeping, and the mother says not to cry. What will the child do? She will start holding her breath, because that is the only way to keep from crying. If you hold your breath, everything stops: crying, tears, everything. Then by and by that becomes a fixed thing—don't be angry, don't cry, don't do this, don't do that.

The child learns that if she breathes shallowly, she remains in control. If she breathes perfectly and totally, as every child is born breathing, then she becomes wild. So she cripples herself.

Every child plays with their genitals because the feeling is pleasant. The child is unaware of the social taboos and nonsense, but if your mother or father sees you playing with your genitals, they tell you to stop it. Such condemnation is in their eyes, you are shocked, and you become afraid of breathing deeply, because if you breathe deeply, it massages your genitals from within. That becomes troublesome, so you don't breathe deeply; your breathing is shallow, so you are cut off from the genitals.

All societies that are sex repressive are shallow-breathing societies. Only people who don't have a repressive attitude about sex breathe perfectly. Their breathing is beautiful; it is complete and whole. They breathe like animals, they breathe like children.

234

239.
WORKAHOLISM

Work is good, but it should not become an addiction. Many people have turned their work into a drug so that they can forget themselves in it—just like a drunkard forgetting himself in alcohol.

One should be as capable of nondoing as of doing—then one is free. One should be capable of sitting, not doing anything, as perfectly and beautifully and blissfully as when one is working hard and doing many things; then one is flexible.

There are two types of people: a few who are glued into their lethargy and at the other extreme, those who are glued into their occupation. Both are in prisons. One should be capable of moving from one to another with no effort, effortlessly. Then you have a certain freedom, a certain grace and a spontaneity to your being.

I am not against work, I am not against anything—but nothing should become an addiction. Otherwise, you are in a very very confused state. If work is an occupation and you are just hiding yourself in it, then it becomes a repetitive thing, a mechanical thing. Work becomes more like an obsession; you are possessed by a demon.

240.

LOVE AND FREEDOM

This is the whole problem of human beings—love and freedom.
These two words are the most important words in the human language.

It is very easy to choose one—to choose love and to drop freedom—but then you will always be haunted by freedom, and it will destroy your love. Love will look as if it is against freedom, inimical to freedom, antagonistic to freedom. How can one leave freedom? It cannot be left, even for love. By and by you will become fed up with love, and you will start moving to the other extreme.

One day you will leave love and rush toward freedom. But just to be free and without loving, how can one live? Love is such a big need. To be loved and to love is almost spiritual breathing. The body cannot live without breath, and the spirit cannot live without love.

This way one moves like a pendulum swings—from freedom to love, from love to freedom. This way the wheel can continue for many lives. This is how it has continued. We call it the wheel of life. It goes on rotating: the same spokes coming up, going down. Liberation comes when one attains a synthesis between love and freedom. Choose the paradox. Don't choose the alternatives that the paradox has given to you. Choose the whole paradox. Don't choose one, choose both; choose together. Move in love and remain free. Remain free, but never make your freedom antilove.

241.
CHILDLIKE

You are bound to become more childlike if you meditate. A little meditation and you will start feeling fresher. And with that comes a sort of irresponsibility—irresponsibility in the sense that you don't consider other people's obsessions any more.

As I see it, becoming childlike is a great responsibility. You start becoming responsible to yourself, but you start dropping your masks, your false faces. Others may start feeling disturbed because they have always had expectations and you were fulfilling those demands. Now they will feel that you are becoming irresponsible. When they say that you are becoming irresponsible, they are simply saying that you are getting out from under their control. You are becoming freer. To condemn your behavior, they call it "childish" or "irresponsible."

In fact, freedom is growing, and you *are* becoming responsible—but responsibility means the ability to respond. It is not a duty that has to be fulfilled in the ordinary sense. It is responsiveness, it is sensitivity. But the more sensitive you become, the more you will find that many people think that you are becoming irresponsible—and you have to accept that—because their interests, their investments, will not be satisfied. Many times you will not fulfill their expectations. But nobody is here to fulfill anybody else's expectations.

242.
VIRGIN SEX

There is a sort of sex that is not sexual at all. Sex can be beautiful,
but sexuality never can.

The focus should be love. You love a person, you share his being,
you share your being with him, you share the space. That is exactly
what love is, to create a space between two people—a space that
belongs to neither or belongs to both, a small space between two
people where they both meet and mingle and merge. That space has
nothing to do with physical space. It is simply spiritual. In that
space you are not you, and the other is not the other. You both
come into that space and you meet.

There is a sort of sex that is not sexual at all. Sex can be beautiful, but sexuality never can. Sexuality means cerebral sex—thinking about it, planning it, managing, manipulating it, but the basic
thing that remains deep down in the mind is that one is approaching the other as a sex object.

When the mind has nothing to do with sex, then it is pure, innocent sex. It is virgin sex. That sex can sometimes be even purer
than celibacy, because if a celibate continuously thinks of sex, then
it is not celibacy.

243.
LIGHT

Feel more and more full of light.
That's the way to come closer to the original source.

Feel more and more full of light. Whenever you close your eyes, just see light streaming all over your being. In the beginning it will be imagination, but imagination is very creative.

So just imagine a flame near the heart and imagine that you are full of light. Keep increasing that light. It becomes almost dazzling! And not only you will start feeling it; others will start feeling it too. Whenever you are close to them, they will start feeling it, because it vibrates.

It is everybody's birthright, but one has to claim it. It is an unclaimed treasure. If you don't claim it, it remains dead, buried under the ground. Once you claim it, you have claimed your own inner being. So wherever you see light, feel deep reverence. Just something ordinary—a lamp is burning, and you feel a deep reverence, a certain awe. In the night there are stars—just watch them and feel connected to them. In the morning, the sun rises. Watch it and let the inner sun rise with it. Whenever you see light, immediately try to make contact with it—and soon you will be able to.

244.

VIRTUE

People become do-gooders. That is not true virtue—it is a camouflage.

Doing good things brings respectability, it gives you a good ego feeling. It makes you feel that you are somebody important, significant—not only in the eyes of the world but also in the eyes of God—that you can stand upright, even encountering God; you can show all the good deeds that you have done. It is egoistic, and religiousness cannot be egoistic.

Not that a religious person is immoral, but he is not moral—he is amoral. He has no fixed character. His character is liquid, alive, moving moment to moment. He responds to situations not according to a fixed attitude, idea, or ideology; he simply responds out of his consciousness. His consciousness is his only character, there is no other character.

245.
LONGING

A desire becomes a longing when you are ready to risk all for it.
A longing is higher than life—one can die for it. Desires are many—
longing can only be one, because it needs your total energy,
it needs you as you are, in your totality.

You cannot withhold any part of yourself, you cannot move toward your longing cautiously, cleverly, calculatingly. It has to be a mad jump.

People are very fragmentary: one desire takes you to the north, another to the south, and all desires are taking you in all directions and driving you mad. Hence people never reach anywhere—it is not possible—because one part moves in this direction, and one part moves in another direction, to the diametrically opposite. How can you arrive? To arrive, your totality will be needed. That's why you see people dragging. They don't have any intensity of life; it is not possible. They are leaking in many directions—they cannot have that energy.

But this longing has to be very blissful; one should not be doing it in a serious way, because the moment you become serious, you become tense. One's longing has to be intense but not tense at all. It has to be playful, it has to be cheerful, it has to be filled with laughter and dance and singing. It should not become a duty. You are not obliging God, or anybody—you are simply living the way you want to live; hence you are blissful. This is the way you have chosen to live, this is the way you want to become aflame... but it has to be a dancing flame.

246.
REFLECTION

It is a good sign, a good indication, when you have started reflecting about yourself—about what you have done, why you have done it.

When one starts inquiring into one's acts, commitments, directions, and goals, great confusion arises. To avoid that confusion, many people never think about what they are doing; they simply go on doing. From one thing to another they simply go on jumping, so there is no time left. Tired, they fall asleep; early in the morning they start chasing shadows again. That process goes on and on, and one day they die without knowing who they were, what they were doing, and why.

Now you will be hesitating about everything. It is the beginning of wisdom. Only stupid people never hesitate. Just see that this is one of the gifts of being a seeker. Many more gifts are on the way.

RESTLESSNESS

The human being is created by nature for almost eight hours' hard work. By and by, as civilization has progressed and technology has taken over much of human labor, we don't have anything that requires hard work, and that has become a problem.

In the past, people suffered because they didn't have enough energy to cope. Now we are suffering from more energy than can be used. That can become restlessness, neurosis, madness. If energy is there and not used rightly it goes sour, becomes bitter. We create energy every day, and it has to be used every day. You cannot accumulate it; you cannot be a miser about it.

In the past, people were working hard as hunters and farmers. By and by that kind of work has disappeared, and societies are more affluent and have more and more energy; so restlessness is bound to be there. Hence the Americans are the most restless people in the world, and part of it is that they are the most affluent society.

We should drop the idea of utility—because that is of the past. When energy was less and work was more, utility had meaning. Now it is no longer a value. So find ways to use your energy— games, jogging, running—and delight in it. Use the energy, and then you will feel very calm. That calmness will be totally different from a forced stillness. You can force yourself, you can have energy and repress it, but you are sitting on a volcano, and there is a constant trembling inside. The more energy you use, the more fresh energy will become available.

248.

OLD HABITS

Old tendencies, old habits, will force into the future and into the past.
The moment you remember, relax—relax in the now.

Laugh at the ridiculousness of old habits. I'm not saying to fight
with them. If you fight you will create anxiety. I am saying simply
to laugh. Whenever you catch yourself red-handed—again in the
future and again in the past—just slip out of it, as a snake slips out
of its old skin. There is no need to fight. Fight never solves anything.
It can create more complexities. Just understand it. Tomorrow will
take its own course. When it comes, you will be there to face it.
And it never comes as tomorrow; it always comes as today. So learn
to be here now.

249.

ADDRESS CHANGE

The morning is very fragile, and the new rays of the sun are not very strong, but they will be proving stronger and stronger every moment. Nourish them, nurture them. And don't identify with the past.

From this moment think of yourself as a newborn child. The night is over, and you are born to the morning. It is not going to be easy, because the hold of the past is deep. The morning is very fragile, and the new rays of the sun are not very strong, but they will be proving stronger and stronger every moment. Nourish them, nurture them. And don't identify with the past. If any old habit comes by, simply watch it. Remain aloof as if it belongs to somebody else, as if the postman has delivered a letter to the wrong house. It is not addressed to you, so you return it to the post office.

The mind will go on believing just because of the old habit, because the mind will take time to know that the address is changed. The mind moves very slowly; then the unconscious moves even more slowly. The body is very lethargic. They have different time systems.

250.
BROKENHEARTED

Heartache is good. Accept it joyously. Allow it, don't repress it.
The natural tendency of the mind is to repress anything that is painful.
But by repressing it you will destroy something that was growing.

The heart is meant to be broken. Its purpose is that——that it should melt into tears and disappear. The heart is to evaporate, and when the heart has evaporated, exactly in the same place where the heart was, you come to know the real heart.

This heart has to break. Once it has fallen apart, suddenly you come to know a deeper heart. Just like an onion, you peel it, and the new layer is there.

251.
THERMOSTAT

We have been taught never to get out of control in anything—
in laughter, in crying, in love, in anger—never to go beyond the limit.

There is a limit to everything, and we have been allowed only up to the limit, and then we have to hold back. After a long conditioning it becomes almost automatic, like a thermostat. You go to a certain extent, then suddenly something happens in the unconscious. Something clicks, and you stop.

I teach how to "uncontrol," because only in uncontrol will you become free. And when the energy is moving spontaneously with no mind behind it to manipulate, to direct, to dictate, then there is tremendous bliss.

The trees exist on a lower plane but are more blissful. And so are the animals; they exist on a lower plane but are more blissful. And the reason is that they don't know how to control. We can be more blissful than the trees and the flowers and the birds, but we have to avoid one trap, the trap of controlling ourselves.

252.

SEX

The depth of your sex experience will decide the depth of all your experiences. If one cannot go deeply into the sexual experience, then one can never go deeper into anything else, because sex is the most fundamental, the most natural experience.

Your biology is ready for sex, you are not expected to learn anything about it. If you learn music, it is not built in; you have to learn it. If you learn poetry or painting or dancing, you have to learn it. Sex is just there—the script is already written in your biology.

So if you cannot go deeply into sex—which is such a natural thing—how can you go deeply into music and how can you go deeply into dancing? If you hold yourself back in sex, you will hold yourself back in dance too. You will not be able to go into any relationship either, because the relationship tends to become sexual. People are so afraid, and the modern mind particularly becomes afraid, because so many things have become known, and the knowledge has not helped you to go deep, it has helped to make you afraid.

Never before in humanity's history was the man afraid, but after Masters and Johnson every man is afraid of whether he will be man enough. The woman is afraid of whether she will be able to have an orgasm. If she cannot have an orgasm, it is better not to go into sex at all, because then it is very humiliating, or she has to pretend. And the man is so afraid and nervous and trembling inside about whether he will be able to prove to the woman that he is the greatest man in the world. What nonsense! Just being yourself is enough.

253.
IMAGINATION

Never deny imagination. It is the only creative faculty in human beings, the only poetic faculty, and one should not deny it.

Denied, imagination becomes very revengeful. Denied, it becomes a nightmare. Denied, it becomes destructive. Otherwise it is very creative. It is creativity and nothing else. But if you deny it, if you disown it, you start a conflict between your own creativity and yourself, then you are going lose.

Science can never win against art, and logic can never win against love. History can never win against myth, and reality is poor compared to dreams, very poor. So if you carry any idea against imagination, drop it. Because we all carry it—this age is very anti-imagination. People have been taught to be factual, realistic, empirical, and all sorts of nonsense. People should be more dreamy, more childlike, more ecstatic. People should be able to create euphoria. And only through that do you reach your original source.

God must be a tremendously imaginative person. Just look at the world! Whoever created it or dreamed it must be a great dreamer... so many colors and so many songs. The whole of existence is a rainbow. It must come out of deep imagination.

DIFFICULTIES

Difficulties are always there. They are part of life.
And it is good that they are there, otherwise there would be no growth.

Difficulties are challenges. They provoke you to work, to think, to find ways to overcome them. The very effort is essential. So always take difficulties as blessings.

Without difficulties, we would be nowhere. Bigger difficulties come—that means that existence is looking after you, it is giving you more challenges. And the more you solve them, the greater challenges will be waiting for you. Only at the last moment, difficulties disappear, but that last moment comes only because of difficulties. So never take any difficulty negatively. Find something positive in it. The same rock blocking the path can function as a stepping stone. If there were no rock on the path, you would never rise up. And the very process of going above it, making it a stepping stone, gives you a new altitude of being. So once you think about life creatively, then everything is useful and everything has something to give you. Nothing is meaningless.

255.
SONG OF GOD

We are all different songs of the same singer,
different gestures of the same dancer.

Each being is a song of God: unique, individual, incomparable, unrepeatable, but still coming from the same source. Each song has its own flavor, its own beauty, its own music, its own melody, but the singer is the same. We are all different songs of the same singer, different gestures of the same dancer.

To start feeling it is meditation. Then conflict disappears, jealousies become impossible, and violence is unthinkable, because there is nobody other than our own reflections all over the world. If we belong to the same source, just like all the waves of the ocean, then what is the point of conflict, competition, feeling superior or inferior, and all that nonsense? Nobody is superior and nobody is inferior: Everybody is simply just himself or herself.

And everybody is so unique that there has never been any other individual like you before, and there is no possibility of there ever being an individual like you again. In fact, you yourself are not the same for two consecutive moments. Yesterday you were a different person, today it is just somebody else. Tomorrow, one never knows.

Each being is a flux, a constant change, a river flowing. Heraclitus says that you cannot step in the same river twice. And I say to you, you cannot step in the same river even once, because the river is constantly flowing. And the river represents life.

256.

HOPELESSNESS

You have all the gadgets that technology has provided for you,
so what can tomorrow give to you that you don't have today?

The future flops, and with the future flopping great hopelessness arises. The world up to now has lived with great hope, but suddenly hopes are disappearing and despair is settling in. To me, this is of immense importance. This crisis in human consciousness is of great import. Either humanity has to disappear from the earth or it will have a totally new being, a new birth. And my work consists of giving a new birth to human consciousness.

The world has failed us; now there is nothing to long for here on the earth. Now the longing can soar high. Now the visible is finished, and we can search in the invisible. Now time is meaningless; we have to move into the nontemporal. Now the ordinary mundane life has no charm; it has lost all joy. We have fulfilled all the desires, all the possible desires, and they have not satisfied us. Now the real discontent is possible, and to be really discontented is a great blessing.

TALK

If you don't feel like talking, don't—don't say a single word that is not coming to you spontaneously. Don't be worried if people think you are going crazy. Accept it. If they think you have become dumb, ccept it, and enjoy your dumbness!

The real trouble is with people who go on talking and don't know what they are talking about and why. They go on talking because they cannot stop. But if you become a little aware of the whole nonsense and the trouble that goes on in the mind, if you become aware that there is nothing to say, that everything seems to be trivia, then you hesitate.

In the beginning it feels as though you are losing the capacity to communicate—it is not so. In fact, people talk not to communicate, but to avoid communication. Soon you will be able to really communicate. Just wait, and don't force anything. Don't be worried about the silence. One does worry, though, because the whole society exists on talking, on language, and people who are very articulate become very powerful in society—leaders, scholars, politicians, writers. One soon becomes afraid that one is losing one's grip on language, but don't be worried. Silence is the grip on God, and once you know what silence is, you have something to talk about.

Once you have gone deeper into silence, then your words carry meaning for the first time. Then they are not just empty words, they are full of something of the beyond. They have a poetry to them, a dance. They carry your inner grace with them.

258.

DREAM

When you go to sleep, one thing should remain in the consciousness
while you are falling into sleep—that everything is a dream, everything,
unconditionally, is a dream.

That which you see with your eyes open—that too, is a dream. That which you see with closed eyes—that too, is a dream. Dream is the stuff life is made of. So with this climate fall into sleep; with this constant remembrance that everything, everything with no exception, is a dream. When everything is a dream, there is nothing to worry about.

That is the whole concept of *maya*—that the world is illusory. Not that the world *is* illusory—it has its own reality—but this is just a technique to help you settle deeply into yourself. Then nothing disturbs you. If everything is a dream, then it is pointless to be disturbed. Just think, if this moment you think that everything is a dream—that the trees, the night, the sound of the night is a dream—suddenly you are transported into a different world. You are there, the dream is there, and nothing is worth worrying about.

So starting tonight just fall into sleep with this attitude. And in the morning too, the first thing you have to remember is that everything is a dream. Let this recur many times in the day, and suddenly you will feel relaxed.

259.
INTIMACY

When you know how to relate—even how to relate with things—
your whole life changes.

When you put on your shoes you can relate with those shoes in a very friendly way, or you can just be indifferent, or even inimical. Nothing will be different for the shoe, but much will be different for you.

Don't miss any opportunity to be loving. Even putting on your shoes, be loving. Those moments of being full of love will be helpful to you. Relate with things as if they are persons. People are doing just the reverse—they relate with people as if they are things. A husband becomes a thing, a child becomes a thing, a wife becomes a thing, a mother becomes a thing.

People completely forget that these are living beings. They use and manipulate. But you can relate even to things as if they are persons—even with the chair you can have a certain loving relationship, and so with the trees and with the birds and with the animals and with people.

When your quality of relating changes, the whole of existence attains a personality. Then it is no longer impersonal, indifferent— an intimacy arises.

260.

LIBERATION
FROM YOURSELF

Enlightenment is not a state of ecstasy; it is beyond ecstasy.

Enlightenment has no excitement in it; ecstasy is a state of excitement. Ecstasy is a state of mind—a beautiful state of mind, but still a state of mind. Ecstasy is an experience. And enlightenment is not an experience, because there is nobody left to experience.

Ecstasy is still within the ego, but enlightenment is beyond the ego. It is not that you become enlightened—you are not, then enlightenment is. It is not that you are liberated, it is not that you remain in that liberation, liberated—it is a liberation from yourself.

261.

RUNNING

If you can do long-distance running, it is a perfect meditation.
Jogging, running, swimming—anything in which you can get
totally involved—is very good.

Only the activity remains, you are not, because the ego cannot function. When you are running there is really only running, there is no runner. And that's what meditation is.

If there is only dance and no dancer, that's meditation. If you are painting and there is only painting and no painter, then it is meditation. Any activity that is total and in which there is no division between the doer and the done becomes meditation.

262.

SELF-CENTEREDNESS

It happens: People who become interested in their own nature and want to know who they are become self-centered; it is just natural.

When you become too self-centered, your very self-centeredness becomes the last barrier; it has to be dropped. Nothing has to be changed in it; rather, something has to be added to it, and that will bring balance.

Buddha used to insist on meditation and compassion together. He used to say, when you meditate and feel ecstasy, immediately shower ecstasy on the whole of existence. Immediately say, "Let my ecstasy be of the whole existence." Don't go on hoarding it, otherwise that will become a subtle ego. Share it, immediately give it, so that you are empty again. Go on emptying, but never hoard. Otherwise, just as you hoard money, so you hoard ecstasies, peak experiences, and the ego can be strengthened very much.

And this second type of ego is more dangerous, because it is more subtle—it is a very pious ego, pure poison.

263.

GOING BACK

There is no going back, and there is no need to go back.
You have to go forward, not back.

Again and again you will think about how to go back. There is no going back; there is no need to go back. You have to go forward. You have to attain your own light; and that can be done. There is no possibility of going back, and even if there were, the same experience wouldn't satisfy you anymore. It would just be a repetition— it wouldn't give you the same thrill: The thrill was in the novelty of it. Now the same experience is not going to give you any joy. You will say, "This I know—but what more is there? What is new in it?" And if it is repeated a few times, you will get bored with it.

One has to go forward, and each day there are new experiences. Existence is so eternally new, that you never have the same glimpse again. It has so many millions of aspects that each day you can have a new vision—so why bother about the old? There is no need.

264.
AWARENESS

There is nowhere to go; we just have to see where we are.
If you become aware, then you suddenly recognize that you were
already there, just where you have been trying to reach.

One is born as one should be—nothing has to be added, and nothing has to be improved. And nothing can be improved. All efforts to improve create more mess and confusion and nothing else. The more you try to improve upon yourself, the more you will be in difficulties, because the very effort goes against your reality. Your reality is as it should be; there is no need to improve it. One simply grows in awareness, not existentially.

It is as if you have not looked into your pocket and you think you are a beggar, so you go on begging, and in your pocket you are carrying a valuable diamond that can give you enough treasures for your whole life. Then one day you put your hand in the pocket, and suddenly you are an emperor. Nothing has changed existentially, the situation is the same—the diamond was there before, the diamond is there now. The only thing that has changed is that now you have become aware that you possess it.

So all growth is growth in awareness, not in being. Being remains exactly as it is. A Buddha or a Christ, you or anybody, have exactly the same state, the same space—but one becomes aware and becomes a Buddha, the other remains unaware and remains a beggar.

265.
NEUROSIS

Neurosis only comes when you cannot accept failure.
It never comes when one is succeeding.

When things are going perfectly well, when one is on top of the world, why should one be neurotic? The problem arises only when you suddenly find that you are no longer at the top. You are in the ditch, dark and dismal, and now things are not succeeding. That is when neurosis enters. The same energy that was becoming ambition, and on which you were riding, turns against you in failure, starts killing you, starts destroying you.

If every neurotic person were to succeed, there would be no more neurosis in the world. When Hitler was successful, nobody ever suspected that he was mad. But in the last moment he himself knew that he was mad—he committed suicide. The problem arises only when you are not succeeding. One has to be just playful while one is succeeding. Develop that attitude of playfulness. Success and failure are not the point—to enjoy whatever you are doing is the point.

Each success is followed by failure, each day is followed by a night, and each love is followed by a darkness. Life is a progression, a movement; nothing is static. Now you are young; one day you will be old. Now you have so many friends, one day you will not have any. Now you have money, one day you will not. If you are playful, nothing is wrong. Just one quality has to be developed—playfulness.

266.

REPETITION

Repetition does not exist. Existence is always fresh, utterly fresh.

Every day is different, and if sometimes you cannot see the difference between one day and another, that simply means that you are not seeing rightly. Nothing is ever repeated. Repetition does not exist. Existence is always fresh, utterly fresh. But if we look through the past, accumulated thoughts, the mind, then it can appear like repetition. And that's why the mind is the only source of boredom. It makes you bored, because it never allows the freshness of life to be revealed to you. It goes on seeing things in the same pattern.

If life seems to be repeating itself, then always remember that it is not life, it is your mind. The mind makes everything dull, flat, one-dimensional. Life is three-dimensional; life is very colorful. The mind is just black and white. Life is like a rainbow. Between black and white there are millions of nuances of light and color and shade. Life is not divided between yes and no. The mind is divided. The mind is Aristotelean. Life is not.

267.

SOFTNESS

The soft always overcomes the hard. The soft is alive; the hard is dead.
The soft is flowerlike, the hard is rocklike. The hard looks powerful but
is impotent. The soft looks fragile but is alive.

Whatever is alive is always fragile, and the higher the quality of
life, the more fragile it is. So the deeper you go, the softer you
become, or the softer you become, the deeper you go. The innermost core is absolutely soft.

That is the whole teaching of Lao Tzu, the teaching of Tao: Be
soft, be like water; don't be like a rock. The water falls on the rock.
Nobody can imagine that finally the water is going to win. It is
impossible to believe that the water is going to win. The rock seems
to be so strong, so aggressive, and the water seems to be so passive.
How is the water going to win over the rock? But in due course the
rock simply disappears. By and by the soft goes on penetrating the
hard.

So let this be a continuous remembrance. Whenever you start
feeling that you are becoming hard, immediately relax and become
soft, whatever the consequence. Even if you are defeated and
momentarily you see that there will be a loss, let it be a loss, but
become soft—because in the long run, softness always wins.

268.

SPEED

We all have our own speeds. We should move with our own speed,
with that which is natural.

Once you find your right rhythm, you will be able to do much more. Your actions will not be hectic, they will run more smoothly, and you will be able to do much more. There are slow workers, but slowness has its own qualities. And in fact, those are better qualities. A fast worker can be quantitatively good. He or she can produce more quantitatively but qualitatively can never be very good. A slow worker is qualitatively more perfect. His whole energy moves into a qualitative dimension. The quantity may not be much, but quantity is not really the point.

If you can do a few things, but really beautiful things, almost perfect, you feel very happy and fulfilled. There is no need to do many things. If you can even do one thing that gives you total contentment, that is enough; your life is fulfilled. You can go on doing many things, with nothing fulfilling you. What is the point?

A few basic things have to be understood. There is no such thing as human nature. There are as many human natures as there are human beings, so there is no one criterion.

269.
ALLOWING

The great secret of spiritual science is allowing something
to happen without doing it. It needs great understanding and
awareness to allow things to happen.

No doing is required on our part, because whatever we do, we do
out of our confused minds. It can't be something really deep,
because the mind itself is very shallow.

Seeing this, understanding it, a new approach arises—the
approach of letting go. The great secret of spiritual science is allowing something to happen without doing it. It needs great understanding and awareness to allow things to happen. The mind is
constantly tempted to interfere. It brings its desires in, it wants
things to be according to it, and that is the whole problem. We are
tiny parts of this vast existence To have some idea of one's own is
to be idiotic. That is exactly the meaning of the word idiot—to
have some idea of one's own.

It is like a wave in the ocean trying to do something on its own.
It is just part of an immense ocean. It is neither independent nor
dependent, because it is not separate at all. The wave exists not—
it is only a manifestation of the ocean. So are we, and if we understand it, then all anxiety disappears. Then there is nowhere to go,
there is no goal to be attained, and there is no possibility to fail or
be frustrated. A great relaxation comes...this is the meaning of
surrendering, of trusting. Then life takes a totally new color. It has
not that tension that ordinarily is always there. One lives relaxedly,
calm and quiet, at home.

270.

MIND TRICKS

This is the problem of all spiritual seekers: sooner or later the mind
starts playing tricks.

Somebody will see lights, somebody will start hearing sounds, somebody will start experiencing something else. And the ego says, "This
is something great—it's only happening to you. It is rare. You are
special, that's why it's happening to you." And you start cooperating.

Don't pay much attention to it—just neglect it! One has to
become utterly empty. The only spiritual experience worth calling
spiritual is the experience of nothingness, of emptiness, what Sufis
call *fana*, the disappearance of the ego. That is the only spiritual
experience—all else is just mind games. And the mind can create
many things. The mind can start hallucinating; it can have visions,
can see Christ and Buddha. The mind has the capacity to dream—
even with open eyes it can dream. When you see Jesus standing in
front of you, how do you not believe? And there is no Jesus standing before you—it is your projection.

That's why Zen masters say, "If you meet the Buddha on the
road, kill him!" They are absolutely right. It sounds sacrilegious,
disrespectful to say if you meet Buddha you should kill him, but
it is true. You will meet Buddha on the way, or Jesus or
Muhammed—that is not the point. You will come across anything
that you had been conditioned for in your childhood. Great spiritual masters and Tibetan lamas will appear, and you will see that
something great is happening. And you will find foolish people
appreciating you. They will say, "Your status is going higher and
higher every day; you are reaching higher stations." Don't listen.

IGNORANCE

Ignoring the inner, one remains ignorant. Not ignoring the inner is the beginning of wisdom. I like this word ignorance. It means something has been ignored, something has been bypassed, you have not taken note of it.

Something is there—it has always been there—but you have been negligent of it. Maybe because it is always there it can be ignored easily. We always ignore that which is always there; we always take note of the new, because the new brings change. The dog can go on sitting if nothing moves around him—he can rest, he can dream. Let anything move and he is immediately alert. Even if a dead leaf moves, he will start barking. That's exactly the state of the mind; it takes note only when something changes, and then it falls asleep again.

And our inner treasure has always been with us. It is very easy to ignore it; we learned to ignore it. That is the meaning of the word *ignorance*. Let your seeking be the beginning of not ignoring the inner, and the awakening comes by itself. And when love is awakened, life has a totally different taste. It has the taste of nectar, of immortality, of deathlessness.

272.
OLD AND MEAN

The mind goes on shrinking—as you grow older, the mind becomes
smaller and smaller and meaner and meaner. It is no accident that old
people start being a little mean.

So many old people are always angry, irritated, annoyed for no particular reason. The reason is that they have missed the heart in their
life. They have lived only by the mind, which knows no way to
expand; it knows only how to shrink. The more you know, the
smaller the mind you have.

The ignorant person has a bigger mind than the knowledgeable
person, because the ignorant person has nothing in the mind. There
is space. The knowledgeable person is too full of knowledge; there
is no space. But the heart is another name for the inner space.

Just as there is outer space—the sky unbounded, there is no
limit to it—exactly in the same way is the inner sky also
unbounded. It has to be—if the outer is infinite, the inner cannot
be finite. It has to balance the outer; it is the other pole of it. The
inner sky is as big as the outer, exactly in the same proportion.

Meditation has not to happen in the head—it cannot happen
there, so whatever happens there is only an imitation of meditation.
Not true, not the real. The real always happens in the heart. So
remember: When I talk of awakening I am talking about the heart's
awakening. It has not to be understood only as a doctrine; it has to
be experienced, it has to become your existential state.

273.
ANGER AND PAIN

Anger arises as a protection against pain. If somebody hurts you,
you become angry as a protection of your being against pain. So every
pain is suppressed by anger—layers and layers of anger on top of pain.

Continue working on anger, and suddenly any moment you will feel the anger has disappeared—that you are becoming sad, not angry. The climate will change from anger to sadness, and when it does you can be certain that now you are close to pain; then the pain will erupt.

It is just as if we dig a hole in the earth to make a well. First we have to remove the earth and many layers of stone, and then the water comes up. At first it is not clean water, it is muddy; then by and by cleaner sources become available. First anger will come—and it has many layers, like earth. Then sadness will come like muddy water, and then pain—clean, pure pain—will be available. And pure pain is tremendously beautiful, because it will give you another birth immediately.

274.
DISILLUSIONMENT

To understand that whatever you have called love up to now
was not love is one of the most meaningful insights.
When it happens, much becomes possible.

People go on thinking that they love, and that becomes their greatest illusion—and the sooner they are disillusioned the better. Love is such a rare thing that it cannot be so easily available to all. It is not; it is as rare as Buddhahood, not less than that.

The insight that you do not know love is good, but it will make you sad, even give you a certain gloom. But don't be worried, because out of a dark night the morning is born. When the night is darkest the morning is closest. You will be very morose, because whatever you were thinking was love was not, and you have lived in dreams and have been missing reality. When this insight dawns on you, you become very sad, almost dead. Don't try to escape from this state. Relax into it, let yourself be drowned in this sadness, and soon you will come out of it completely new.

The human tendency is not to allow it, to escape from it—to go to the restaurant, to the cinema hall, to find friends—anything so that you can escape from this state. But if you escape, you again miss something that was going to happen. So relax into it.

275.
THE FALSE AND THE TRUE

The first time that mind becomes meditative, love seems like
a bondage. And in a way it is true, because a mind that is not
meditative cannot really be in love. That love is false, illusory,
more an infatuation than love.

You have nothing to compare false love to unless the real happens, so when meditation starts, the illusory love by and by dissipates, disappears. Don't be disheartened, and don't make disappointment a permanent attitude.

If somebody is a creator and meditates, all creativity will disappear for the time being. If you are a painter, suddenly you will not find yourself in it. You can continue, but by and by you will have no energy and no enthusiasm. If you are a poet, poetry will stop. If you have been in love, that energy will simply disappear. If you try to force yourself to move into a relationship, to be your old self, that enforcement will be very dangerous. Then you are doing a contradictory thing: On one hand you are trying to go in, on the other you are trying to go out. It is as if you are driving a car, pressing the accelerator and at the same time pressing the brake. It can be a disaster, because you are doing two opposite things at the same time.

Meditation is only against false love. The false will disappear, and that's a basic condition for the real to appear. The false must go, the false must vacate you completely; only then are you available for the real. Many people think that love is against meditation, and meditation is against love—that's not true. Meditation is against false love, but is totally for true love.

276.

HELPLESSNESS

The world is vast, and human beings are helpless. It is difficult, very difficult, but once you accept basic human suffering you will become absolutely calm.

It is easier to accept one's own misery than to accept another's. It is even possible to accept another's suffering, but the misery of a child—innocent, helpless, suffering for no reason at all; he cannot retaliate, cannot even protest or defend himself—it seems so unjust, so ugly, horrible, that it is difficult to accept.

But remember that not only is the child helpless; you are too. Once you understand your own helplessness, acceptance will follow as a shadow. What can you do? You are also helpless. I am not saying become hard like a stone. Feel, but know that you are helpless. The world is vast, and human beings are helpless. At the most we can feel compassion. And even if we do something, there is no certainty that our doing is going to help—it may cause even more misery.

So I am not saying to lose your compassion. Only lose your judgment that human suffering is wrong. And drop the idea that you have to do something about it, because once the doer comes in, the witness is lost. Compassion is good, and helplessness is good. Cry, there is nothing wrong in it. Let tears come, but allow them knowing that you are also helpless; that is why you are crying. The very idea that we can make any change is very egoistic, and the ego goes on disturbing things. So drop that ego and just watch.

277.
UNCHANGING

Always remember that you are not the momentary but the eternal,
not the changing but the unchanging.

In a flower there are two constituents: one that is constantly changing—the body part, the form—and then, hidden behind the form, the formless, which is unchanging. Flowers come and go, but their beauty remains. Sometimes it is manifested in a form, sometimes it dissolves back into the formless. Again there will be flowers, and beauty will assert itself. Then the flowers will fade and the beauty will move into the unmanifest.

And the same is happening with human beings, with birds, with animals, with everything. We have two dimensions: the day part when we become manifested, and the night part when we become unmanifested—but we are eternal. We have been always, and we will be always. Being is beyond time and beyond change.

In the beginning just remember it "as if," then you will start feeling the reality of it.

278.
CHANGE

We want to change if there is no risk, and that's impossible. That
condition—that there be no risk—makes it impossible to change,
because everything has to be at stake, only then is change possible.

Change cannot be partial. Either it is or it is not—it can only be
total. So the decision is between to be or not to be. It is a jump, not
a gradual process. If you are really fed up with the life that you
have lived, if you are really fed up with your old patterns, then
there is no trouble. It is easy, very easy to change if you understand
that you have been living a life that was not worth much, that has
not brought anything, that has never allowed you to flower.

It is not a question of worldly recognition. People may think
that you have succeeded, that you have all the qualities they would
like themselves, but that's not the point. Deep down you feel a
stagnancy, a frozenness, a shrunkenness, as if you are already dead,
as if something has closed. The flavor of life, the poetry and flow,
the song has disappeared; the fragrance is there no more. You go
on because you have to. What can you do? You seem almost a victim of circumstance, chance—like a puppet—not knowing what
you are doing, where you are going, from where you have come,
who you are.

If you really think that this has been so, then change is very
easy. It is so spontaneous a phenomenon that in fact nothing is
needed to be done about it; just the very understanding brings
change. Understanding is radical revolution, and there is no other
revolution.

NONATTACHMENT

I am not for renunciation. Enjoy everything that life gives, but always remain free. If times change, if things disappear, it makes no difference to you. You can live in a palace, you can live in a hut... you can live as blissfully under the sky.

The constant awareness that one should not start clinging to anything makes life blissful. One enjoys tremendously whatever is available. It is always more than one can enjoy, and it is always available. But the mind is too attached to things—we become blind to the celebration that is always available.

There is a story of a Zen monk who was a master. One night a thief entered his hut, but there was nothing there to steal. The master became very worried about what the thief would think. He had come at least four or five miles out of the town, and on such a dark night....

The monk had only one blanket that he was using—that was his clothing and bedcover and everything. He put the blanket in the corner, but the thief could not see in the dark, so the master had to tell him to take the blanket, begged him to take it as a gift saying that he should not return empty-handed. The thief was much puzzled; he felt so awkward that he simply escaped with the blanket.

The master wrote a poem saying that if he had been able, he would have given the man the moon. Sitting under the moon that night, naked, he enjoyed the moon more than ever before.

Life is always available. It is always more than you can enjoy; you always have more than you can give.

280.

GLIMPSES

*It always starts with glimpses, and it is good that it does; a sudden
opening of the sky will be too much, unbearable. One can go mad
if a realization happens too suddenly.*

Sometimes you can be foolish enough to go into some realization
too suddenly, which can be dangerous, because it will be too much
for you; you will not be able to absorb it. The question is not of
realization itself, but how to digest it by and by, so that it is not an
experience but becomes your being. If it is an experience it will
come and go; it will remain a glimpse. No experience can remain
permanent—only your being can be permanent.

And don't be greedy about inner matters. It is bad even in outward matters, and very bad in inward matters. It is not so dangerous when you are greedy about money and power and prestige.
Because those things are just futile, and whether you are greedy or
not does not make much difference. But greed inside, when you
move on the inward path, can be very dangerous. Many people
have gone almost mad. It can be too dazzling to their eyes, and
they can go blind.

It is always good to come and go. Let it be a constant rhythm so
that you are never out of the world and never in the world. By and
by you will realize that you transcend it. This process has to be so
gradual—just as a flower opens so gradually that you cannot see
when the opening really happened.

281.

THE BODY

Always listen to your body. It whispers, it never shouts.

Only in whispering does the body give you messages. If you are alert, you will be able to understand it. And the body has a wisdom of its own, which is very much deeper than the mind. The mind is just immature. The body has remained without the mind for millennia. The mind is a late arrival. It does not know much yet. All the basic things the body still keeps in its control. Only useless things have been given to the mind—to think about philosophy and God and hell and politics.

So listen to the body, and never compare yourself to anyone else. Never before has there been a person like you, and never will there be. You are absolutely unique—in the past, present, and future. So you cannot compare notes with anybody, and you cannot imitate anybody.

282.

POLAR STAR

The polar star is the most permanent, unmoving star. Everything goes on moving, but this is the only star that doesn't move.

Love is the polar star. Everything moves except love. Everything changes; only love remains permanent. In this changing world only love is the unchanging substance. Everything else is a flux, momentary. Only love is eternal.

So these two things you have to remember. One is love, because that is the only thing that is nonillusory. That is the only reality; everything else is a dream. So if one can become loving, one becomes real. If one attains total love, one has become oneself, the truth, because love is the only truth.

And the second thing is that when you are walking, remember that something in you never walks. That's your soul, your polar star. You eat, but something in you never eats. You become angry, but something in you never becomes angry. You do a thousand and one things, but something in you remains absolutely beyond doing. That is your polar star. So walking, remember that which never walks. Moving, remember the immobile. Talking, remember silence. Doing things, remember being.

Always remember that which is absolutely permanent, which never flickers, never wavers, which knows no change. That unchanging one within you is the real. And love is the way to find it.

283.
BACK TO THE CENTER

If you feel a sort of wavering left and right and you don't know
where your center is, that simply shows that you are no longer
in contact with your hara, so you have to create that contact.

In the night when you go to sleep, lie down on the bed and put both
your hands two inches below the navel, and press a little. Then start
breathing deeply, and you will feel that center coming up and down
with the breathing. Feel your whole energy there as if you are
shrinking and shrinking and shrinking and just existing there as a
small center, as very concentrated energy. Just do this for ten,
fifteen minutes, and then fall asleep. If you fall asleep doing this, it
will be helpful. Then the whole night that centering persists. Again
and again the unconscious goes and centers there. So the whole
night without your knowing, you will be coming in many ways in
deep contact with the center.

In the morning, the moment that you feel that sleep has gone,
don't open your eyes right away. Again put your hands below
your navel, push a little, and start breathing; again feel the *hara*.
Do this for ten or fifteen minutes and then get up. Do this every
night, every morning. Within three months you will start feeling
centered.

284.
UNCONDITIONING

Love is an unconditioning. It simply takes away the old patterns and does not give you new ones.

It almost always happens that lovers become childlike—because love accepts you. It makes no demands on you. Love does not say, "Be this, be that." Love simply says, "Be yourself. You are good as you are. You are beautiful as you are." Love accepts you. Suddenly you start dropping your ideals, "shoulds," personalities. You drop your old skin, and again you become a child. Love makes people young.

The more you love, the younger you will remain. When you don't love you start becoming old, because when you don't love you lose contact with yourself. Love is nothing but coming in contact with yourself via the other, somebody who accepts you, who mirrors you as you are.

Love can be the right situation in which to drop all conditioning. Love is an unconditioning. It simply takes away the old patterns and does not give you new ones. If it gives you a new pattern, it is not love, but politics.

285.
WONDER

Knowledge destroys the capacity to wonder. Wonder is one of the most valuable things in life, and knowledge destroys it. The more you know, the less you wonder, and the less you wonder, the less life means to you.

You are not exhilarated with life. You are not surprised—you start taking things for granted. The innocent heart is continuously in wonder like a small child collecting seashells or colored stones on the beach or just running hither and thither in a garden after butterflies and being surprised by everything. That's why children ask so many questions.

If you go for a morning walk with a child you start feeling exhausted, because the child goes on asking about this and that, asking questions that cannot be answered: "Why are the trees green?" and "Why is the rose red?" But why is the child asking? He is intrigued. He is interested in everything. The word *interest* comes from a root that means to be involved in—*inter-esse*. The child is involved in everything that is happening.

The more you become knowledgeable, the less and less you remain involved in life. You simply pass by—you are not concerned with the cow and the dog and the rose bush and the sun and the bird; you are not concerned. Your mind has become very narrow; you are just going to your office or back to your home. You are just running after money more and more, that's all. Or after power, but you are no longer related to life in its multi-dimensionality. To be in wonder is to relate with everything, and to be constantly receptive.

286.

ANY TIME, ANY PLACE

Meditation has nothing to do with time or place. Rather, it has something to do with you, your inner space. So whenever you are free of the day-to-day routine, relax and allow it to happen. It can happen any place, any time, because it is nontemporal and nonspatial.

The right meditation knows no limitation, and slowly, slowly the flow becomes more and more conscious. Then whatever you are doing remains on the surface; deep down, the river goes on flowing. Even in the marketplace, surrounded by all kinds of turmoil, you are utterly silent. Even when somebody is insulting you, offending you, trying to provoke you, deep down there is a calmness; something remains undisturbed. Even when there are a thousand and one distractions, at the center nothing is distracted. But that meditation cannot be managed by the mind; it can only be allowed by the heart.

This moment is meditation—it is here! You have not done anything for it to happen; it is happening on its own. In this moment there is no time. In this moment you are transported. In this moment you can feel that quiet, that serenity, that transcendence.

287.
SOCIALIZING

*Ninety percent of people's activities are utterly useless; and they are
not only useless but harmful too. What you call socializing, meeting
with people, relating, talking, conversation, is almost all rubbish.
It is good that it drops; when one becomes a little alert, it drops!*

It is as if you have been suffering from a high fever—105 degrees—
and have been shouting and thrashing about in your bed. Then the
fever cools down to ninety-eight—normal—and you think that all
of life is gone, because you are no longer thrashing, no longer saying that your bed is flying into the sky, that ghosts are standing
around. You are no longer in a delirium. Certainly it will feel a little poor, because all those people were surrounding you, and you
were flying in the sky and talking to gods, and now all is gone and
you are just normal!

That's what happens when socializing drops: The delirium is
gone—you are becoming normal. Rather than talking the whole
day, unnecessarily gossiping, you will be talking telegraphically. You
may not speak a lot—you may become a person of few words, but
those few words will be significant. And now only real relationships will remain, and they are worth something.

One need not have a crowd around oneself. A few deep, intimate
relationships are enough; they are really fulfilling. In fact, because
people don't have intimate relationships, they have many relationships to substitute. But there is no substitution for real intimacy. You
can have one thousand friends—that will not make for one real
one. But that's what people are doing: They think that quantity can
become a substitute for quality. It never does. It cannot.

288.

LETTING GO

Once one knows how to let go, for the first time life starts happening.
We are unnecessarily striving to attain something; in fact, the very effort
to attain it is the hindrance.

Life happens—it cannot be attained. The more one strives for it,
the less one has it. One need not go to it; it comes on its own. All
that is needed is a total state of receptivity, of openness. One has
to become a host to life. Life need not be chased. In chasing is
misery; the more you chase it, the farther away it goes.

And life contains all. It contains God, it contains bliss, it contains
benediction, it contains beauty, good, truth, whatever you want to
call it—it contains all; there is nothing other than life. Life is the
name of the totality of existence.

One has to learn to be patiently relaxed, and then the miracle
of miracles happens: One day when you are really relaxed, something suddenly changes. A curtain disappears, and you see things as
they are. If your eyes are too full of desires, expectation, longing,
they cannot see the truth. The eyes are covered with the dust of
desire. All search is futile. Search is a byproduct of the mind. To be
in a state of nonsearch is the great moment of transformation.

All the meditations are just preparations for that moment. They
are not real meditations but just preparations so that one day you
can simply sit, doing nothing, desiring nothing.

289.
THE GUIDE

Every river reaches to the ocean without any guide, without any map.
We too can reach to the ocean, but we become entangled on the way.

The guide, the master, is not needed to take you to the ocean—that can happen on its own—the master is needed to keep you alert not to get entangled on the way, because there are a thousand and one attractions.

The river goes on moving. It comes to a beautiful tree; the river enjoys the tree and moves on; it does not become attached to the tree, otherwise the movement will stop. It comes to a beautiful mountain but it goes on, utterly thankful, grateful to the mountain, for the joy of passing through the mountain and all the song that happens, and the dance. The river is grateful, certainly grateful, but not attached at all. It goes on moving; its movement doesn't stop.

The problem with human consciousness is that you come across a beautiful tree and you want to make your home there; now you don't want to go anywhere. You come across a beautiful man or a woman and become attached. The master is needed to remind you again and again not to become attached to anything. I don't mean not to enjoy anything. In fact, if you become attached you will not be able to enjoy; you can enjoy only if you remain unattached, untethered.

290.
RIGHT MOMENTS

When you are feeling happy, loving, floating—these are the right
moments when the door is very close. Just a knock will be enough.

It almost always happens that when people are miserable, anxious,
tense, and nervous, they try meditation—but then it is hard to
enter. When you are feeling hurt, angry, or sad, then you think of
meditation, but that is almost going against the current and will be
difficult.

When you are feeling happy, loving, floating—these are the right
moments when the door is very close. Just a knock will be enough.
Suddenly one morning you are feeling good, for no visible reason.
Something must have happened deep in the unconscious. Something
must have happened between you and the cosmos, some harmony;
maybe it happened in the night, in deep sleep. In the morning you
are feeling good; don't waste that time. Just a few minutes of meditation will be worth more than a few days of meditation when you
are miserable.

Or suddenly at night lying on the bed, you feel at home…cozy
surroundings, the warmth of the bed. Just sit for five minutes;
don't waste that moment. A certain harmony is there—use it, ride
on it, and that wave will take you far away, farther than you can go
on your own. Learn how to use these blissful moments.

291.
ONENESS

Outside and inside are just false divisions, as all divisions are.
They are useful—because it is difficult to talk without words.
But then you come to understand that there is only one. It has no
outside to it and no inside. It is one, and you are that.

This oneness is the meaning of the Upanishads' *Tattwamasi Swetaketu*— "that art thou." *That* means the outside, *thou* means the inside; they are bridged. That becomes thou, and thou becomes that. Suddenly there is no division.

There *is* no division—death is life, and life is death. All divisions exist because the mind is incapable of seeing that the contradictory can be one. It is because of its logic that the mind cannot see how a thing can be both. The mind thinks of either/or; it says either this or that. And life is both, existence is both together—so much so that to say that existence is both things together is not right. It is a tremendous oneness.

MASKS

Whatever you are doing, just be conscious. If you are wearing a mask,
be conscious; wear it knowingly. It should not be an automatic thing.

If you are in a sad mood and somebody comes and you remain sad, you will make him sad too. And he has not done anything. He has not deserved it in any way, so why make him sad unnecessarily? You smile and talk, and you just manage, knowing well that this is a mask. When your friend goes you become sad again. That was just a social formality. If you use it consciously there is no problem.

If you have a wound, there is no need to go and show it to everybody; it is none of their affair. Why create misery in their minds about your wound? Why be an exhibitionist? Let it be there; take care of it, try to heal it. Show it to the doctor, but there is no need to show it to every passerby on the road. Just be conscious.

One has to use many masks; they function as lubricants. Somebody comes and asks how you are, and you start telling her all your problems. She did not ask for it; she was just saying hello. Now for one hour she has to listen to you. That will be too much! Next time she will not even say hello; she will escape.

In life many formalities are needed, because you are not alone, and if you don't live according to the formal patterns of the society, you will create more misery for yourself, nothing else.

293.
SURPRISE

All that is beautiful and true always comes as a surprise. So retain
the capacity to be surprised. That is one of the greatest blessings of life.

Once you lose the capacity to be surprised, you are dead. If things
can surprise you, you are still alive. And the more you are surprised by things, the more alive you are. That is the aliveness of
children; they are surprised by trivia. One cannot even believe they
are surprised—by just an ordinary tree, or bird, or dog, or cat, or
a pebble on the shore. Children are even more surprised than you
would be if you were to find a Kohinoor, a great diamond—even
then you won't be surprised. But because children have the capacity to become surprised, each pebble becomes a diamond. If you
are not surprised, even a diamond becomes an ordinary pebble.

Life carries as much meaning as you carry the capacity to be
surprised, the capacity to wonder. So always remain open. Remind
yourself again and again that life is infinite. It is always an ongoing
process; it never comes to an end. It is an eternal journey, and each
moment is new, each moment is original. When I say each moment
is original, I mean each moment throws you back to your origin,
each moment makes you a child again.

294.
THE UNKNOWABLE

The mind is the known, meditation is to stand in the unknown,
and godliness is the unknowable—like a horizon just bordering
on the unknown. The closer you come, the further away it recedes.
It is always a rainbow; you can never catch hold of it.

You can try to reach the unknowable—every effort should be made
to reach it—but it is always unreachable.

God is unknowable, and because the unknowable exists, life is
beautiful. Because the impossible exists, life is a tremendously
beautiful adventure of discovery. When a thing becomes known,
possible, it loses its meaning. That's why in the West life is losing
more meaning than in the East. Because science has made you more
knowledgeable, and because of the dust science has poured on you,
the capacity to be surprised is becoming less and less. You are
becoming almost insensitive to the unknowable. This is the only
grave, the only death—that you think that you have known. Always
remain available to the unknown and the unknowable.

295.
THE CRITICAL VOICE

This critical voice is never yours. When you were a child, your father said, "Don't do this," and your mother said, "Don't do that." Whatever you wanted to do was always wrong, and whatever you never wanted to do was what they wanted you to do, was right.

You are in a double bind. You know what the "right" thing to do is, but you don't want to do it, so if you end up doing it, you do it as a duty. Then there is no joy; you feel that you are destroying yourself, that you are wasting your life. If you do what you like, you feel guilty, you feel that you are doing something wrong. So you have to get rid of your parents, that's all. And it is a very simple thing, because now you are grown-up, and your parents are no longer there; they are just inside your mind.

I don't mean to go and kill your parents—I mean kill this hangover from the past. You are no longer a child: Recognize this fact. Take the responsibility into your own hands; it is your life. So do whatever you like to do, and never do anything that you don't like to do. If you have to suffer for it, then suffer. One has to pay the price for everything; nothing is free in life.

If you enjoy something and the whole world condemns it, good! Let them condemn. Accept that consequence; it is worth it. If you don't like something and the whole world calls it beautiful, it is meaningless, because you will never enjoy your life. It is your life— and who knows? Tomorrow you may die. So enjoy it while you are alive! It is nobody else's business—neither your parents nor society's nor anybody else's. It is your life.

296.
TECHNIQUE

Love is what works; the technique is just an excuse. The therapist works, not the therapy.

Sometimes with a man like Fritz Perls, the founder of Gestalt therapy, something starts happening. It is not Gestalt, it is the personality of the man—his tremendous courage, his tremendous compassion. He tries to help; he tries to reach the other person.

But our logical minds say that it must be the Gestalt therapy that is helping; and that has been the fallacy through the ages. It is not Christianity that helps, it was Christ. It is not Buddhism, but Buddha. For twenty-five hundred years people have been thinking that it was Buddhism that helped people, but it was Buddha. If Buddha had been saying something different, that too would have been of help. Even if he had said just the opposite of whatever he said, then too it would have helped. It was the life force of that man, his compassion and his love and his understanding that helped.

But our minds immediately catch hold of the techniques, of the superficial. Then the superficial becomes important, and we lose contact with the essential. And there are problems: The essential cannot be taught, only the non-essential can be taught. So you cannot teach Fritz Perls—you can only teach Gestalt. A Fritz Perls happens when he happens; there is no way to teach that! But society wants to be certain about something, so it starts teaching, and only the nonessential can be taught.

So all teaching goes against the teacher, because the teacher brings the essential, and the teaching teaches the nonessential.

297.
PRISON BREAK

I may be wrong. I may not really be out of jail, maybe I am just pretending. I may even be the jailer himself! Nobody can ever be certain about it. So it is a gamble, a matter of trust. Trust is always a gamble.

If you decide on your own to quit smoking, and you say nothing to anybody, there are ninety-nine chances out of a hundred that you will smoke. Someone else decides that he will not smoke, and he tells his friends. There is a ninety percent chance that he will still smoke. The third possibility is that he joins a society of nonsmokers where nobody smokes. Now there is a ninety-nine percent chance that he will not smoke.

Gurdjieff used to say that if you want to do something, find a few friends so that you can do it together. It is almost as if you are imprisoned in a jail: You want to escape, but to escape alone will be very difficult. If you make a gang the possibility is greater: together you can kill the guard, but alone it will be very difficult. Together you can break the wall, but alone it will be very difficult. But there is still a possibility that you may not be able to succeed, because your gang will be a small gang of helpless prisoners. The forces that manage the jail are bigger than you.

The best thing is to make contact with people who are outside, who are already free, who are not in the jail, who can supply things to you, who can give you the map, who can bribe the guards, who can take the jailer away for a picnic.

298.
BODY RHYTHM

Body rhythm is very important to understand. And it cannot be changed.
It settles the moment you are born.

Just watch your rhythm. If you feel like going to bed early, then go to bed early and get up early in the morning. And once you have understood what time suits you, it is better to be regular about it. If it is possible, then be regular; if sometimes it is not possible, that's okay, but don't make irregularity a routine.

Now much research has been done on body rhythm, and there seems to be no possibility to change it. It is something in the very cells; the cells are programmed. There are birds that fall asleep as the sun sets. Once these birds were put in artificial chambers and deceived. When it was night outside there was light in the chamber, and when it was day outside there was night in the chamber. The birds were in these chambers for months. They became neurotic—they started committing suicide or killing one another—but their body rhythm could not be changed. They would fall asleep while it was day in the chamber and they would become awake when it was night. And of course it was very strange for their bodies to be awake in the night—they started feeling something eerie, something weird, and that started telling on their systems.

So simply follow your own rhythm.

299.
SHADOW

Nobody can kill the ego, because the ego is not. It is a shadow—
you cannot kill a shadow.

Even to fight with a shadow is foolish, you will be defeated—and not because the shadow is very powerful but because the shadow is not! If you start fighting with a shadow, how can you win? It is nonexistential; and so is the ego.

The ego is the shadow of the self. Just as the body creates a shadow, the self also creates a shadow. You cannot fight with it, and you cannot kill it; in fact, the one who wants to kill it is the ego.

One can only understand. If you want to kill the shadow, bring light in, and the shadow will disappear; bring in more awareness, and the ego will disappear.

300.
THE MASTER KEY

Total acceptance is the key. It is the master key; it opens all the doors.

There is no lock that cannot be opened by acceptance. It is simply the key that fits all the locks—because the moment you accept something, a transformation has started in your being because now there is no conflict. You are not two. In acceptance you have become one, you have become a unity.

Remember your unity, your complexity. It is beautiful. Desires are beautiful. Passion is good—if you accept it, it will become compassion. If you accept the desires, by and by you will see that the same energy is becoming desirelessness. It is the same energy that was involved in the desires. When you accept the desires, by and by you relax, and energy starts streaming more naturally. You start seeing things as they are. You are not too involved with this desire or that. You have accepted, so there is no problem.

Whatever you call desire will become desirelessness. Right now is like coal. It can be transfigured into diamonds; it can become precious. Just think of the man who is desireless—he will be impotent. In fact, she will not be alive, because how will he live without desire? So desirelessness is not negative. It is the ultimate positivity of all desires. When desires are known, understood, lived, and experienced, you have gone beyond them. You have come of age.

3OI.
PARENTS

It is always good to come to an understanding with your parents.

Gurdjieff used to say, "Unless you are in good communion with your parents, you have missed your life." If some anger persists between you and your parents, you will never feel at ease. Wherever you are, you will feel a little guilty. You will never be able to forgive and forget.. Parents are not just a social relationship. It is out of them that you have come. You are part of them, a branch of their tree. You are still rooted in them.

When parents die, something very deep-rooted dies within you. When parents die, for the first time you feel alone, uprooted. So while they are alive, do everything that you can so that an understanding can arise and you can communicate with them and they can communicate with you. Then things settle and the accounts are closed. Then when they leave the world—and they will leave someday—you will not feel guilty, you will not repent; you will know that things have settled. They have been happy with you; you have been happy with them.

302.

REINCARNATION

The Eastern concept of reincarnation is beautiful. Whether or not it is true is not the point. It gives you a very relaxed attitude toward life. That is the real thing.

In the West there is too much hurry because of the Christian concept that there is only one life, and with death you are gone and will not be able to come back. That has created a very crazy idea in people's minds. So everybody is in a hurry, running fast.

Nobody worries about where they are going; they just think about going faster, that's all. So nobody is enjoying anything, because how can you enjoy things at such a speed? All of life has become a hit-and-run affair.

To enjoy anything one needs a very relaxed attitude. To enjoy life one needs eternity. How can you enjoy when death is going to come so soon? One tries to enjoy as much as one can, but in that very effort all peace is lost, and without peace there is no enjoyment. Delight is possible only when you are savoring things very slowly. When you have enough time to waste, only then only is delight possible.

The Eastern concept of reincarnation is beautiful. Whether or not it is true is not the point. It gives you a very relaxed attitude toward life. That is the real thing. I am not worried about metaphysics. It may be true, it may not be true; that's not the point at all. To me it is irrelevant. But it gives you a beautiful background.

303.
HISTORY

History is so ugly. Man has not reached the level at which history should start. It has all been nightmares.

Humanity has nothing yet to write about itself—just a very few cases somewhere a Buddha, somewhere a Jesus, just like faraway stars.

Humanity has lived in violence and wars and madness, so it's good, in a way, to forget the past. The past is too heavy and it does not help. In fact, it corrupts the mind. Looking at the past, it seems that humanity cannot grow. It makes things look very hopeless.

History is not yet worth writing or reading. And the very interest in history is not good. History is concerned with the past. It is concerned with the dead. It is concerned with that which is no more. The whole concern should be with that which is right now, this very moment.

Don't only forget history, but forget your biography also, and each morning start your day as if it were completely new, as if you have never existed before. That's what meditation is all about: to start each moment anew, fresh like dew, not knowing anything of the past. When you don't know anything of the past and you don't carry anything of it, you don't project any future. You have nothing to project. When the past disappears, the future also disappears. They are joined together. Then pure present is left. That is pure eternity.

304.
ROOTED

If you are rooted in love, you are rooted.
There is no other way to be rooted.

You can have money, you can have a house, you can have security, you can have a bank balance; those things will not give you rootedness. They are just substitutes, a poor substitute for love. They may increase your anxiety even more, because once you have physical security—money, a social status—you become more and more afraid that these things may be taken from you. Or you become worried about having more and more of these things, because discontent knows no limit. And your basic need was of being rooted.

Love is the earth where one needs to be rooted. Just as trees are rooted in the earth, human beings are rooted in love. Our roots are invisible, so anything visible is not going to help. Money is very visible, a house is very visible, social status is very visible. But we are trees with invisible roots. You will have to find some invisible earth—call it love, call it godliness, call it prayer—but it is going to be something like that, something invisible, intangible, elusive, mysterious. You cannot catch hold of it. On the contrary, you will have to allow it to catch hold of you.

305.
DEDICATION

Life has to become a dedication; only then is there meaning.
Meaning comes through dedication, and the greater the object
of dedication, the greater will be the meaning.

There are people who are dedicated to countries—the fatherland, the motherland. A country is a very tiny thing to surrender to, and foolish, and some Adolf Hitler will exploit this surrendering.

Then there are people who are dedicated to churches— Hinduism, Christianity, Islam. These are better than countries, but they are still a dogma, a creed, a manmade thing, and something that basically divides humanity. One becomes a Christian, another becomes a Hindu, and there is division, there is conflict, there is violence—and the irony of it is that the violence is in the name of love!

So never dedicate yourself to anything that divides.

306.
EMPTY-FULL

With one hand create emptiness, with another create fullness, so that
when you are really empty, your fullness can descend into it.

Sometimes it happens that you become addicted to one sort of
meditation. That addiction brings about a sort of impoverishment.
You should allow many dimensions to penetrate you. You should
allow at least two meditations: one inactive, one active. That is a
basic requirement; otherwise the personality becomes lopsided.

Watching is a passive process. There is nothing to do. It is not a
doing; it is a sort of nondoing. It is a Buddhist meditation—very
good, but incomplete. So Buddhists have become very lopsided.
They became very quiet and calm, but they missed something—
what I call bliss.

Buddhism is one of the most beautiful approaches—but it is
incomplete. Something is missing. It has no mysticism in it, no
poetry, no romance; it is almost bare mathematics, a geometry of
the soul but not a poetry of the soul. And unless you can dance,
never be satisfied. Be silent, but use your silence as an approach
toward blissfulness.

Do a few dancing meditations, singing meditations, music, so at
the same time, your capacity to enjoy, your capacity to be joyful,
also increases.

307.
BOUNDARIES

Love means dropping territorial boundaries. That invisible line has to disappear, hence fear arises, because it is our animal heritage. That's why, once you are in a loving state of mind, you go beyond animal heritage. For the first time you become human, really human.

If you really want to live a rich, fulfilled, tremendously vibrant life, then there is no other way but to drop boundaries. The only way is to make more and more contact with people. Allow more and more people to trespass your being, allow more and more people to enter you.

One can be hurt—that's the fear—but that risk has to be taken. It is worth it. If you protect yourself your whole life and nobody is allowed near you, what is the point of your being alive? You will be dead before you are dead. You will not have lived at all. It would be as if you had never existed, because there is no other life than relationship. So the risk has to be taken.

All human beings are just like you. Essentially the human heart is the same. So allow people to come close. If you allow them to come close to you, they will allow you to come close to them. When boundaries overlap, love happens.

308.

THEORIZING

The philosopher invents the truth; it is not a discovery.
It is the philosopher's own intellectual invention.

Truth is not to be invented. All that is invented will be untrue.
Truth is already here. One has to uncover it, to discover it. There
is no need to invent it, because whatever you invent is going to be
false. You don't know what truth is; how can you invent it? In ignorance, whatever is invented will be just a projection of ignorance.
Truth cannot be invented; it can only be discovered, because it is
already the case.

The second thing is that no curtain is covering truth. The curtain is on your eyes. The truth is not hidden. The truth is absolutely
clear, right in front of you. Wherever you look, you are looking at
the truth. Whatever you do, you are doing to the truth. You know
or you know not; that is not the point.

A real seeker of truth is one who will not invent, one who will
not guess, one who will not infer, one who will not make a logical
syllogism, one who will simply be receptive, open, responding,
vulnerable, and available to truth. A seeker of truth has to learn
one thing, and that is how to be infinitely passive and patient and
waiting. Truth happens to you whenever you are open.

309.
ATOMIC MOMENT

Each moment is atomic.
There is no need for two moments to have any sequence.

It is the one-dimensional mind that continuously asks for some meaning, some meaning that runs through all moments, that wants everything to be connected by a cause-and-effect chain, that wants everything to move somewhere, to reach somewhere, to conclude somewhere. That is the logical mind, the one-dimensional mind.

Life is multidimensional. It has no goal really, no destiny. And it has no meaning, in fact—meaning in the sense that all the moments are following each other in a queue, reaching somewhere. No, life is not moving anywhere. It is simply dancing here. The right word is *dance,* not *movement.*

Each moment is a dance, and one should enjoy each moment as it comes, as it happens. Then your burden will disappear completely. That's what freedom is—to be in the moment, to be of the moment, never worried about the past, never worried about that which has not come yet, and never trying to make a logical sequence out of anything.

3IO.
TWILIGHT

Many people have entered into existence through twilight.

In India, the word s*andhya*—twilight—has become synonymous with prayer. If you approach an orthodox Hindu who is praying, he will say, "I was doing *sandhya*—I was doing my twilight." When the sun rises, just before sunrise, there is a great change. The whole passive existence becomes active. Sleep is broken; dreams disappear. The trees and birds and life everywhere arise again. It is a resurrection. It is a miracle every day. If you allow yourself to float with it in that moment, you can rise to a very high peak.

And the same change happens again when the sun sets. Everything quiets, calms. A tranquility, a deep silence, pervades existence. In that moment, you can reach to the very depths. In the morning you can reach to very great heights; in the evening you can reach to very deep depths, and both are beautiful. Either go high or very deep. In both ways you transcend yourself.

311.
INNER MOUNTAIN

When one is utterly silent and still, and there is no movement in the
mind, one starts feeling like a great peak of the mountain, snowcapped.

The mountain has always attracted meditators. There is something in the mountains—the silence, the stillness, the absolute
unmoving, almost a timelessness. The mountain remains almost
permanent, and the way the mountain sits represents a kind of centering. It is as if the mountain is in deep centering; all is centered
within. Buddha sitting under a tree looks like a mountain. And it
is no accident that the first statues ever made in the world were
made of Buddha and were made of stone—of just a rock, unmoving, timeless, deathless, centering in its self.

   The movements of the mind—thought, desire, imagination, and
memory—all these create misery. When there is no movement of
thought and desire, the mind has disappeared. You are, but there is
no mind in it. That state of no-mind will give you the glimpse of the
inner mountain.

312.
METAPHYSICS

The word meta means beyond. Physics is not all, and matter is not all,
and those who think that it is are satisfied with the circumference of life.
They will keep moving round and round, but they will never come home,
because home exists at the center.

Metaphysics means coming home, knowing that you are consciousness, knowing that the whole of existence is full of consciousness, that consciousness is not a byproduct of matter. It is not. Matter is only the body of consciousness—its clothing, its shelter, its abode, its temple—but the deity is consciousness. And the temple is created for the deity, not vice versa. Matter exists because consciousness exists, not vice versa.

Matter is consciousness asleep; consciousness is matter become awakened. There is ultimately only one thing—call it x, y, or z or God or truth or whatever you wish. Ultimately there is one thing, but that one thing can have two states: one of sleep and one of awakeness. When matter becomes aware of itself it is consciousness. When consciousness forgets itself it is matter.

So those who think that matter is all remain asleep. Their lives remain just a groping in darkness. They never know what light is, they never reach the dawn. And naturally in darkness they stumble much and hurt themselves and others too, and their whole life consists only of conflict, friction, violence, war. They never come to know what love is, because love is possible only when you are full of light.

Metaphysics is a kind of sweet wisdom. Logic is bitter, quarrelsome; philosophers continuously quarrel. The one who has known himself is sweet; his very presence is like honey.

313.
A KNACK

*Real meditation consists of a knack, not an art—the knack of falling into
spontaneous silence. If you watch, in twenty-four hours, every day, you will
find a few moments in which you are falling automatically into silence.
These moments come on their own; it is just that we have not watched.*

The first thing to be aware of is when these silent moments come.
And when they come, simply stop all that you are doing. Sit silently,
and flow with the moment. And they do come—they are natural.
A few windows always open on their own, but we are so occupied
that we never notice that the window has opened and the breeze is
coming in and the sun has penetrated; we are so occupied with our
work.

So watch... early in the morning when you are fresh after a long,
deep sleep, and the world is just awakening and the birds have
started singing and the sun is rising. If you feel a moment surrounding you, a space growing in you, just fall into it. Sit silently
under a tree, by the side of the river, or in your room, and just
be... nothing to be done. Just cherish that space—and don't try to
prolong it.

Once you have known the knack of it, it will come more and
more. Then you start falling into a kind of harmony with it. A love
affair starts between you and that space called silence, serenity,
tranquility, stillness. And the bond becomes deeper and deeper.
Finally, ultimately, it is always there. You can always close your eyes
for a moment and look at it; it is there. You can almost touch it—
it becomes tangible. But it is a knack, not an art. You cannot learn
it: You have to imbibe it.

314.
UNSTRUCK MUSIC

In Sanskrit the word nada means "music," but in Spanish it means
"nothing." That too is a beautiful meaning, because the music I am
talking about is the music of nothingness, it is the music of silence.
The mystics have called it unstruck music.

There is a music that is uncreated, that is just there as an undercurrent in our being; it is the music of inner harmony. There is also a music in the outer sphere—the harmony of the stars, the planets; the whole of existence is like an orchestra. Except for human beings, nothing is out of tune; everything is in tremendous harmony. That's why trees have so much grace, and the animals and the birds. Only humanity has become ugly, and the reason is that we have tried to improve on ourselves; we have tried to become something.

The moment the desire to *become* arises, one becomes ugly, one falls out of tune, because existence knows only *being;* becoming is a fever in the mind. Human beings are never contented. That discontent creates ugliness, because people are full of complaints, only complaints and nothing else. People want this, they want that, and they are never fulfilled; even if they get, they want more. The "more" persists—the mind goes on asking for more and more. Becoming is the disease of man.

The moment one drops becoming, suddenly a music is heard. And when that music starts overpouring, starts flowing all over you and then beyond you to other people, it becomes a sharing. That is the grace of the Buddhas. They are full of inner music, harmony, and the harmony goes on overflowing; it reaches other people also.

315.
FEARLESSNESS

To grow to your destiny requires great courage and fearlessness. Fearlessness is the most religious quality.

People who are full of fear cannot move beyond the known. The known gives a kind of comfort, security, and safety because it is known. One is perfectly aware. One knows how to deal with the situation. One can remain almost asleep and go on dealing with it—there is no need to be awake; that's the convenience of the known.

The moment you cross the boundary of the known fear arises, because now you will be ignorant, now you will not know what to do, what not to do. Now you will not be so sure of yourself, now mistakes can be made; you can go astray. That is the fear that keeps people tethered to the known, and once a person is tethered to the known, he or she is dead.

Life can only be lived dangerously—there is no other way to live it. It is only through danger that life attains maturity, growth. One needs to be an adventurer, always ready to risk the known for the unknown. That's what being a seeker is all about. But once one has tasted the joys of freedom and fearlessness, one never repents because then one knows what it means to live at the optimum. Then one knows what it means to burn your life's torch from both ends together. And even a single moment of that intensity is more gratifying than a whole eternity of mediocre living.

316.
SEEKING

Lao Tzu has said, "Seek and you will miss. Do not seek and you will find."
Now, this is one of the most significant statements ever made. In the very
seeking you have missed.

If you seek, you have taken a wrong standpoint. In the very seeking you have accepted one thing—that you don't have that which you seek. That is where the fault lies. You have it; you already have it. The moment you start searching for something, you will become neurotic, because you cannot find it—there is nowhere to look, because it is already there.

It is like a man who is searching for his glasses. His glasses are already on his eyes, on his nose, and he is looking through those glasses and searching! Now he will never find them, unless he remembers that all search is futile, unless he remembers, "If I can see, then my glasses must be already there in front of my eyes, otherwise how could I see?"

In our very seeing, the truth is hidden. In our very search, the treasure is hidden. The seeker is the sought—that is the problem, the only problem that human beings have been trying to solve and about which they have been growing more and more puzzled.

The sanest attitude is that of Lao Tzu. He says, "Stop searching and be." Just be, and you will be surprised: You will find it!

317.
FUNDAMENTAL
ALONENESS

We cannot run away from ourselves. There is no way—you are you.
And the aloneness is so fundamental that there is no way to escape it.

The more you try to escape from aloneness, the lonelier you will feel. If you start accepting aloneness, if you start being in love with it, if you start enjoying it, then all loneliness will disappear. And then aloneness has beauty, tremendous beauty.

We are made alone. That aloneness is our freedom. And it is not against love. In fact, only a person who is alone and knows how to be alone will be able to love. This is the paradox of love: That only the person who is alone can love, and only the person who loves becomes alone. They come together. So if you are not capable of being alone, you will not be capable of being in love either. Then all your so-called love will be just an escape from yourself. It will not be real love, it will not be real relating. Who will relate with whom? You have not even related with yourself; how can you relate with the other? You are not there—who is going to relate with others? So a false kind of love exists in the world: You are trying to escape from yourself, the other is trying to escape from herself or himself, and you are both seeking shelter in each other. It is a mutual deception.

The first thing is to know one's celibacy, one's fundamental celibacy—to know that our aloneness is our very individuality. Function from that aloneness. Even your love has to function from that base. Then you will be able to love.

318.
CHILDREN'S LIBERATION

Children's liberation is needed. It is the greatest need in the world,
because no other slavery is so deep and so dangerous and so destructive.
children are not allowed to know themselves.

Society creates false selves, says that children are this or that, that
they should behave this way or that. The society gives ideals, ideas,
and very soon the child becomes accustomed to the fact that he is
a Christian, that he is a man and he has to behave in a manly way,
that he should not cry because that is sissy. The girl starts behaving
in a feminine way—she learns that she should not climb trees, that
that is boyish. Slowly, there are more and more boundaries, and
they go on becoming narrower; then everyone feels suffocated.
That is the situation: Everybody is suffocated, and deep down
everybody hankers to be free. But how?

It seems that the walls that surround one are really very powerful and strong. And people live in this kind of imprisonment their
whole lives. They live in prison and they die in prison, never having known what life was, what life was meant to be, never knowing the glory and the grandeur of existence.

This is the conditioned state of mind. The whole process of meditation is to uncondition it, to withdraw those walls. What the parents and the society and the priests and the politicians have done has
to be undone by meditation.

319.
ABSURDITY

Society has been suppressing three things: sex, death, and the absurd.
And the absurd is the most suppressed.

There are Freuds against the suppression of sex, and they have created a little atmosphere so that people can be freed of that. More than sex, death is the taboo. Death still needs a Freud to fight against its suppression so that people can allow their feelings about death, so that they can think about and meditate on it, and he fact that death exists so it is no longer a taboo. But even deeper than the taboo against death is that against the absurd. My whole fight is against this taboo.

I would like you to be absurd, because that's how existence is. It is meaninglessly meaningful, illogically logical. All the contradictions, all the paradoxes, are in an inner coherence. Are you yourself not absurd? How can you prove that you are needed here in any way? Does existence need you? Existence would do fine without you, perfectly fine. You were not, existence was; you will not be, and existence will, so what is the point of your being here?

If you allow laughter and you feel that it is absurd, just hidden behind it is the real absurdity—not the laughter, but the one who is laughing. Allow it, and soon you will see that it releases you to the infinite sky. Even the confinement of logic is dropped. Then you simply live; you don't ask for meaning. Then each moment is intrinsically meaningful—or meaningless; they are the same.

320.
DELIGHT

Fun is not the right word. Delight goes a little deeper.
Rejoice in life; celebrate it.

You go to a circus—that is fun, silly, in a way. It never touches your depths, never touches your heart; it is clownish. People seek fun just to pass time; it is superficial.

So delight more, rejoice more, celebrate it. Move gracefully through it. Fun is a little profane, and delight is sacred—so move on holy ground. If you laugh, your laughter should come out of your rejoicing, not out of a ridiculing mind that says that these people are ridiculous andwhat foolish things they are doing. If there is even a slight notion lingering in your unconscious that the whole thing is ridiculous, then you will feel a little sad, a little empty.

But if you have delighted in it, then you will feel very very silent, not sad; very very silent, but not empty. That silence will have a quality of fullness in it.

321.
GUILT

Guilt is part of the egoistic mind; it is not spiritual. Religions have been exploiting it, but it has nothing to do with spirituality. Guilt simply tells you that you could have done otherwise. It is an ego feeling; as if you were not helpless, as if everything were in your hands.

Nothing is in your hands. You yourself are not in your hands. Things are happening; nothing is being done. Once you understand this, guilt disappears. Sometimes you can cry and weep for something, but deep down you know it had to happen, because you are helpless, a part of such a great totality—and you are such a tiny part. It is like when there is a leaf on a tree and a strong wind comes and the leaf is separated from the tree. Now the leaf thinks a thousand and one things—that it could have been that way and not this way; that this separation could have been avoided. What could the leaf do? The wind was too strong.

Guilt goes on giving you the wrong notion that you are powerful, that you are capable of doing everything. Guilt is the shadow of the ego: You could not change the situation, and now you are feeling guilty about it. If you look deep into it, you will see that you were helpless, and the whole experience will help you become less egoistic.

If you go on watching the shape things take, the forms that arise, and the happenings that happen, by and by you drop your ego. Love happens—separation too. We cannot do anything about it. This is what I call a spiritual attitude: when you understand that nothing can be done; when you understand that you are just a tiny part of such a tremendous vastness.

322.
MASTERY

To conquer the world is not real bravery; to conquer oneself is.

To be a fighter in the world, to be a warrior, is nothing extraordinary. Everybody is a warrior, more or less, because the whole world is fighting. It is a continuous war, sometimes hot, sometimes cold.

Every individual is fighting, because everyone is brought up in ambition, everybody is poisoned with it. And wherever there is ambition, there is fight, there is competition. Everyone is too ambitious, because all societies that have existed up to now have lived on ambition. All the educational systems do nothing but condition children to be ambitious and to be successful.

The real bravery, the real fight, is not outside. The real fight is inside, it is an inner conquest. Although Alexander may have been a great warrior, but as far as his own instincts were concerned, he was a slave. Napoleon may have been a great soldier, but as far as his own anger, lust, and possessiveness were concerned, he was just as ordinary as anybody else.

The really brave ones are Jesus, Buddha, Patanjali—these types of people. They have overcome themselves. Now no desire can pull them here and there, now no unconscious instinct can have any power over them. They are masters of their own lives.

323.
BONDAGE

You will have to take 100 percent responsibility. And whenever you accept 100 percent responsibility, you become free, and then there is no bondage in this world.

In fact, anger is a kind of bondage. I cannot be angry, because I am not in a bondage. I have not been angry with anybody for years, because I don't make anybody else responsible. I am free, so why should I be angry? If I want to be sad, it is my freedom. If I want to be happy, it is my freedom. Freedom cannot be afraid, freedom cannot be angry. Once you know that you are your world, you have penetrated into a different kind of understanding. Then nothing else matters—all else is games and excuses.

324.
SABOTAGE

Take twenty-four hours and write down everything that you can
remember of how you have been sabotaging—everything in detail.
Look at them from every angle, and then don't repeat them.
It will become a meditation.

If you decide beforehand that you cannot do something, you will
not be able to. Your decision will affect your life. If will become an
autosuggestion. It will become a seed. It will sabotage your whole
life. Even you cannot decide what you can and cannot do—you
have to do it, you have to see for yourself. Only life decides. So it
is simply foolish, childish, to decide beforehand—but many childish things continue. The tape keeps playing itself, and if you play it
too much, it becomes habitual.

It is a trick of the mind to avoid. Once you decide that you cannot make it, then why bother? Why struggle? Why so much
conflict, effort? You know already that you cannot make it. It is the
mind that is finding a rationalization so that you can avoid struggle.
And of course, if you avoid effort, you will not make it, so you fall
back on your decision. You say it was right, it was always right; you
knew it beforehand. These are self-perpetuating things in the mind.
They fulfill themselves, and the circle goes on moving, the wheel
goes on moving.

325.
DEPTH

A single moment can become eternity, because it is not a question of length but of depth. This has to be understood: Time is length, meditation is depth.

Time is length: one moment following another moment following another moment. It is a row, a line, a linear process—but one moves horizontally on the same plane. Tick…tick…moments pass…but the plane remains the same.

In moments of depth suddenly you slip down, or if you allow me to use other words, you slip up. Both are the same, but you are no longer horizontal—you become vertical. You make a turn, and suddenly you are slipping out of the linear process. One becomes afraid, because mind exists only on the horizontal plane. The mind becomes scared. Where are you going?

It looks like death. It looks like madness. Only two interpretations are possible for the mind: Either you are going mad, or you are dying. Both scenarios are scary, and in a way, both are true. You are dying to the mind—so your interpretation is right—and you are dying to the ego. And in a certain way you are going mad, because you are moving beyond the mind, which monopolizes all sanity, which thinks that only that which is within the mind is sane, and that which is beyond it is insane. You are crossing the boundary, you are crossing the danger line, and who knows?—once you have crossed the line you may not come back.

But when you slip beyond the horizontal line, there is eternity; time disappears. One moment can be equal to eternity, as if time stops. The whole movement of existence stops because motivation stops.

326.
NO

No is like a rock on the fountain; the spring is being crushed by it,
and that spring is you. With no you remain crippled and paralyzed.

Go on hammering on the rock of no, and one day the rock will give way, and when it does, then the yes, the authentic yes, will arise. So I am not saying to pretend yes, or to say yes when it is not coming to you. If it is not coming to you, there is nothing to worry about. Go on hammering on the rock.

Don't accept the no, because one cannot live in a no. You cannot eat no food, you cannot drink no water. Nobody can live in no—you can only suffer and create more and more miseries. No is hell. Only yes brings heaven close, and when there arises a real yes out of your total being, nothing remains behind. In that yes you become one, and your whole energy moves upward and says yes, yes, yes!

That is the meaning of the word *amen*. Each prayer is to be closed with "amen"—it means yes, yes, yes. But it should come out of your very guts. It should not be a mind affair, it should not be just in the thoughts. I am not telling you to say it; I am saying to make way for it to come.

327.
LUNATIC

Everybody is a lunatic. Once you realize that you are a lunatic,
sanity has started; it is already on the wing.

The moment you understand that you're a lunatic, you go beyond
it; the first step toward sanity has been taken. People never realize
that they are mad, and because they don't, they remain mad. Not
only do they not realize it, but if you say it to them they will defend
themselves. They will argue and try to tell you it is you who is mad,
not they. Once you realize that you are a lunatic, sanity has started;
it is already on the wing. By the very realization that you are insane,
you have dropped your madness.

328.
YOUR DECISION

All the love in the world can be given to you, but if you decide
to be miserable, you will remain miserable. And one can be happy,
tremendously happy, for no reason at all—because happiness and
misery are your decisions.

It takes much time to realize that happiness and misery are up to
you, because it is very comfortable for the ego to think that others
are making you miserable. The ego goes on making impossible
conditions, and it says that first these conditions have to be
fulfilled and only then can you be happy. It asks how can you be
happy in such an ugly world, with such ugly people, in such an
ugly situation?

If you see yourself rightly you will laugh about yourself. It is
ridiculous, simply ridiculous. What we are doing is absurd. Nobody
is forcing us to do it, but we go on doing it—and crying for help.
And you can simply come out of it; it is your own game—to
become miserable, and then to ask for sympathy and love.

If you are happy, love will be flowing toward you…there is no
need to ask for it. It is one of the basic laws. Just as water flows
downward, and fire flows upward, love flows toward happiness…
happinesswards.

329.
HELPING

Just be as happy as you can. Don't think about others. If you are happy, your happiness will help others. You cannot help, but your happiness can.

You cannot help—you will destroy—but your happiness can help. Happiness has its own ways of working—very indirect, very subtle, feminine. When you start working your energy becomes aggressive, and if you start trying to help others they will resist. They will resist unknowingly, because it seems as if somebody has the upper hand, and nobody wants to be liberated by anybody else. Nobody wants to be made happy by anybody else, because that seems to be a dependence, so a deep resistance comes in.

Simply don't be worried about it. That is the other person's business. You have done nothing to cause anybody else's problems. They have earned them through many lives, so they have to drop them. Just be happy, and your happiness will give others courage. Your happiness will give them impetus and a stimulation, a challenge. Your happiness will give them some idea of what it will be like when they say yes. That's all....

330.
CLINGING

Mind always clings—and it is good to drop this clinging. Each day is new, each moment is new. And after each moment we move in a different world, and one should be prepared so that nothing has a hold on one.

Buddha used to tell his disciples to never stay in a house for more than three days, because by the fourth day one starts feeling at home. Before one feels at home, one should move on.

Mind always clings—and it is good to drop this clinging. Each day is new, each moment is new, and after each moment we move in a different world, and one should be prepared so that nothing has a hold on one. The past should simply disappear; you should die continually to the past. So don't waste time. Die to what is gone; it is no more.

Otherwise, as you are clinging to that which is no more, even when a new thing arrives you will be clinging to the old. This is how the mind goes on missing. Always remain true to the present. Remain committed to this moment—there is no other commitment.

One commitment is enough: commitment to this moment, to here-now.

331.
PRAYER

Prayer should be unlearned; it should be spontaneous.

Many people pray in the churches, in the temples, and nothing happens; nothing is going to happen. They can go on praying for lives together and nothing will happen, because their prayer is not spontaneous. They are managing it; it is through the mind. They are too wise, and for a prayer to function you have to be a fool.

Prayer is foolish—you may even feel awkward that you are talking to God. It is foolish, but it works. There are times when foolishness is wisdom, and wisdom is foolishness. So whenever you feel a moment when prayer is needed, use it. The more you use it, the more it will become available. And out of meditation your prayer will deepen.

You pray inside, and if something happens in the body, allow it, whatever it is. If any movement comes to the body, any energy starts waving in the body or if you become like a small leaf in a strong wind, just pray and allow it.

332.
THE ANSWER

There is no answer. There are only two ways for the mind to be: full of questions and empty of questions.

Maturity is coming to a point where you can live without answers; that is what maturity is. And to live without answers is the greatest and most courageous act. Then you are no longer a child. A child goes on asking questions, wanting answers for everything. A child believes that if he can formulate a question, then there must be an answer, there must be somebody to supply the answer.

I call this immaturity. You think that because you can formulate a question, there is bound to be an answer; maybe you don't know it, but somebody must know the answer, and some day, you will be able to discover it. That's not so. All questions are man-created, manufactured by man.

Existence has no answer. Existence is there, with no answers, completely silent. If you can drop all questions, a communication happens between you and existence. The moment you drop questions, you drop philosophy, you drop theology, you drop logic, and you start living. You become existential. When there are no questions, that state itself is the answer.

333.
SHAME

Whatever you are ashamed of, you hide inside, in the unconscious. It moves deeper into your being, circulates in your blood, goes on manipulating you from backstage.

If you want to repress, repress something beautiful. Never repress something you are ashamed of, because whatever you repress goes deep and whatever you express will evaporate into the sky. So whatsoever you are ashamed of, express it so you are finished with it. Whatever is beautiful keep as a treasure inside, so it goes on influencing your life.

But we do just the opposite. Whatever is beautiful we go on expressing—in fact too much—we express more than is there. You go on saying, "I love, I love, I love," and you may not even mean it that much. You go on suppressing anger, hatred, jealousy, possessiveness, and by and by you find that you have become all that you have suppressed, and then deep guilt arises.

There is nothing to be ashamed of; everything is perfect as it is. There cannot be any more perfect a world than this. Right now, this moment, is the climax of the whole existence, the very matrix around which everything revolves. Nothing can be more perfect, so simply relax and enjoy.

Open your doors to the sun and the air and the sky. Then new fresh air is always passing you, new sun rays are always passing you. Allow the traffic of existence to pass through you. Never be a closed road, otherwise only death and dirt gathers. Just drop all notions of shame, and never judge anything.

334·
TOTALITY

Whatever is of the total becomes beautiful. The partial is ugly,
and the total is beautiful. So whatever is you, be total in it,
and your being total will transform the very quality of it.

This is the alchemy of transformation, of inner transformation. Accept and move with the moment. If you really move, there will be no hangover. If you really go into anger you finish with it, because when you go into it totally it is finished. And then you are out of it, completely out of it, uncorrupted by it.

Watch a small child who is not yet corrupted by the society. When he is angry, he is really angry; he explodes. A tiny child, but he becomes so powerful—as if he will destroy the whole world. He becomes red hot, as if he is on fire. Just watch the child, how beautiful he is—so alive. And the next moment he is playing and laughing—the anger is no more there. You cannot even believe that he was angry just a moment before. Now he is so loving, so flowerlike—and just a moment before he was a flame!

This is the way to live. You are, so totally, that there is never any hangover left from any moment. You are always fresh and young, and the past is not like a load on you. This is what I call a spiritual life. A spiritual life is not a life of discipline. It is a life of spontaneity.

335.
DESIRE

Become such an intense desire that the very fire of the desire burns you completely and nothing is left.

Desire can have two forms: you can desire something but you remain away from the desire. You can drop the desire or you can fulfill it, but you are separate. If it is not fulfilled you will feel frustrated, but when you are separate, the desire is just accidental to you.

Abheepsa means when the desire has become your very soul. You cannot drop it, because if you do, you are dropped in it. When it becomes so existential that there is no separation between you and the desire, then desire has tremendous beauty. Then it takes a new dimension, moves into the timeless.

336.
INNER ANGER

*One part of anger is understandable because it is related to people,
to situations. But when this superficial layer of anger is thrown away,
then suddenly you come on a source of anger that is not related to the
outside at all, which is simply part of you.*

We have been taught that anger comes only in certain tense situations. That's not true. We are born with anger, it is part of us. In certain situations it comes up, in certain other situations it is inactive, but it is there.

So one first has to throw out the anger that is related, and then one comes on the deeper source of anger that is unrelated to anybody else—that one is born with. It is unaddressed, and that's the trouble in understanding it. But there is no need to understand it. Just throw it—not on anybody, but on a pillow, on the sky, on God, on me.

This is going to happen with every emotion. There is a part of love that is related to someone. Then if you go deeper, one day you will come to the source of love that is unaddressed. It is not moving toward anybody, it is simply there, there inside. And the same is true of everything you feel. Everything has two sides.

One side, the unconscious, the deeper side, is simply with you, and the superficial is the functioning of this deeper layer in relationship. People who remain superficial always completely forget their inner treasures. When you throw out the inner anger, you come face-to-face with inner love, inner compassion. The rubbish has to be thrown out so that you can come to the purest gold within you.

337.
PARENTHOOD

A few parents are needed to change the whole world. But it is difficult—
you follow the pattern that your parents have forced on you.
This is the problem that we can't see at all: You cannot tolerate your
parents, but you are following the same pattern as they did.

The world will be totally different if parents can become a little more understanding. They are not, and nobody can tell them anything because they are so loving—that's the trouble. Behind love, so much that is not love goes on hiding. Love becomes a shelter for many things that are not love at all.

Your parents might have been very loving and must have done whatever they could. They must have been thinking that they were creating a happy life for you. But nobody can make anybody happy, nobody.

So allow your children to grow in freedom. Of course it is risky, but what can be done? Life is a risk, but every growth is possible in danger and risk. Don't protect them too much or they will become hothouse plants—almost useless. Let them be wild. Let them struggle in life, let them grow on their own, and they will always be grateful to you. And you will always be happy, because later on you will see an aliveness in them.

338.
SOLITUDE

All that is beautiful has always happened in aloneness; nothing has happened in a crowd. Nothing of the beyond has happened except when one is in absolute solitude, alone.

The extrovert mind has created conditioning all around that has become very ingrained: that when you are lonely you feel bad. It tells you to move around, meet people, because all happiness is in being with people. That's not true. The happiness that is with people is very superficial, and the happiness that happens when you are alone is tremendously deep. So delight in it.

When aloneness happens, enjoy it. Sing something, dance something, or just sit silently facing the wall and waiting for something to happen. Make it an awaiting, and soon you will come to know a different quality. It is not sadness at all. Once you have tasted from the very depth of aloneness, all relationship is superficial. Even love cannot go so deep as aloneness goes, because even in love the other is present, and the very presence of the other keeps you closer to the circumference, to the periphery.

When there is nobody, not even a thought of anybody and you are really alone, you start sinking, you drown in yourself. Don't be afraid. In the beginning that drowning will look like death, and a sadness will surround you, because you have always known happiness with people, in relationships.

Just wait a little. Let the sinking go deeper, and you will see a silence arising and a stillness that has a dance to it, an unmoving movement inside. Nothing moves, and still everything is tremendously speedy, empty, yet full. Paradoxes meet, and contradictions dissolve.

339.
FACING THE WALL

Just sit facing the wall. The wall is very beautiful. There is nowhere to go.

Bodhidharma sat for nine years just facing the wall, doing nothing—just sitting. The tradition has it that his legs withered away. To me that is symbolic. It simply means that all movements withered away, because all motivation withered away. He was not going anywhere. There was no desire to move, no goal to achieve—and he achieved the greatest that is possible. He is one of the rarest souls that has ever walked on earth. And just sitting before a wall he achieved everything, by not doing anything, using no technique, no method, nothing. This was the only technique.

So whenever you sit, just sit facing the wall. The wall is very beautiful. There is nowhere to go. Don't even put a picture there; just have a plain wall. When there is nothing to see, by and by your interest in seeing disappears. By just facing a plain wall, inside you parallel emptiness and plainness arise. Parallel to the wall another wall arises—of no-thought.

Remain open and delight. Smile; hum a tune or sway. Sometimes you can dance—but go on facing the wall; let it be your object of meditation.

340.
DRUGS

It is better not to use drugs, because sometimes they can give you certain experiences, and that's the problem. Once you have the experiences this way, it is very difficult to reach them naturally—without drugs. And to have an experience is not the basic thing; to grow through it is.

You can have an experience through a drug, but you don't grow. The experience comes to you; you don't go to the experience. It is as if you have seen the Himalayas in a vision—beautiful as far as it goes, but it does not go very far. You remain the same. By and by, if the vision becomes your reality, you are losing something, because you will become addicted to it.

No, it is better to go to the Himalayas. It is hard; it is a long journey. Drugs make it too short. They are almost violent; they force something premature. It is better to go the long way, because only through struggle do you grow. An integration arises in you, and you become crystallized. That's the real thing—experience is irrelevant. The real thing is growth. Always remember that my whole emphasis is on growth, not on experiences. The mind is always asking for more and new experiences; it is infatuated with experiences—and we have to go beyond the mind.

So the real spiritual dimension is not the dimension of experience. In fact, there is nothing to experience. Only you—not even you, just pure consciousness with no limit, with no object to it—just pure subjectivity, just being. Not that you experience beautiful things. You are beautiful, but you don't experience beautiful things. You are tremendously beautiful, but nothing happens. All around is tremendous emptiness.

341.

SPIRITUAL EXPERIENCE

Finally one has to remember that everything has to be dropped so you
remain, in your total purity. Even a spiritual experience corrupts;
it is a disturbance.

Something happens, and a duality arises. When something happens
that you like, the desire to have it more arises. When something
happens that makes you feel beautiful, the fear that you may lose it
arises, so all corruption comes in—greed, fear. With the experience, everything of the mind comes back and again you are
trapped.

My whole effort here is to take you beyond—beyond the experience—because only then are you beyond the mind, and there is
silence. When there is no experience, there is silence. When there
is no bliss, then there is bliss—because bliss is not an experience;
you don't feel that you are blissful. If you feel, it is just happiness.
It will go, will wither away, and you will be left in the dark.

If you understand the point, then no technique is spiritual,
because all techniques will give you experiences. And one day this
should be the goal—that everything has been dropped. You are
alone in your house—with no furniture, with no experiences—
and then you experience the ultimate. But it is not an "experience,"
that is just a way of saying it.

342.
COMMITMENT

Commitment cannot be forced. Make the person happy so he feels
there is no need for any other relationship. But on the contrary,
most people make such trouble that even if the other was not thinking
of another relationship, he will have to think of it—just to escape.

This is one of the deep-rooted problems in any man-woman relationship. Man has more need of freedom than of love, and woman
has more need of love than of freedom. It is a problem all over the
world with every couple. The woman is not worried about freedom
at all. She is ready to become a slave if only she can make the other
a slave also. She is ready to move into any commitment if the other
is also forced into a commitment. She is ready to live in a prison if
the other is ready to live in a dark cell.

And the man is ready even to sacrifice love if it becomes too
risky to his freedom. He would like to live in the open sky, even
alone. He would like to be in a loving relationship, but it becomes
dark and an imprisonment. So this is the trouble.

One has to become aware that this asking for too much commitment or for too much freedom are both immaturities. Somewhere one has to come to terms with the other person. Once you
understand that the man needs more freedom, you put down your
demands for commitment. Once the man understands that the
woman needs commitment, he puts down his demand for freedom, that's all. If you love, you are ready to sacrifice a little. If you
don't love, it is better to separate.

343.
RESISTANCE

Resistance is one of the most basic problems, and out of that all other problems are created. Once you resist something, you are in trouble.

Jesus has said, "Resist not evil." Even evil should not be resisted, because resistance is the only evil, the only sin. When you resist something it means you are separating yourself from the whole. You are trying to become an island, separate, divided. You are condemning, judging, saying this is not right, that should not be so. Resistance means you have taken a posture of judgment.

If you don't resist, then there is no separation between you and the energy that is moving around. Suddenly you are with it—so much so that you are not; only the energy is moving. So learn to cooperate with things that are going on; don't put yourself against the whole. By and by you start feeling a tremendous new energy that comes by walking in step with the whole, because in resistance you dissipate energy. In nonresistance you absorb energy.

That is the whole Eastern attitude about life: Accept and don't resist, surrender and don't fight. Don't try to be victorious, and don't try to be the first. Lao Tzu has said, "Nobody can defeat me, because I have accepted defeat and I am not hankering for any victory." How can you defeat anyone who is not hankering for any victory? How can you defeat an unambitious person? How can you kill a person who is ready to die? It is impossible. Through this surrender, one comes to be victorious.

Let this be an insight: Don't waste time in resisting.

344.
PATIENCE

*Love is patient, and everything else is impatient. Passion is impatient,
love is patient. And once you understand that to be patient is to be
loving, and to be patient is to be in prayer, then everything is understood.
One has to learn how to wait.*

There are some things that cannot be done; they only happen.
There are things that can be done, but those things belong to the
world. Things that cannot be done belong to God or belong to the
other world, or however you name it. But things that cannot be
done—only these are the real things. They always happen to you;
you become the receiving end—and that is the meaning of surrender.

Become a receiving end... be patient and just wait. Wait with
deep love, prayerfulness, gratitude—gratitude for that which has
already happened, and patience for that which is going to happen.
Ordinarily the human mind does just the opposite. It is always
grumbling for that which has not happened, and it is always too
impatient for it to happen. It is always complaining, never grateful.
It is always desiring, and never creating the capacity to receive. A
desire is futile if you don't have the capacity to receive.

345.
HOMELESS

Bliss is always homeless, it is a vagabond. Happiness has a home,
unhappiness also has a home, but bliss has none. It is like a white cloud,
with no roots anywhere.

The moment you get roots, bliss disappears and you start clinging
to the earth. Home means security, safety, comfort, convenience.
And finally, if all these things are reduced to one thing, home means
death. The more alive you are, the more you are homeless.

That is the basic meaning of being a seeker: It means to live life
in danger, to live life in insecurity, to live life not knowing what is
coming next. It means always remaining available and always being
able to be surprised. If you can be surprised, you are alive. *Wonder*
and *wander* come from the same root. A fixed mind becomes incapable of wondering, because it has become incapable of wandering.
So be a wanderer, like a cloud, and each moment brings infinite
surprises. Remain homeless. Homelessness doesn't mean not to
live in a home. It simply means never become attached to anything.
Even if you live in a palace, never become attached. If a moment
comes to move, you move—without looking back. Nothing holds
you. You use everything, you enjoy everything, but you remain the
master.

346.
HUMBLENESS

Love is essentially humbleness—there is no other kind of humbleness.
If humbleness is cultivated without love, it is just another trick of the ego.

When humbleness comes naturally out of love, then it is tremendously beautiful. So fall in love with existence—and the beginning is to fall in love with yourself.

Once you are in love with yourself you start feeling in love with many people, and by and by that space becomes bigger and bigger. One day you suddenly find that the whole of existence is included in it, that love is now no longer addressed to anybody in particular, that it is simply there for anybody to take—it is simply flowing. Even if nobody is there to take it, it is flowing.

Then love is not a relationship, it is a state of being. And in that state of being lies humbleness, true humbleness. Jesus is humble in that way; the pope is not humble. Somebody can cultivate poverty and become very egoistic about it, somebody can cultivate humbleness and become egoistic about it. To me, real humbleness arises as a fragrance of love. It cannot be cultivated, you cannot practice it, there is no way to learn it. You have to go into love and one day suddenly you find that love has flowered—spring has come and love has bloomed and there is a certain fragrance that was never there before: You are humble.

347.
COOPERATION

When Charles Darwin wrote his thesis about evolution and the survival of the fittest, another man, Prince Kropotkin of Russia, was writing a quite diametrically opposite thesis: that evolution happens through cooperation.

People have not heard much about Prince Kropotkin, and his thesis is far superior to Darwin's. It will take time, but he will win over Darwin.

The very idea that one evolves through conflict is violent; it is a very lopsided idea. If you look through the eyes of Darwin, life is just a survival of the fittest. And who is the fittest? The most destructive, the most aggressive is the fittest. So the fittest has no value; it is not even human—the fittest is the one who is the most animal-like. Christ cannot survive, he is not the fittest. Buddha cannot survive, he is not the fittest. Buddha will be the most helpless man—and Jesus. Then Alexander survives, Hitler survives, Stalin survives, Mao survives; these are the fittest. Then only violence survives, not love. Only murder survives, not meditation.

The Darwinian vision is a very inhuman meditation about life. If you go into the forest and look through Darwinian eyes, you will see conflict everywhere: species destroying other species, everybody in conflict. It is a nightmare. And if you go to the same forest and look through the eyes of Kropotkin, there is tremendous cooperation. These species have been living in deep cooperation, otherwise nobody would have survived.

Violence may be part, but is not the whole; deep down is cooperation. And the higher you grow, the less and less violence the more and more cooperation there is. That is the ladder of growth.

348.
ONE'S OWN TEMPLE

A public temple is a public temple; one needs one's own temple,
it is a private phenomenon.

In the East we used to have a separate room for meditation. Each
family who could afford it would have a small temple of their own.
And people would go there only to pray or meditate, not for anything else.

Everything about the place—the incense burning, the colors,
the sounds, the air—becomes associated with the idea of meditation. If you have been meditating in the same room, the same place,
every day at the same time, then the moment you enter the room
and you take your shoes off, you are already in meditation.

The moment you enter the room and you at the walls—the
same walls, the same color, the same incense burning, the same
fragrance, the same silence, the same time—your body, your vitality, your mind, start falling into a unity. They all know that this is
the time to meditate. And they help; they don't fight with you.
One can simply sit there and go into it easily—more easily, more
silently, more effortlessly.

So if you can manage, have a small place—just a corner will
do—and don't do anything else there. Otherwise the space
becomes confused, mm? This is difficult to explain, but the space
also becomes confused. Make a small corner, meditate there, and
every day try to do it regularly at the same time. If sometimes you
miss, there's nothing to feel guilty about—it's okay. But even if out
of 100 days you can make it regularly for sixty days, that will be
enough.

349.
CONCENTRATION

Concentration follows interest; it is a shadow of interest.

If you feel that concentration is missing, nothing can be done directly about concentration; something will have to be done about interest. For example, a child sitting in the school suddenly starts listening to birds chirping outside the window and completely concentrates on listening to that. The teacher shouts, "Concentrate!" and the child cannot concentrate on the blackboard, his mind returns again and again to the birds. They are so joyful and he is really interested in them, so his concentration is there.

The teacher says, "Concentrate!" He *is* concentrating—in fact the teacher is distracting him from his concentration. But the teacher wants his concentration for something for which he has no interest; that's why he finds it difficult to concentrate.

So always remember: If you feel that you go on forgetting things, that simply means that somewhere interest is missing, or you have some other interest. Maybe you want to earn money out of it, your interest is in the money but not in the workthen you will start forgetting things. So just watch your interest.

And whatever you are doing, if you are doing it with deep interest, there is no need to worry about remembrance—it simply comes. So just start taking more interest. Remain in the moment, take more interest in whatever you are doing. And after two or three months you will see that the memory simply follows.

350.
LIVING AT THE MINIMUM

Human beings are not aware of their potential, and they go on living at the minimum. Now psychologists say that even very great geniuses use only fifteen percent of their intelligence—so what about the ordinary, the average person?

The average person uses about five to seven percent of his or her intelligence. But that is intelligence; nobody has bothered about love. When I look at people, I see that rarely do they use their love energy. And that is the real source of joy.

We use seven, or at the most fifteen, percent of our intelligence. So even our greatest genius lives at the minimum; eighty-five percent of intelligence will be a sheer waste; he will never use it. And one never knows what would have become possible if he had used 100 percent.

And we are not using even five percent of our love. We go on pretending at the game of love, but we do not use our love energy. Intelligence brings you closer to the outside reality, and love brings you closer to the inner reality. There is no other way; love is the only way of knowing the inner.

351.
FREEDOM AND LOVE

When two people are in love they are free, individuals.
They have freedom; love is not a duty. It is out of their freedom
that they give to each other, and they are free to say no.

If people in love say yes to each other, that is their decision—it is not an obligation, it is not a fulfillment of any expectation. Because you enjoy giving love, you give. And any moment you can change, because no promise has been made, no commitment has been made. You remain two free individuals—meeting out of freedom, loving out of freedom, but your individuality and your freedom are intact. Hence the beauty of love!

The beauty is not only of love; it is more of freedom than of love. The basic ingredient of beauty is freedom; love is a secondary ingredient. Love is also beautiful with freedom, because freedom is beautiful. Once the freedom is gone, love becomes ugly. Then you will be surprised at what has happened. Where has all that beauty gone?

352.
NAMELESS

Tao is the name for that which cannot be named, a name
for the nameless—just like God or dharma or truth or logos.
These are just names for human helplessness.

We have to call it something; we have to address it. Tao is one of the
most beautiful names given to the unknown, because it is utterly
meaningless. The word *God* has become very meaningful; hence it
has lost significance.

You can worship God, you cannot worship Tao; there is no
image. You may not worship a stone image, but the moment you say
"God," a subtle image arises in you: somebody sitting there on a
golden throne, controlling the whole world, a very wise man with
a white beard and all that, a father figure. But with "Tao" no figure
arises. That is the beauty of the name, that it simply gives you no
clue. It gives you no excuse to go into imagination.

Tao is the greatest name given to the unknown. It is significant
because it is meaningless; it means nothing. All that it means is the
way—not a way to any goal but just the way things are.

353.
DON'T DISSECT
THE FLOWERS

When something unfolds inside you, don't jump on it intellectually.
Otherwise you will kill the flower. You will take the petals apart to see
what is inside, but in that very dissection the flower is gone.

The irony is that if you want to know what a flower is and you take
its petals off, you will never know what the flower is. Whatever
you come to know about it this way will be about something else—
maybe about the chemical constituents of the flower, the physical
constituents of the flower, the color, and this and that, but it will
have no reference to beauty. That beauty disappeared the moment
you you dissected and destroyed it.

Now what you have is just a memory of the flower, it is not the
real flower. And whatever you know about it, you know about a
dead flower, not about an alive one. And that aliveness was the very
stuff, the real thing; that alive flower was growing, unfolding,
releasing fragrance. And so is the case with the inner unfolding.

Meditation will bring many new spaces that are very good. But
if you start thinking about it—what it is, why it happened, what
it meant in the first place—you bring in the mind. And the mind
is poison. Then rather than watering the flower, you have poisoned it. Meditation is just the diametrically opposite dimension
to the mind. So don't bring the mind in. Enjoy! They have been
good experiences. More and more experiences of far more
significance will be coming—this is just a beginning. Remain open
and available

354.
DO-IT-YOURSELF

In itself life is neutral. We make it beautiful, we make it ugly; life is what energy we bring to it.

If you pour beauty into life, it is beautiful. If you simply sit there and you want it to be beautiful, then it will not be—you have to create beauty. Beauty is not there like an object, like a rock. Beauty has to be created. You have to give a vision to reality, you have to give color to reality, you have to give a song to reality—then it is beautiful.

So whenever you participate in creating beauty, it is there; whenever you stop creating, it is not. Beauty is a creation; so is ugliness. Happiness is a creation; so is misery. You get only that which you create, and you never get anything else. That is the whole philosophy of karma: You get only that which you do. Life is just a blank canvas—you can paint a beautiful scene, a landscape, or you can paint black ghosts and dangerous people. It's up to you. You can make a beautiful dream or a nightmare.

Once this is understood, things are very simple. You are the master; it is your responsibility. Ordinarily we think that life has some objective beauty and objective ugliness. No! Life is just an opportunity. It gives you all that is needed: Now do it yourself! It is a do-it-yourself affair.

355.
THE LAST LUXURY

When there is no need, love flowers.

Love flowers only when needs have disappeared. A love happens only between a king and a queen—neither is in any need.

Love is the most luxurious thing in the world. It is not a need—it is the last luxury, the ultimate in luxuries. If you are needing it, it is just as other needs; one needs food, one needs shelter, one needs clothes, one needs this and that. Then love is also part of this world. When there is no need and you are simply flowing with energy and would like to share with somebody, and somebody is also flowing with energy and would like to share with you, then you both offer your energies to an unknown God of love.

And it is sheer luxury, because it is purposeless. It has no business to do. It is intrinsic—it is not a means to anything else. It is a great play.

356.
WALL OF WORDS

Ninety percent of language is just an avoidance of relationship. We create a great wall of words to hide the fact that we don't want to relate.

If you are feeling sad, then why say it? Be sad! People will know what you mean without language. If you are very, very happy, then why say it? Be happy! And happiness is neither Italian nor English nor German—everybody will understand it. You can dance when you are happy, and they will understand. When you are angry you can simply hit somebody—why say it? That will be more authentic and real. People will understand immediately that you are angry.

Language is a way of saying things that we really don't want to say. For example, I am angry at you and I don't want to be angry, so I simply say, "I am angry." It is a very impotent way of saying that I am angry. I love you and I don't want to really say it, so I simply say, "I love you." Just words! If I love you I will say it in some more real way—why through words?

Try expressing through a gesture, through the face, through the body, through touch, through expression, but not through language. And you will enjoy it, because you will have a new feeling and you can innovate.

357.
MUSIC

This existence is an orchestra, and we have to be in tune with it.
That is why music has so much appeal to the human mind, to the
human heart—because sometimes listening to beautiful music,
you start slipping into that universal harmony.

Listening to Beethoven or to Mozart, to classical Eastern music, one starts moving into a different world; a totally different gestalt arises. You are no longer in your thoughts—your wavelength changes. That great music starts surrounding you, starts playing on your heart, starts creating a rhythm that you have lost.

That's the definition of great music: that it can give you a glimpse of how one can exist, totally, with the whole—even for a few moments. Great peace descends, and there is great joy in the heart. You may not understand what has happened, but the great master, the great musician, is simply playing on a very fundamental base. The fundamental base is that existence has a certain rhythm. If you can create music according to that rhythm, those who participate in listening to that music will also start falling into it.

And you can do it in many ways. For example, if you are sitting by a waterfall just listen to the sound of the waterfall and become one with it. Close your eyes and feel that you have become one with the waterfall—start falling with the water, deep inside. And there will be moments, a few moments, when suddenly you will find that there has been a participation, that you could get the chanting of the waterfall, and you were in tune with it. Great ecstasy will arise out of those moments. Listening to the birds, do the same.

358.
FANTASY

Fantasy can do one thing: It can either create hell or it can create heaven.
Fantasy is very consistent; it cannot create the paradox.

Fantasy is very logical, and reality is very illogical. So whenever reality erupts, it will have both the polarities in it—that is one of the criteria of reality. If it has not both polarities together, then it is a mind construction.

The mind plays safe and always creates a consistent thing. Life itself is very inconsistent and contradictory—it has to be, it exists through contradiction. Life exists through death, so whenever you are really alive you will feel death too. Any moment of great life will also be a great moment of death. Any moment of great happiness will also be a great moment of sadness. This has to be so.

So let this be remembered always: Whenever you have a contradictory experience—two things that don't fit together, that are diametrically opposite to each other—they must be real; you could not have imagined them. Imagination is never so illogical.

359.
CREATIVITY

Creativity is a food, and people who are not creative rarely grow—
because they are starved.

We come close to God only when we create. If God is the creator, then to be creative is the way to participate in God's being. We cannot create this universe, but we can create a small painting—we can create small things. And it does not make any difference whether you create a big thing or a small thing. Creativity knows no difference.

So creativity is not concerned with quantity, it is concerned with quality. And it has nothing to do with what others say about your creations—that is irrelevant. If you enjoyed doing your work, that's enough; you have been already paid for it.

360.
UNDERSTANDING

Lovers can separate, but the understanding that has been gained in the company of the other will always remain as a gift. If you love a person, the only valuable gift that you can give to him or her is some quantity of understanding.

Talk to each other, and understand that sometimes your partner will need to be alone. And this is the problem: This need may not happen at the same time to both of you. Sometimes you want to be with her, and she wants to be alone—nothing can be done about it. Then you have to understand and leave her alone. Sometimes you want to be alone, but he wants to come to you—then tell him that you are helpless!

Just create more and more understanding. That's what lovers miss: They have enough love, but understanding, none, none at all. That's why on the rocks of misunderstanding their love dies. Love cannot live without understanding. Alone, love is very foolish; with understanding, love can live a long life, a great life—of many joys shared, of many beautiful moments shared, of great poetic experiences. But that happens only through understanding.

Love can give you a small honeymoon, but that's all. Only understanding can give you deep intimacy. And each honeymoon is followed by depression, anger, frustration. Unless you grow in understanding, no honeymoon is going to be of any help; it will be just like a drug.

So try to create more understanding. And even some day if you separate, the understanding will be with you, that will be a gift of your love to each other.

361.
THE MYSTERIOUS

Listen to the mysterious; don't deny it. Don't say offhandedly that it
doesn't exist. All the people who have walked on the earth in a conscious
way agree—that the mysterious exists.

The world is not finished at the visible. The invisible is there, and
it is far more significant because it is far deeper. The visible is only
a wave in the invisible. The invisible is the ocean. So when something strange happens, don't deny it and don't close yourself to it.
Open up; let it come in. And there are many, many moments every
day when the mysterious knocks at the door.

Suddenly a bird starts calling: Listen to it, and listen through
the heart. Don't start analyzing it. Don't start talking inside about
it. Become silent, let it penetrate you as deeply as possible. Don't
hinder it by your thoughts. Allow it an absolute passage. Feel it—
don't think it.

You may feel different the whole day because you encountered
a rose in the early morning. You may feel totally different the whole
day if you have seen the sun rising in the morning and were over-
whelmed by it. You will feel like an utterly new person if you have
seen birds on the wing and you have been with them for a moment.
Your life has started changing.

This is the way one becomes a seeker. One has to absorb
the beauty of existence, the sheer joy of it, the overwhelming
blessing of it.

362.

REMAIN ADVENTUROUS

Always remain adventurous. Never forget for a single moment that life
belongs to those who are explorers. It does not belong to the static; it
belongs to the flowing. Never become a reservoir; always remain a river.

The mind cannot cope with the new. It cannot figure out what it is,
it cannot categorize it, it cannot put labels on it; it is puzzled by the
new. The mind loses all its efficiency when it confronts something
new.

With the past, with the old, with the familiar, the mind is very
at ease, because it knows what it is, how to do, what to do, what
not to do. It is perfect in the known; it is moving in well-traveled
territory. Even in darkness it can move; the familiarity helps the
mind to be unafraid. But this is one of the problems to be understood: Because the mind is always unafraid only with the familiar,
it does not allow you growth. Growth is with the new, and the
mind is only unafraid of the old. So the mind clings to the old and
avoids the new. The old seems to be synonymous with life, and the
new seems to be synonymous with death; that is the mind's way of
looking at things. You have to put the mind aside.

Life never remains static. Everything is changing: Today it is
there, tomorrow it may not be. You may come across it again; who
knows when? Maybe it will take months, years, or lives. So when
an opportunity knocks at the door, go with it. Let this be a fundamental law: Always choose the new over the old.

363.
MADHOUSE

Always remember one thing: that as you are, as everybody is,
you are already mad. Humanity is mad; this earth is a madhouse.
So you can only go sane, you cannot go mad.

If you are afraid of becoming sane, that is one thing, but don't be afraid of going mad, because what else can happen? The worst has happened already! We are living in the worst kind of hell. So if you fall you may fall into heaven. You cannot fall anywhere else.

But people are afraid, because whatever they have been living, they think that is the normal thing. Nobody is normal. It is only very rarely that there is a normal man like Jesus or Buddha: All others are abnormal. But the abnormal are in the majority, so they call themselves normal; Jesus looks abnormal. And naturally the majority can decide; they have the votes to decide who is normal and who is not. It is a strange world: Here normal people appear abnormal, and the abnormal are thought to be normal.

Watch people, watch your own mind: It is a monkey, a mad monkey. For thirty minutes just write down whatever comes into your mind, and then show it to someone. Anybody will certify you as mad! Don't be afraid. Go with the feeling that comes to you, go with that call, follow that hint. And if you disappear, disappear! What have you got to lose?

364.
CHALLENGE OF THE WILD

This is just a beginning. You will have to pass through more and more strange lands. Truth is stranger than any fiction. But be courageous.

Before you start entering inside yourself, you don't know how much of yourself was never known to you. You were living with just a fragment of your being. You were living like a drop of water, and your being is like an ocean. You were identified with just the leaf of the tree, and the whole tree belongs to you.

Yes, it is very strange, because one starts expanding. New realities have to be absorbed. Each moment one has to come across facts that one has never come across, so each moment there is an unsettlement, and the chaos becomes continuous. You can never settle. You can never become certain, because who knows what is going to be opened to you in the next moment?

That's why people never go in. They live a settled life. They have cleared a small land of their being and made their house there. They have closed their eyes and have made big fences and walls, so they think, "This is all." And just beyond the wall is their real, wild being waiting for them. That is the challenge, the call of the wild.

365.
BEGINNING

Wherever you are, it is always at the beginning.
That's why life is so beautiful, so young, so fresh.

Once you start thinking that something is complete, you start becoming dead. Perfection is death, so perfectionistic people are suicidal. Wanting to be perfect is a roundabout way of committing suicide. Nothing is ever perfect. It cannot be, because life is eternal. Nothing ever concludes; there is no conclusion in life—just higher and higher peaks. But once you reach one peak, another is challenging you, calling you, inviting you.

So always remember that wherever you are is always a beginning. Then one always remains a child, one remains virgin. And that's the whole art of life—to remain a virgin, to remain fresh and young, uncorrupted by life, uncorrupted by the past, uncorrupted by the dust that ordinarily gathers on the roads on the journey. Remember, each moment opens a new door.

It is very illogical, because we always think that if there is a beginning, then there must be an end. But nothing can be done. Life is illogical. It has a beginning but no end. Nothing that is really alive ever ends. It goes on and on and on.

ABOUT THE AUTHOR

The Osho teachings defy categorization, covering everything from the individual quest for meaning to the most urgent social and political issues facing society today. His books are not written but are transcribed from audio and video recordings of extemporaneous talks given in response to questions from visitors over a period of thirty-five years. Osho has been described by the *Sunday Times* in London as one of the "1,000 Makers of the 20th Century" and by the *Sunday Mid-Day* in India as one of the ten people—along with Gandhi, Nehru, and Buddha—who have changed India's India.

About his own work Osho has said that he is helping to create the conditions for the birth of a new kind of human being. He has often characterized this new human being as "Zorba the Buddha"—capable of enjoying both the earthy pleasures of a Zorba the Greek and the silent serenity of a Gautama the Buddha. Running like a thread through all aspects of the work is a vision that encompasses both the timeless wisdom of the East and the highest potential of Western science and technology.

Osho is also known for his revolutionary contribution to the science of inner transformation, with an approach to meditation that acknowledges the accelerated pace of contemporary life. His unique "active meditations" are designed to first release the accumulated stresses of body and mind, making it is easier to experience the thought-free and relaxed state of meditation.

ABOUT OSHO COMMUNE INTERNATIONAL

Osho Commune International is a meditation resort that was created to help people directly to experience a new way of living—with more alertness, relaxation, and humor. Located about 100 miles southeast of Bombay in Pune, India, the resort offers a variety of programs to the thousands of people who visit each year from more than one hundred countries.

The campus is spread over forty acres in the tree-lined residential area of Koregaon Park. Although accommodation for visitors is limited, there is a variety of nearby hotels and private apartments available for stays of a few days up to several months.

The programs at the meditation resort, which take place in an elegant pyramid complex adjoining a fifteen-acre Zen garden, are designed to provide contemporary people with the tools they need to transform their lives. The aim of the programs is to give people access to a new lifestyle, one of relaxed awareness, an approach they can take home with them into their everyday life. A selection of self-discovery and meditative classes are offered throughout the year. In the main meditation hall, the daily schedule includes meditation methods that are active and silent, contemporary and traditional. For exercising the body and keeping fit, there is a beautiful outdoor resort facility where one can experiment with a Zen approach to sports and recreation.

Every evening visitors to the resort have the opportunity to participate in a unique two-hour meditation meeting of music, dance, and silence. Following this meeting, the nightlife in this multicultural resort is alive with entertainment, including concerts, and outdoor eating areas serving traditional Indian fare and a choice of international dishes. The plaza café fills with friends, and there is often dancing, with a DJ or live music.

The commune has its own supply of safe, filtered drinking water, and the food served is made from organically grown produce from the commune's own farm. An online tour of the meditation resort, as well as travel and program information, can be found at www. osho.com, a comprehensive website in different languages that also includes an online magazine, audio and video webcasting, and a complete archive of Osho talks plus a catalog of all Osho publications, including books, magazines, audios, and videos. You can also email Osho International, New York, at osho-int@osho.com.

ALSO BY OSHO:

Autobiography of a Spiritually Incorrect Mystic
Awareness: The Key to Living in Balance
The Book of Secrets: 112 Keys to Unlock the Mystery Within
Courage: The Joy of Living Dangerously
Creativity: Unleashing the Forces Within
Love, Freedom and Aloneness: A New Vision of Relating
Meditation: The First and Last Freedom